Running with the Devil

MUSIC / CULTURE

A series from Wesleyan University Press

Edited by Robert Walser and Susan Fast

ORIGINATING EDITORS:

George Lipsitz, Susan McClary, and Robert Walser

(continued on page 223)

ROBERT WALSER

✻

Running with the Devil

POWER, GENDER,

AND MADNESS IN HEAVY

METAL MUSIC

✻

WESLEYAN UNIVERSITY PRESS

Middletown, Connecticut

Published by Wesleyan University Press, Middletown, CT 06459
www.wesleyan.edu/wespress

Originally produced in 1993 by Wesleyan/
University Press of New England, Hanover, NH 03755

Printed in the United States of America
15 14 13 12 11 10 9 8

CIP data appear at the end of the book

ISBNs for the paperback edition:
ISBN–13: 978–0–8195–6260–9
ISBN–10: 0–8195–6260–2

Acknowledgments for song lyrics quoted:

"Electric Eye": Words and music by Glenn Tipton, Rob Halford, and K. K. Downing,
© 1982 EMI APRIL MUSIC, INC. / CREWGLEN LTD. / EBONYTREE LTD. / GEARGATE LTD.
All rights controlled and administered by EMI APRIL MUSIC, INC. International copyright
secured. All rights reserved. Used by permission.

"Suicide Solution": Words and music by John Osbourne, Robert Daisley, and Randy
Rhoads, TRO—© Copyright 1981 Essex Music International, Inc. and Kord Music Publishers, New York, N.Y. Used by permission.

Contents

✳

Photographs follow page 107

Acknowledgments

✳

I am grateful for the generosity of the nearly two hundred heavy metal fans from Minnesota, California, Michigan, and Illinois who discussed their music and their lives with me. Through interviews, casual conversations, and questionnaires, their assistance was invaluable in helping me to understand heavy metal. In contrast to the common stereotype of metal fans as sullen and inarticulate, I was surprised by the friendliness and enthusiasm I found among fans and musicians alike. Most fans were pleased to find someone taking their music seriously; they were eager to fill out the questionnaires I circulated at concerts, and far from having to persuade people to let me interview them, I received many more requests to do interviews than I could accommodate. In particular, I thank Peter Del Valle for helping me to set up my first interview with a group of fans.

I have learned from conversations about heavy metal and popular culture with many other people, particularly Chris Kachian, Csaba Toth, and Metal Mark of GMS. I thank Gary Thomas and the members of his Gay Studies class for an evening spent discussing heavy metal videos and gender construction. My work has benefited from the ideas and criticisms of my students at the University of Michigan, the University of Minnesota, and Dartmouth College, especially those in my Contemporary Popular Music Studies course at Michigan. Thanks also to my metal guitar teacher, Jeff Loven, and to the many other rock musicians I have performed with and learned from, especially Gene Retka, Steve Cekalla, James Capra, Dave Michel, John Helgen, and Gregg Ramseth.

William Shurk at Bowling Green State University is the knowledgeable curator of an enormous archive of popular music, including heavy metal recordings and fan magazines (many confiscated from fans by parents or police). I thank him for his assistance and for granting me access to materials that I found useful. For travel funds that enabled me to carry out that research and to present papers on heavy metal at a number of academic conferences, I thank the University of Minnesota, especially Vern Sutton and the School of Music, as well as the School of Music at the University of Michigan, and Dartmouth College. And I am pleased to have an opportunity to acknowledge the influence of Bruce Lincoln, who introduced me to cultural criticism and changed my life nearly fifteen years ago.

Several non-metal-fan friends were brave enough to overcome strong misgivings and accompany me to heavy metal concerts; I thank Bruce Holsinger, Chris Kachian, George Lipsitz, Susan McClary, and John Mowitt for the pleasure of their company and for their insights concerning what they saw and heard. It is regrettable that the only violence I ever witnessed at a heavy metal concert was committed by one of these people.

For their helpful comments on drafts and portions of this book, I thank Andrew Goodwin, Wendy Kozol, Carolyn Krasnow, Richard Leppert, John Mowitt, and Christopher Small. I am particularly grateful to those who read the entire book and provided much-needed corrections, provocations, and encouragement: Simon Frith, Dave Marsh, Terry Cochran, Charles Hamm, and Ross Chambers.

Finally, I owe my largest intellectual debts to Susan McClary and George Lipsitz. To put it simply, Susan taught me how to think about music, and George taught me how to think about popular culture. I feel proud and fortunate to have been their student and friend, and it is to them that I dedicate *Running with the Devil*.

November 1992 R.W.

Introduction

*

In the catacombs of a nineteenth-century warehouse, hulking in a run-down riverfront district, passageways wind through rough stonework to connect small rooms, each fronted by a sturdy iron door. Behind these doors musicians compose and rehearse through all hours of the day and night. Wandering the crooked hallways, I hear waves of sound clashing and coalescing: powerful drums and bass, menacing and ecstatic vocals, the heavy crunch of distorted electric guitars. In some rooms, lone guitarists practice scales, arpeggios, heavy metal riffs, and Bach transcriptions. Occasionally, I pass an open door, and musicians who are taking a break consider my presence with cool curiosity.

I am struck by the resemblance of these underground rehearsal spaces to the practice rooms of a conservatory. The decor is different, but the people are similar: musicians in their late teens and early twenties, assembled for long hours of rigorous practice. There is a parallel sense of isolation for the sake of musical craft and creativity, a kindred pursuit of technical development and group precision. And like conservatory students, many of these heavy metal musicians take private lessons, study music theory, and practice scales and exercises for hours every day. They also share the precarious economic future faced by classical musicians; in both cases, few will ever make enough money performing to compensate them for the thousands of hours they have practiced and rehearsed.

There are important differences from the conservatory environment, too, not the least of which is the grungy setting itself, which underlines the fact that this music does not enjoy institutional prestige or receive governmental subsidy. The musicians must pool their funds to pay for rental of the rooms, and the long hair that marks them as members of a heavy metal subculture also ensures that they are not likely to have access to jobs that pay well. On the other hand, many of these people are actually working as musicians, at least part-time. Unlike most of their peers in the academy, they know a great deal about the commercial channels to which they hope to gain access. Some talk of not compromising their art for popular success, but there is little evidence of the music academy's pretense that art can be pursued apart from commerce. This is in part because they are more closely connected with their potential audiences, through their own fan activities and those of their friends, while relatively few aspiring classical musicians actually belong to the moneyed class that underwrites the performance of classical music. Heavy metal musicians are, in fact, strongly influenced by the practices of the musical academy, but their activities also retain the priorities of collective creation and orality derived from traditions of popular music making.

The noisy vaults of that warehouse and the musicians who haunt them evoke images and raise issues that will be central to my discussions of heavy metal. If metal could be said to have gotten started in any single place, it would be Birmingham, England, the industrial city whose working class spawned Ozzy Osbourne, Black Sabbath, and Judas Priest in the late 1960s and early 1970s. That heavy metal bands now labor in spaces abandoned by industry is particularly appropriate for a music that has flourished during the period of American deindustrialization. And just as the labor of industrial production is invisible in mass media representations of consumer products, the musical labor that sustains and reinvents mass-mediated popular music often takes place in such marginal locations. Heavy metal is perhaps the single most successful and enduring musical genre of the past thirty years; yet it is in such dank cellars that many of its future stars serve their apprenticeships. This noisy basement is a good analogy for the position heavy metal occupies in the edifice of cultural prestige.

When I began writing about heavy metal in 1986, it seemed a strange thing for a cultural critic—let alone a musicologist—to do. Metal has been ignored or reviled, not only by academics of all stripes but even by most rock critics. Yet in the United States and many other countries, heavy metal was arguably the most important and influential musical genre of the 1980s; throughout the decade, it became increasingly clear that, between them, hip hop and heavy metal were redefining American popular music. Moreover, the debates surrounding heavy metal and the people who make it—over meaning, character, behavior, values, censorship, violence, alienation, and community—mark metal as an important site of cultural contestation. This is most obvious when attacks come from groups with overt moral missions, such as the Parents' Music Resource Center, Christian fundamentalist groups, rock critics, or academics. But intense reactions to heavy metal are widespread: a recent marketing survey found that ten million people in the United States "like or strongly like" heavy metal—and that nineteen million strongly dislike it, the largest backlash of any music category.[1] People care deeply about heavy metal, one way or another, which suggests that it engages with some fundamental social values and tensions.

Such strong reactions, along with heavy metal's sheer popularity, might seem sufficient justification for the study of heavy metal, since the genre embraces such a significant portion of the musical activity of our time. However, I was initially drawn to writing about metal not because of such a sociological or political mandate. Rather, I became interested in exploring heavy metal because I found the music compelling. Already active as a professional musician on other instruments, I began playing guitar in the late 1970s. I moved among bands and musical styles for several years, learning on stage rather than in a practice room, from other musicians instead of from sheet music or recordings, and in 1980 I found myself playing heavy metal before I had actually listened to much of it. As a performer, metal granted me access to its power almost immediately—it doesn't take long to learn to play power chords—yet its musical subtleties and technical demands continued to inspire and challenge me a decade later.

I once heard a prominent sociologist of popular music tell an audience that he actually had no interest in the music he had been studying for years. The reason he gave for having become involved with studying popular music, rather than some other "product," was that all of the other industries were taken. He was not embarrassed by this admission; rather, he seemed to take it as a point of pride, perhaps because he thought such objectivity would enhance his scholarly rigor. It seemed appropriate to have no particular investment in the products of the industry he studied; he thought it no more important to discuss or discriminate among musical texts than it would be to analyze individual tires or refrigerators.

To be sure, scholars who interpret cultural texts should notice the commercial processes and power struggles that make those texts available to their attention, as well as the social structures and tensions that make them meaningful. But to analyze popular culture only in terms of the commercial structures that mediate it is to "imagine markets free of politics."[2] Economics becomes an autonomous abstraction from a conflicted society, and the hard-nosed study of institutions and monetary power is but a false veneer of political engagement, masking a refusal to confront the political dimension of economic choices. As Christopher

Small asks those who discuss popular culture only in terms of production and consumption,

How do you "consume" music, when (a) music isn't a thing and (b) it's still there after you've used it—or you think you've used it. Just because the industry markets it as commodity doesn't mean we have to accept their terms of reference. It's time people stopped talking about "consuming" art and culture and so on and started thinking of art as an activity, something you do. Even buying and playing records are activities; the record is only the medium through which the activity takes place.[3]

Just as important, most scholars of popular music assume that recent mass-mediated music is somehow more "compromised" than earlier music by its involvement with commercial structures and interests. This is simply not true. Music has always been "commercial," at least since the Renaissance; that is, music has always been supported by the interests and patronage of particular social groups and enmeshed in institutional politics, mechanisms of distribution, and strategies of promotion.[4] If it makes sense to study specific operas as sites of the exchange and contestation of social meanings, rather than as interchangeable epiphenomena of a patronage structure, it makes equal sense to treat more recent popular texts with similar specificity and care.

As a musician, I cannot help but think that individual texts, and the social experiences they represent, are important. My apprenticeships as a performer—conservatory student and orchestral musician, ethnic outsider learning to play Polish polkas, jazz trumpeter, pop singer, and heavy metal guitarist—were periods spent learning musical discourses. That is, I had to acquire the ability to recognize, distinguish, and deploy the musical possibilities organized in styles or genres by various communities. Each song marshals the options available in a different way, and each musical occasion inflects a song's social meanings. Becoming a musician in any of the styles I have mentioned is a process of learning to understand and manipulate the differences intrinsic to a style, which are manifested differently in each text and performance. Unlike many scholars, I think it is possible to analyze, historicize, and write about these processes.

Moreover, I find some songs powerfully meaningful and others not; so do all of the fans and musicians I know. Some of us are better than others at explaining why we care about this song and not that one, but for most people, music is intimately involved with crucial feelings of identity and notions of community. This is where sociological approaches to the study of popular music have so often failed. For while I do not suggest that either technical training or performing experience are necessary prerequisites for insightful writing about popular music, one must be able to experience—not just discern—differences among musical texts, in order to avoid imposing an interpretation of monotony and singularity of meaning that fans and musicians do not recognize.

Accordingly, I have integrated methods of musical analysis, ethnography, and cultural cricitism in this study. Following the example of scholars of popular culture such as Janice Radway and ethnomusicologists like Steven Feld, I have tried to find out what real listeners hear and how they think about their activities. Along with those working in cultural studies, like John Fiske and George Lipsitz, I want to situate the texts and practices I study within a forthrightly politicized context of cultural struggle over values, power, and legitimacy. And finally, I owe an important debt to the few musicologists, such as Susan McClary and Christopher Small, who have discussed musical structures as social texts imbued with political significance.[5]

My interest is less in explicating texts or defining the history of a style than in analyzing the musical activities that produce texts and styles and make them socially significant. I find Christopher Small's notion of "musicking" helpful. Small revives the idea of music as a verb rather than a noun in order to challenge our common practice of analyzing and understanding music in terms of objects, which encourages abstract stylistic description and effaces the social activity that produces musical texts and experiences.[6] "Musicking" embraces composition, performance, listening, dancing—all of the social practices of which musical scores and recordings are merely one-dimensional traces. To understand heavy metal as musicking, I studied it from many aspects. I attended concerts, studied recordings, interviewed fans and musicians, took heavy metal guitar lessons, and read fan magazines, industry reports, and denunciations.[7] My goal was to find answers through a kind of cultural triangulation, using ethnography as a check on textual interpretation and developing ethnographic strategies out of my own and others' cultural analyses.

I have chosen to focus on the most popular examples of heavy metal —the bands with multiplatinum record sales and arena-filling concert tours, the bands named as exemplary by fan magazines and by the fans I consulted through questionnaires and interviews: Ozzy Osbourne, Iron Maiden, Judas Priest, Poison, Van Halen, Megadeth, Guns N' Roses, etc. While much interesting work could be done on less popular, "underground" metal subcultures, this study concentrates on massively popular heavy metal because that focus enables engagement with important contemporary debates over music, mass mediation, morality, and censorship. Like Stuart Hall, I see "the popular" as an important site of social contestation and formation, and I find unconvincing the common assumption that culture that exists either at the margins of society or among a prestigious elite is necessarily more important, interesting, complex, or profound than the culture of a popular mainstream.[8] Popular culture is important because that is where most people get their "entertainment" and information; it's where they find dominant definitions of themselves as well as alternatives, options to try on for size.

I have elected to concentrate primarily on music of the 1980s, since that is the music both my informants and I know best, and because that is the decade of heavy metal's greatest popularity and influence. I have not tried to write a full history of heavy metal, nor have I attempted a comprehensive study of its most important artists or works. Neither have I pursued a more tightly focused study of a particular style or performer. Rather, I have tried to begin establishing an analytic context within which such work could be undertaken by examining several aspects of heavy metal that I feel are crucial to its success and meaningfulness—to its power.

Most important, perhaps, I have tried to pay particular attention to the *music* of heavy metal, in ways that are both textually specific and culturally grounded. For like most musicians and fans, I respond more intensely to music than to words or pictures. Before I knew any lyrics, before I had even seen any of the major performers, I was attracted to heavy metal by specifically musical factors. Within the context of the other kinds of music I knew, I found the "language" of heavy metal— the coherent body of musical signs and conventions that distinguished it as a genre—powerful and persuasive. Much of this book will be concerned with what has been conspicuously absent from discussions of popular music, whether academic, journalistic, or moralistic: analysis of the specific musical choices embodied in individual songs and organized by genres. Musicians take such conventions and details seriously, and fans respond to them; critics and scholars cannot justify continuing to ignore them.[9]

Chapter 2 prepares for such discussions by sketching the terms of heavy metal as a discursive practice, as a coherent, though always changing, universe of significant sonic options. I examine heavy metal music as a social signifying system rather than an autonomous set of stylistic traits, employing an approach to musical analysis that construes musical details as significant gestural and syntactical units, organized by narrative and other formal conventions, and constituting a system for the social production of meaning—a discourse. This chapter dissects and discusses heavy metal music as a discourse, with reference to an example that is in many ways paradigmatic for the genre. Both this and the following chapter are fairly "guitarocentric," since the point is to get "beyond the vocals," and guitarists have been the primary composers and soloists of heavy metal music.

Chapter 3 focuses on the intersection of heavy metal and classical music, an example of what I call "discursive fusion." Makers of popular culture have always thrived on borrowing, customizing, and reinterpreting other peoples' cultural property; yet this aspect of popular music has received little analytical attention, for many critics remain influenced by ideologies of authenticity that accord a higher place to supposedly pure popular creations (e.g., "folk music"). Heavy metal musicians have appropriated musical materials from eighteenth- and nineteenth-century concert music, reworking what is now the most prestigious of musical discourses to serve the interests of what is now the least prestigious of musical communities. Chapter 3 examines this appropriation of musical signs as a case study in cultural politics, comparing means and ends across the sacrosanct boundaries of classical/popular and high/low culture.

In comparing the techniques of heavy metal musicians to those of classical musicians, I am not simply making a bid for academic legitimacy on behalf of the former. The point of such comparisons is to pursue what Bakhtin called "interillumination," his method of "de-privileging languages," or what Marcus and Fischer characterize as "defamiliarization by cross-cultural juxtaposition," part of their plan for remaking "anthropology as cultural critique."[10] It is to contribute to demystifying classical music's aura of transcendent autonomy and to debunking stereotypical notions of heavy metal's musical crudity. Arguing for the worth of popular music in the terms of valuation used for more prestigious music is not without risk: jazz has gained a certain amount of academic respectibility through such toil by its defenders, but at the cost of erasing much of the music's historical significance, its politics, its basis in non-European modes of musical thinking and doing. (Indeed, this is precisely what has happened to the many different kinds of historical music making that have been collapsed into "classical music" by our century.) However strange it might seem to compare heavy metal and classical music, heavy metal musicians themselves have already accomplished this juxtaposition, and we must reach beyond accepted cultural categories to understand what they are doing. Such comparisons reveal much about both musics and challenge hegemonic assumptions about "trained" musicians and "serious" music.

Chapter 4 takes up issues of gender in heavy metal. Since the social contexts within which heavy metal circulates (primarily Western societies in the late twentieth century) are highly patriarchal, it is not surprising to find that an important concern of metal is to represent male power and female subordination. Music, lyrics, visual images, and behavior serve to construct gender identities, infusing them with power and implying that they are natural and desirable. These representations primarily serve the interests of the male musicians who dominate heavy metal performance and the male fans who until recently were their primary constituency. Through discussion of heavy metal songs and videos, I trace four strategies for dealing with the "threat" women embody to patriarchy. But as a genre that now boasts a gender-balanced audience, heavy metal depictions of gender identities and relationships must offer credible positions for women. In small part this is accomplished by female metal musicians, who search for a style that will articulate their contradictory position as women and performers. But women are more often offered heavy metal empowerment through adaptations of the ideology of romance, the ambiguous implications of androgyny, and their increasing ability to identify with constructions of power that had previously been understood as inherently male. This chapter, more than the others, explicitly analyzes music videos because of the connections that exist in contemporary Western cultures among music, gender, and spectacularity.[11]

Chapter 5 assesses the significance of violence and mysticism in heavy metal. I begin with recent critiques, controversies, and court cases involving heavy metal, including debates over suicide and censorship. Through discussions of selected songs, I argue that while it is clear that some heavy metal music does articulate struggle, madness, violence, and disorientation, metal does not invent or inject these affective states; instead, it mediates social tensions, working to provide its fans with a sense of spiritual depth and social integration. Many people who condemn heavy metal accept historically contingent formations of youth, socialization, and deviance as absolutes: "Heavy metal's subject matter is simple and virtually universal. It celebrates teenagers' newfound feelings of rebellion and sexuality. The bulk of the music is stylized and formulaic."[12] But such characterizations essentialize the category of youth, removing it from history and depoliticizing it. Heavy metal fans do tend to be young, and this is surely relevant to any explanation of its appeal; but youth itself must be understood within a larger social framework, as a category constructed by ideological labor. And the rebellious or transgressive aspects of heavy metal, its exploration of the dark side of social life, also reflect its engagement with the pressures of a historical moment.

For rebellion and escapism are always movements away from something, toward something else. Rebellion is critique; whether apparently effectual or not, it is politics. But even more important, what seems like rejection, alienation, or nihilism is usually better seen as an attempt to create an alternative identity that is grounded in a vision or the actual experience of an alternative community. Heavy metal's fascination with the dark side of life gives evidence of both dissatisfaction with dominant identities and institutions and an intense yearning for reconciliation with something more credible.[13] To explain this side of metal as the pathological imprint of malicious musicians or as adolescent socialization gone awry (as is often done) is to dehistoricize the specific forms and practices of heavy metal.

For I simply don't find persuasive arguments that explain heavy metal in terms of deviance. The context for this study is the United States during the 1970s and 1980s, a period that saw a series of damaging economic crises, unprecedented revelations of corrupt political leadership, erosion of public confidence in governmental and corporate benevolence, cruel retrenchment of social programs along with policies that favored the wealthy, and tempestuous contestation of social institutions and representations, involving formations that had been thought to be stable, such as gender roles and the family. This social climate, besides shaping lyrical concerns and distributive networks, provided the context within which heavy metal became meaningful for millions of people. Heavy metal is intimately embedded in the social system of values and practices that its critics defend.

Chapter 1, then, situates heavy metal as a cultural practice that is historically constituted and socially contested; it examines how "heavy metal" means different things to the variety of people who are involved with it—fans, musicians, historians, critics, academics, censors. I trace the history of heavy metal as it has been assembled by critics, fans, and musicians and then discuss ongoing disputes over the boundaries of the genre, emphasizing the divergent interests of fans, musicians, critics, fan magazines, and other commercial mediators. A summary of the characteristics, activities, and beliefs of heavy metal fans is followed by discussion of the very different interpretations of those activities provided by academics and rock critics.

I have intersected the texts and debates of metal fans and musicians with analytical and historical perspectives that are sometimes foreign to that experience but find common ground in my arguments for the cultural coherence of that experience. This study is organized around the issues that fans and musicians, through their activities and statements and the music itself, have indicated are central to the power and meaning of heavy metal. But it also reflects my own position as an academic and cultural critic, and it engages with ongoing arguments about music and culture that not all readers will find interesting or important. In some circles, for example, it is still necessary to argue that music can be analyzed as having social meaning; readers who are willing to grant this point may wish to skip over parts of chapter 2.

In my attempts to make sense of heavy metal, I have learned from and taken issue with the arguments of sociologists, musicologists, rock critics, and cultural theorists because I have found such interdisciplinary inquiry the only adequate approach to the study of something as complex as popular music. While heavy metal appears as the object of study of my cultural and musicological investigation, I have tried through my engagement with heavy metal to raise larger questions about the politics of culture, recent American history, "classical" music, and the nature of musical discourses, experience, and analysis.

The specific sites of metal activity—concert arenas, clubs, record stores, warehouse rehearsal rooms, fans' bedrooms and cars—may be distant and unfamiliar to many people. Similarly, the musical discourses of metal are grounded in semiotic codes that are widely shared but often drawn upon by metal musicians precisely to articulate alienating noise and exclusivity. *Running with the Devil* attempts to resituate heavy metal within contemporary debates over music and cultural politics without muting that noise. It offers some explanations of how heavy metal works and why people care about it.

Running with the Devil

CHAPTER ONE

Metallurgies

Genre, History, and the Construction of Heavy Metal

✷

I have been invited to try my hand at explaining heavy-metal music.
First, heavy metal is power. . . .   —Rob Halford of Judas Priest[1]

The Oxford English Dictionary traces "heavy metal" back through nearly two hundred years. In the late twentieth century, the term has two primary meanings: for chemists and metallurgists, it labels a group of elements and toxic compounds; for the rest of us, it refers to a kind of music. But these meanings are not unrelated. Even in the nineteenth century, "heavy metal" was both a technical term and a figurative, social one:

1828   Webster s.v., *Heavy metal*, in military affairs, signifies large guns, carrying balls of a large size, or it is applied to the balls themselves.

1882   Ogilvie s.v., *Heavy metal*, guns or shot of large size; hence, *fig.* ability, mental or bodily; power, influence; as, he is a man of heavy metal; also, a person or persons of great ability or power, mental or bodily; used generally of one who is or is to be another's opponent in any contest; as, we had to do with heavy metal. (Colloq.)[2]

"Heavy metal," in each of its parts and as a compound, evoked power and potency. A "man of heavy metal" was powerful and daunting, and the *OED* vividly confirms a long-standing social conflation of power and patriarchal order. The long history of "heavy metal" in the English language resonates with modern usage, even as contemporary musicians converse with the musical past in their work. "Heavy metal" is not simply a recently invented genre label; its meaning is indebted to the historical circulation of images, qualities, and metaphors, and it was applied to particular musical practices because it made social sense to do so.

"Heavy metal" now denotes a variety of musical discourses, social practices, and cultural meanings, all of which revolve around concepts, images, and experiences of power. The loudness and intensity of heavy metal music visibly empower fans, whose shouting and headbanging testify to the circulation of energy at concerts.[3] Metal energizes the body, transforming space and social relations. The visual language of metal album covers and the spectacular stage shows offer larger-than-life images tied to fantasies of social power, just as in the more prestigious musical spectacles of opera. The clothing and hairstyles of metal fans, as much as the music itself, mark social spaces from concert halls to bedrooms to streets, claiming them in the name of a heavy metal community. And all of these aspects of power provoke strong reactions from those outside heavy metal, including fear and censorship.

The names chosen by heavy metal bands evoke power and intensity in many different ways. Bands align themselves with electrical and mechanical power (Tesla, AC/DC, Mötorhead), dangerous or unpleasant animals (Ratt, Scorpions), dangerous or unpleasant people (Twisted Sister, Mötley Crüe, Quiet Riot), or dangerous and unpleasant objects (Iron Maiden). They can invoke the auratic power of blasphemy or mysticism (Judas Priest, Black Sabbath, Blue Öyster Cult) or the terror of death itself (Anthrax, Poison, Megadeth, Slayer). Heavy metal can even claim power by being self-referential (Metallica) or by transgressing convention with an antipower name (Cinderella, Kiss). Some bands add umlauts (Motörhead, Mötley Crüe, Queensrÿche) to mark their names as archaic or gothic.[4]

If there is one feature that underpins the coherence of heavy metal as a genre, it is the power chord. Produced by playing the musical interval of a perfect fourth or fifth on a heavily amplified and distorted electric guitar, the power chord is used by all of the bands that are ever called heavy metal and, until heavy metal's enormous influence on other musical genres in the late 1980s, by comparatively few musicians outside the genre. The power chord can be percussive and rhythmic or indefinitely sustained; it is used both to articulate and to suspend time. It is a complex sound, made up of resultant tones and overtones, constantly renewed and energized by feedback. It is at once the musical basis of heavy metal and an apt metaphor for it, for musical articulation of power is the most important single factor in the experience of heavy metal. The power chord seems simple and crude, but it is dependent upon sophisticated technology, precise tuning, and skillful control. Its overdriven sound evokes excess and transgression but also stability, permanence, and harmony.

But what is the nature of this power? Where does it come from, how is it generated, mobilized, circulated? How can heavy metal music articulate claims to power, and what social tensions are addressed or mediated by it? These are the issues that animate this book. In chapter 2, I will take up the problem of defining heavy metal structurally, as a musical discourse comprising a coherent system of signs such as power chords. In this one, I will be concerned with a more functional view of heavy metal as a genre, with the processes of definition and contestation that go on among those concerned with the music. In other words, I will be focusing here on how heavy metal gets construed—by fans, historians, academics, and critics.[5] The essential characteristics of heavy metal not only vary according to these different perspectives, but the very existence of something called heavy metal depends upon the ongoing arguments of those involved. Heavy metal is, like all culture, a site of struggle over definitions, dreams, behaviors, and resources.

Genre and Commercial Mediation

Discursive practices are characterized by the delimitation of a field of objects, the definition of a legitimate perspective for the agent of knowledge, and the fixing of norms for the elaboration of concepts and theories. Thus, each discursive practice implies a play of prescriptions that designate its exclusions and choices. —Michel Foucault[6]

I hate that term "heavy metal." —Angus Young, AC/DC

Heavy metal began to attain stylistic identity in the late 1960s as a "harder" sort of hard rock, and a relatively small but fiercely loyal subculture formed around it during the 1970s. Because heavy metal threatened to antagonize demographically targeted audiences, metal bands received virtually no radio airplay, and they had to support their album releases by constant touring, playing to an audience that was mostly young, white, male, and working class.[7] The 1980s was the decade of heavy metal's emergence as a massively popular musical style, as it burgeoned in both commercial success and stylistic variety. The heavy metal audience became increasingly gender-balanced and middle-class, and its age range expanded to include significant numbers of preteens and people in their late twenties. By 1989, heavy metal accounted for as much as 40 percent of all sound recordings sold in the United States, and *Rolling Stone* announced that heavy metal now constituted "the mainstream of rock and roll."[8] By then, metal had diversified into a number of styles and influenced other musical discourses. The term "heavy metal" itself became an open site of contestation, as fans, musicians, and historians struggled with the prestige—and notoriety—of a genre name that seemed no longer able to contain disparate musical styles and agendas.

Thus, heavy metal is not monolithic; it embraces many different musical and visual styles, many kinds of lyrics and behaviors. "Heavy metal" is a term that is constantly debated and contested, primarily among fans but also in dialogue with musicians, commercial marketing strategists, and outside critics and censors. Debates over which bands, songs, sounds, and sights get to count as heavy metal provide occasions for contesting musical and social prestige. "That's not heavy metal" is the most damning music criticism a fan can inflict, for that genre name has great prestige among fans. But genre boundaries are not solid or clear; they are conceptual sites of struggles over the meanings and prestige of social signs.

Fans care, often passionately, about difference; they find certain bands and songs meaningful and relevant to their lives, while others leave them indifferent or repulsed. But there are institutional pressures for a kind of generic coherence that effaces such distinctions. Fan magazines try to apply "heavy metal" very broadly, to attract as many readers as possible. But their editors must negotiate discursive boundaries cautiously. Magazines that define themselves as wholly or primarily about heavy metal strive to appear as inclusive as possible, in part to advise fans on new bands or even to market those new bands for the sake of record company sponsors, but also because every fan wants to read about (and look at pictures of) his or her favorites in every issue. On the other hand, to include bands that fans do not accept as metal would weaken the magazine's credibility and the fans' enjoyment of the heavy metal "world" portrayed.[9]

Record clubs ("Grab Ten Headbanging Hits for 1¢!") and fan merchandisers work to produce a notion of heavy metal that is inclusive and indiscriminate, just as in classical music, where orchestra advertising, music appreciation books, and record promoters campaign to erase historical specificity in order to stimulate consumption. And just as the promoters of classical music offer encounters with unspecified "greatness," those who market heavy metal present it vaguely, as participation in generalized rebellion and intensity.[10] But in both cases the coherence of the genre and the prestige of its history are crucial concerns of the music industry. An executive for Polygram Records describes the company's success in mobilizing a sense of heavy metal history as a marketing tool: "We used an in-store campaign for Deep Purple that emphasized peer pressure. Many of the potential buyers of DP records are too young to remember the band in its previous incarnation. So we had to instill in these young metal fans that they were not really hip, not dedicated headbangers until they knew about Deep Purple. The campaign was very successful."[11]

Rigid genre boundaries are more useful to the music industry than to fans, and the commercial strategy of hyping cultural genres while striving to obliterate the differences that make individual choices meaningful often works very effectively to mobilize efficient consumption (nowhere more so than in classical music). But not always. The consequences of such a coarse view of heavy metal can be seen in the failure of the biggest metal concert tour of 1988. Touted as the heavy metal event of the decade, the Monsters of Rock tour during the summer of 1988 was a mammoth disappointment for fans and promoters alike. At the moment of heavy metal's greatest popularity ever, several of the world's most successful heavy metal bands were assembled for a U.S. tour: Van Halen, Scorpions, Metallica, Dokken, and Kingdom Come. These were some of the biggest names in metal, yet attendance throughout the tour was surprisingly light, and it became clear that the promoters who had assembled the tour suffered substantial losses because they had misunderstood the genre of heavy metal: they saw it as monolithic, failing to realize that heavy metal and its audience are not homogeneous, that fans' allegiances are complex and specific. Many fans came to the Monsters of Rock concerts just to hear one or two bands; many Metallica fans, for example, despise bands like Scorpions and Kingdom Come. Waves of partisan arrivals and departures at the concert helped defuse the excitement normally generated in full arenas, and the fans' selective attendance undercut the concession and souvenir sales that are so important to underwriting tour expenses and profits.[12]

The crude assumptions about genre that sank the Monsters of Rock tour are also endemic in writings about metal, from the rectitudinous denunciations of would-be censors to sociologists' "objective" explanations—nearly everywhere, in fact, but in the magazines read by the fans themselves, where such totalizing errors could never be taken seriously. Outsiders' representations of heavy metal as monolithic stand in stark contrast to the fans' views, which prize difference and specificity. Because the magazines present heavy metal as exciting and prestigious at the same time that they apply the term more broadly than most fans can accept, the magazine itself becomes a site for contestation of the term. Writers of record reviews and articles gain credibility with their readers by arguing for distinctions that may contradict the inclusive stance of the magazine itself. But fans also contribute their perspectives directly through the letters columns that begin each issue. For example, one fan wrote to offer his canon of the best metal bands; his letter is emphatic about the importance of genre, and he sees "heavy metal" as a distinction of great value, something that can be attained and then lost:

Some other good groups are Accept, from Germany, and Exciter, Heaven, Twisted Sister, Girls School, Wild Dogs and so many others. Van Halen was once Heavy Metal but they got stuck on themselves. Van Halen is now what we refer to as "Bubblegum" hard rock. Loverboy, ZZ Top and Zebra are all hard rock. There is a difference between hard rock and Heavy Metal. Heavy Metal is actually a "New Wave" music for the 80s.[13]

Another fan addressed the controversial split between glam and speed metal, rebutting the many hostile letters that disparage one side or the other. She takes a liberal stance that retains the label "heavy metal" for her favorite band but acknowledges the merit of its incompatible cousins: "Poison and Metallica shouldn't even be compared really. Poison is heavy metal. Metallica is speed metal. Poison is good at what they do, and Metallica is good at what they do."[14] The letters columns of magazines like *RIP* or *Hit Parader* also serve as forums for other kinds of debates, including discussions of sexism, homophobia, and racism. Fans often write in to critique the representations of gender and race they find in heavy metal lyrics, interviews with musicians, and journalism.[15]

Musicians who are considered heavy metal by their fans may vary greatly in their allegiance to the genre. Judas Priest's goal has been "to achieve the *definition* of heavy metal," while members of AC/DC and Def Leppard claim to hate the term, even though all three bands are mainstay subjects of heavy metal fandom.[16] Many writers and fans consider Led Zeppelin the fount of heavy metal: "Quite simply, Led Zeppelin is, was, and will always be the ultimate heavy metal masters."[17] But Zeppelin's lead singer, Robert Plant, rejects that characterization, saying, for example, of the band's first album, "That was not heavy metal. There was nothing heavy about that at all. . . . It was ethereal."[18]

There are many reasons for bands to position themselves carefully with respect to a genre label. Their account of their relationship to heavy metal can imply or deny historical and discursive connections to other music. But more important, it situates them with respect to audiences, interpretative norms, and institutional channels. Guitarist Yngwie Malmsteen denies any connection with metal out of contempt for a genre that he views as technically and aesthetically inferior to his own music. Malmsteen hopes to gain greater prestige as an artist than is normally granted to metal musicians, but he is also bidding for the radio play that is often denied them.[19] Iron Maiden has always depended on selling tickets and albums to hard-core metal fans; they have no other audience. Yet the group's singer, Bruce Dickenson, affects nonchalance when discussing the genre and their place in it: "What is your viewpoint? I wouldn't call UFO a heavy metal band, but if you happen to be a fan of Human League, they probably are. And if you're a fan of

Motorhead, UFO aren't heavy metal. If we said we are heavy metal, it wouldn't matter much in the way we sound. It's a category."[20] Many artists bridle at genre categories because they see them as restrictive stereotypes, implying formulaic composition. Dickenson resists being pigeonholed by pointing to the relative, rather than absolute, nature of genre distinctions. But he must feign indifference to the meaningfulness of genre to fans and institutions in order to claim this appearance of artistic freedom.

The music of Rush meets the criteria of the definition of heavy metal held by most outsiders but fails the standards of most metal fans. Geddy Lee, the band's singer and bass player, muses on the problematic status of his band: "It's funny. When you talk to metal people about Rush, eight out of ten will tell you that we're not a metal band. But if you talk to anyone outside of metal, eight out of ten will tell you we *are* a metal band. *Metal* is a very broad term."[21] There is, of course, a great deal of coherence in the genre of heavy metal; there are many bands that would be considered metal by virtually all fans. But genres are defined not only through internal features of the artists or the texts but also through commercial strategies and the conflicting valorizations of audiences. These debates over heavy metal are grounded in historical formations of meaning and prestige. To understand the priorities and values of heavy metal musicians and fans, we will need to examine their history.

Casting Heavy Metal

The term "heavy metal" has been applied to popular music since the late 1960s, when it began to appear in the rock press as an adjective; in the early 1970s it became a noun and thus a genre. The spectacular increase in the popularity of heavy metal during the 1980s prompted many critics and scholars of popular music to begin to write metal's history. In histories of rock and of American music, in encyclopedias of popular music, in books and periodicals aimed at the dedicated metal fan or the quizzical outsider, writers began to construct a history of the genre. These historians have all understood their task similarly: they have attempted to define the boundaries of a musical genre and to produce a narrative of the formation and development of that genre, usually in the context of the history of rock music. The best of these histories, such as Philip Bashe's *Heavy Metal Thunder* or Wolf Marshall's articles in *Guitar for the Practicing Musician*, are insightful and lucid, written by journalists with intimate knowledge of the bands and their fans.[22]

Histories typically begin with a problem most writers regard as essential: the question of the origin of the term "heavy metal." The first appearance of "heavy metal" in a song lyric is generally agreed to be in Steppenwolf's "Born to Be Wild," a hit motorcycle anthem of 1968, celebrating the "heavy metal thunder" of life in the fast lane. But the term "heavy metal," we are usually told, had burst into popular consciousness in 1962, with the U.S. publication of William S. Burroughs's novel *Naked Lunch*, a beat junkie's fantasies and confessions of drugs, sleaze, and violent sex. Burroughs is often credited with inventing the term and sometimes even with inspiring the genre. Some sources claim that Steppenwolf lifted the phrase directly from Burroughs's book, although no one has provided any evidence for that link.

This story of the origin of "heavy metal" appears in nearly every recounting of metal's history.[23] It is, however, not only simplistic but wrong, since the phrase "heavy metal" does not actually appear anywhere in *Naked Lunch* (although a later novel by Burroughs, *Nova Express* (1964), introduces as characters "The Heavy Metal Kid" and the "Heavy Metal People of Uranus"). At some point this notion of origin got planted in rock journalism, and the appeal of a clear point of origin led others to perpetuate the error.[24] But as we are reminded by *The Oxford English Dictionary*, "heavy metal" enjoyed centuries of relevant usage as a term for ordnance and poisonous compounds. The longstanding use of the phrase as a technical term in chemistry, metallurgy, and discussions of pollution suggests that the term did not spring full-blown into public awareness from an avant-garde source. "Heavy metal poisoning" is a diagnosis that has long had greater cultural currency than Burroughs's book has had, and the scientific and medical uses of the term "heavy metal" are even cognate, since they infuse the music with values of danger and weight, desirable characteristics in the eyes of late 1960s rock musicians. The evidence suggests that the term circulated long before Steppenwolf or even Burroughs and that its meaning is rich and associative rather than an arbitrary label invented at some moment. Eventually, "heavy metal" began to be used to refer specifically to popular music in the early 1970s, in the writings of Lester Bangs and Dave Marsh at *Creem*.

A heavy metal genealogy ought to trace the music back to African-American blues, but this is seldom done. Just as histories of North America begin with the European invasion, the histories of musical genres such as rock and heavy metal commonly begin at the point of white dominance. But to emphasize Black Sabbath's contribution of occult concerns to rock is to forget Robert Johnson's struggles with the Devil and Howlin' Wolf's meditations on the problem of evil. To trace heavy metal vocal style to Led Zeppelin's Robert Plant is to forget James Brown's "Cold Sweat." To deify white rock guitarists like Eric Clapton or Jimmy Page is to forget the black American musicians they were trying to copy; to dwell on the prowess of these guitarists is to relegate Jimi Hendrix, the most virtuosic rock guitarist of the 1960s, to the fringes of music history. The debt of heavy metal to African-American music making has vanished from most accounts of the genre, just as black history as been suppressed in every other field.

Rock historians usually begin the history of heavy metal with the white (usually British) musicians who were copying urban blues styles. Mid-1960s groups like the Yardbirds, Cream, and the Jeff Beck Group combined the rock and roll style of Chuck Berry with the earthy blues of Muddy Waters and Howlin' Wolf. Along with Jimi Hendrix, these British blues bands developed the sounds that would define metal: heavy drums and bass, virtuosic distorted guitar, and a powerful vocal style that used screams and growls as signs of transgression and transcendence. The Kinks released the first hit song built around power chords in 1964, "You Really Got Me." Some credit Jimi Hendrix with the first real heavy metal hit, the heavily distorted, virtuosic "Purple Haze" of 1967. Blue Cheer, a San Francisco psychedelic band, extended the frontiers of loudness, distortion, and feedback (but not virtuosity) with their defiantly crude cover version of "Summertime Blues," a hit single in 1968, the same year Steppenwolf released "Born to Be Wild."

We had a place in forming that heavy-metal sound. Although I'm not saying we knew what we were doing, 'cause we didn't. All we knew was we wanted more power. And if that's not a heavy-metal attitude, I don't know what is.
—Dick Peterson, singer/bass player with Blue Cheer [25]

These groups of the late 1960s, now identified as early heavy metal bands, favored lyrics that evoked excess and transgression. Some, such as MC5 and Steppenwolf, linked their noisiness to explicit political critique in their lyrics; others, like Blue Cheer, identified with the San Francisco–based psychedelic bands, for whom volume and heaviness aided an often drug-assisted search for alternative formations of identity and community. Inspired by the guitar virtuosity and volume of Jimi Hendrix and Eric Clapton, late 1960s rock bands developed a musical language that used distortion, heavy beats, and sheer loudness to create music that sounded more powerful than any other.[26] Groups like Iron Butterfly and Vanilla Fudge added organ to the musical mix; like the electric guitar, the organ is capable of sustained, powerful sounds as well as virtuosic soloing, and the combination of both resulted in an aural wall of heavy sound. Iron Butterfly's *In-A-Gadda-Da-Vida* (1969), featuring the seventeen-minute title tune with its interminable drum solo, became the biggest-selling album Atlantic Records had ever had. Drummers of the late 1960s hit their drums very hard, resulting in a sound that was not only louder but heavier, more emphatic. Their drum sets grew ever larger and more complicated, along with the expansion of concert amplification and guitar distortion devices.

The sound that would become known as heavy metal was definitively codified in 1970 with the release of *Led Zeppelin II*, Black Sabbath's *Paranoid*, and *Deep Purple in Rock*. Joe Elliot, now lead vocalist for Def Leppard, recalls this moment, which he lived as a young fan: "In 1971, there were only three bands that mattered. Led Zeppelin, Black Sabbath, and Deep Purple."[27] Led Zeppelin's sound was marked by speed and power, unusual rhythmic patterns, contrasting terraced dynamics, singer Robert Plant's wailing vocals, and guitarist Jimmy Page's heavily distorted crunch. Their songs were often built around thematic hooks called riffs, a practice derived from urban blues music and extended by British imitators such as Eric Clapton (e.g., "Sunshine of Your Love").[28] In their lyrics and music, Led Zeppelin added mysticism to hard rock through evocations of the occult, the supernatural, Celtic legend, and Eastern modality. Deep Purple's sound was similar but with organ added and with greater stress on classical influences; Baroque figuration abounds in the solos of guitarist Ritchie Blackmore and keyboardist Jon Lord.[29] Black Sabbath took the emphasis on the occult even further, using dissonance, heavy riffs, and the mysterious whine of vocalist Ozzy Osbourne to evoke overtones of gothic horror.

A "second generation of heavy metal," the first to claim the name unambiguously, was also active throughout the 1970s: Kiss, AC/DC, Aerosmith, Judas Priest, Ted Nugent, Rush, Motörhead, Rainbow, Blue Öyster Cult. Scorpions, from Germany, became the first heavy metal band from a non-English-speaking country to achieve international success. Heavy metal shows became increasingly spectacular as musicians performed in front of elaborate stage sets to the accompaniment of light shows, pyrotechnics, and other special effects. Incessant touring of these impressive shows built the metal audience in the 1970s. Kiss, between 1974 and 1984, made nineteen albums, seventeen of which went gold (thirteen went platinum) with virtually no radio airplay.[30] Many of the most successful performers of heavy metal, like Judas Priest and Iron Maiden, have never had a Top 40 single.

The rise of heavy metal was simultaneous with the rise of professional rock criticism, but their relationship was not cordial. Flushed with enthusiasm for the artistic importance of rock music, critics were deeply suspicious of commercially successful music, which smacked of "sell-out" because it appealed to too many people. Many critics were also hostile toward visual spectacle, which they saw as commercial artifice, compromising rock music's "authenticity." With the exception of some writers at *Creem*, they abhorred the face paint and fantastic costumes of Kiss, the macabre theatricality of Alice Cooper, and the fireworks, smoke, and unearthly props of everyone else in heavy metal. The pronouncements of the critics had little effect on the loyalties of heavy metal fans, for whom the concert experience remained primary: Led Zeppelin's 1973 tour of the United States set new concert attendance records, breaking the previous records held by the Beatles. However, critics contributed to the establishment of heavy metal as a genre, since such labels were useful to them, as they were to the music industry, then in a phase of commercial growth and diversification (including increasingly specialized radio formats).

Heavy metal record sales slumped severely during the second half of the 1970s, as attention shifted to disco, punk, and mainstream rock bands like Fleetwood Mac. Writing for posterity in 1977, Lester Bangs summarized: "As the Seventies drew to a close, it appeared that heavy metal had had it." Bangs described metal's obsolescence: "What little flair and freshness remained in heavy metal has been stolen by punk rockers like the Ramones and Sex Pistols, who stripped it down, sped it up and provided some lyric content beyond the customary macho breast-beatings, by now not only offensive but old-fashioned."[31] Bangs's description of that moment was a fair one, but the 1980s saw the growth of heavy metal on a scale none had imagined.

Heavy Metal in the 1980s

During the 1980s, heavy metal was transformed from the moribund music of a fading subculture into the dominant genre of American music. Eddie Van Halen had revolutionized metal guitar technique with the release of Van Halen's debut album in 1978, fueling a renaissance in electric guitar study and experimentation unmatched since thousands of fans were inspired to learn to play by Eric Clapton's apotheosis in the late 1960s and Jimi Hendrix's death in 1970. But the real boom occurred with what became known as the "new wave of British heavy metal," around the turn of the decade. The United States was overrun by another "British invasion," as important for metal as the Beatles and Rolling Stones had been fifteen years earlier for pop music. Singer Joe Elliot recalls: "As years went on, hard rock did feel a certain loss of popularity with record audiences. But around 1979 or '80, it came back again. Suddenly, there was us [Def Leppard], Iron Maiden and Saxon doing really well."[32] Bands like Iron Maiden and Motörhead exported very different styles of music, but they all were experienced as a wave of renewal for the genre of heavy metal. For the most part, the new wave of metal featured shorter, catchier songs, more sophisticated production techniques, and higher technical standards. All of these characteristics helped pave the way toward greater popular success.

The next wave of metal came out of Los Angeles around 1983–84. Mötley Crüe and Ratt spearheaded a revival of "glam" metal androgyny, and other L.A. bands, like Quiet Riot, Dokken, and W.A.S.P., gained international attention. Southern California emerged as the center of heavy metal music for the 1980s, and bands from other parts of the country, among them Poison and Guns N' Roses, flocked to Los Angeles in hopes of getting signed to a major label contract. In 1983, Def Leppard released *Pyromania*, the album that brought them stardom, leading the metal boom of the following year. In 1983, heavy metal records accounted for only 8 percent of all recordings sold in the United States; one year later, that share had increased phenomenally, to 20 percent.[33] Dokken, Iron Maiden, Mötley Crüe, Ratt, Twisted Sister, and Scorpions rode the crest of this new success.

The following year, bands from around the world joined in the metal boom: Japan's Loudness, Sweden's Europe, and Germany's Scorpions all achieved widespread acceptance, not only in their homelands but also among English-speaking fans. Swedish guitar virtuoso Yngwie Malmsteen had comparatively less commercial success with his albums of 1984–88, but his extension of metal's neoclassical tendencies greatly influenced other heavy metal guitarists. Malmsteen's fusion of heavy metal with Baroque musical rhetoric upped the ante for technical prowess and inspired legions of young imitators.[34] Heavy metal fan magazines proliferated in France (*Hard Force, Hard Rock*), Italy (*HM, Heavy Metal, Rockstar, Flash*), and Germany (*Rock Hard, Horror Infernal, Metalstar, Breakout, Metal Hammer*), just as new magazines appeared in the United States and Britain (*RIP* and many others), and already established rock and pop magazines began focusing exclusively on metal (*Hit Parader, Circus*).

The popularity of heavy metal continued to increase throughout the decade. *Billboard* attributed this trend in the economy of American popular music to a shift in the subcultural support of metal: "Metal has broadened its audience base. Metal music is no longer the exclusive domain of male teenagers. The metal audience has become older (college-aged), younger (pre-teen), and more female."[35] The release of Bon Jovi's third album, *Slippery When Wet*, in 1986 was an important moment in this transformation of the metal audience, for Bon Jovi fused the intensity and heaviness of metal with the romantic sincerity of pop and the "authenticity" of rock, helping to create a huge new gender-balanced audience for heavy metal.[36] Bon Jovi's success not only reshaped metal's musical discourse and sparked imitations and extensions, but it also gained metal substantial radio airplay for the first time. A *Billboard* writer summarized: "Many credit the mass-appeal success of Bon Jovi's 'You Give Love a Bad Name' last summer with opening programmers' ears to the merits of metal. Others give a nod to Motley Crue's "Smokin' in the Boys Room" for dispelling the notion that top 40 and hard rock don't mix. Metal and hard rock have fallen between the programming cracks because of their predominantly teen appeal."[37]

In December 1986, MTV significantly increased the amount of heavy metal it programmed, initiating a special program called "Headbangers' Ball" and putting more metal videos into their regular rotation. The response was tremendous; "Headbangers' Ball" became MTV's most popular show, with 1.3 million viewers each week.[38] Heavy metal's spectacular live shows made it a natural for television, where its important visual dimension could be exploited and presented virtually unchanged. Once heavy metal achieved access to the airwaves, its popularity and influence increased sharply. In June 1987, the number-one album on the *Billboard* charts was by U2, but the next five places were held by metal bands: Whitesnake, Bon Jovi, Poison, Mötley Crüe, and Ozzy Osbourne/Randy Rhoads. For the rest of the decade, metal usually accounted for at least half of the top twenty albums on the charts.[39]

The expansion of the metal scene during the 1980s, however, was accompanied by its fragmentation. Genres proliferated: magazine writers and record marketers began referring to thrash metal, commercial metal, lite metal, power metal, American metal, black (satanic) metal, white (Christian) metal, death metal, speed metal, glam metal—each of which bears a particular relationship to that older, vaguer, more prestigious term "heavy metal."[40] Just as one of the major musical debates of nineteenth-century Europe was over who should be considered Beethoven's musical heir (Wagner versus Brahms), metal bands and fans continually position the music they care about with respect to a lineage dating back to the late 1960s founders: Led Zeppelin, Black Sabbath, and Deep Purple. Though allegiances were often complex and genre boundaries blurred, two main camps formed during the 1980s.

On the one hand, there was the metal of the broad new audience forged during the mid-1980s by bands like Mötley Crüe and Bon Jovi. This was the heavy metal on the sales charts, with radio play, the metal seen on MTV and at huge arena concerts. On the other hand, a different camp disparaged the newfound popularity of what they call lite metal or the music of "posers." These fans and bands attempted to sustain the marginal status metal enjoyed during the 1970s; they shunned the broad popularity that they saw as necessarily linked to musical vapidity and subcultural dispersion. The "underground" metal scene was, until the late 1980s, based in clubs rather than arenas, in subcultural activity rather than mass-mediated identity. Its literature often took the form of local, self-published fanzines instead of slick, full-color, national publications like *Hit Parader* or *Circus*. Sometimes lumped together as "speed metal" or "thrash," these underground styles of metal tended to be more deliberately transgressive, violent, and noisy.

The thrash metal style coalesced in the San Francisco Bay area and Los Angeles in the early 1980s, with groups like Metallica, Slayer, Testament, Exodus, Megadeth, and Possessed. The musicians who created thrash were influenced by both heavy metal and punk; Motörhead, an important pioneer of speed metal, has played for both punk and metal audiences since the 1970s. The punk influence shows up in the music's fast tempos and frenetic aggressiveness and in critical or sarcastic lyrics delivered in a menacing growl. From heavy metal, thrash musicians took an emphasis on guitar virtuosity, which is usually applied more generally to the whole band. Thrash bands negotiate fast tempos, meter changes, and complicated arrangements with precise ensemble coordination. Speed metal was in part a reaction against the spectacular dimension of other metal styles; thrash bands appealed to "a new generation for whom Zeppelin and Sabbath were granddads but Quiet Riot and Mötley Crüe were too glam."[41] However, though it is often compared to punk rock because of its speed, noise, and violence, thrash metal contrasts with punk's simplicity and nihilism, both lyrically and musically. The Ramones and the Sex Pistols placed musical amateurism at the aesthetic core of punk rock; but to be considered metal, bands must demonstrate some amount of virtuosity and control.

Bubbling underground since the mid-1970s, thrash or speed metal broke through to the surface of popular music in the late 1980s, with successful major-label releases by Metallica, Megadeth, Anthrax, and Slayer, at that time the Big Four of thrash metal.[42] The breakthrough came in 1986, when Metallica's *Master of Puppets*, their first album on a major record label, began to receive the acclaim that would make it thrash metal's first platinum album. Metallica's success sparked increased interest in speed metal among the major record companies, who developed promotional tactics to help bring underground bands to mainstream attention. Until then, speed metal bands had recorded on independent labels like Combat, Megaforce, and Metal Blade, relying on a loyal underground of fans to spread the word. In 1989, MTV sponsored their "Headbanger's Ball Tour," which gained wide exposure for Anthrax, Exodus, and Helloween.

By the end of the decade, thrash metal had successfully challenged the mainstream of metal and redefined it. Metallica and a few other bands were able to headline arena concerts and appear regularly on MTV, although radio play remained incommensurate with their popularity. Other styles of metal coexisted, despite a slump in heavy metal record and ticket sales in 1990, which was explained by music industry figures as the result of the economic recession and overexploitation of the metal market—too many bands signed, too many records released, too many concert tours—as the industry scrambled to cash in on the boom of the late 1980s.[43]

Throughout the 1980s, the influence of heavy metal on other kinds of popular music was pervasive and substantial. On what became the best-selling record of all time, Michael Jackson (or his producer Quincy Jones) brought in guitarist Eddie Van Halen for a cameo heavy metal solo on the song "Beat It" (1982). Just as Jackson and Jones used Vincent Price's voice on "Thriller," on the same album, to invoke the scary thrills of horror films, Van Halen's noisy, virtuosic solo fit well in a song about danger and transgression. As the 1980s went on, heavy metal guitar sounds became well enough known to be used in all sorts of contexts, to evoke danger, intensity, and excitement. Rappers Run-D.M.C. brought metal guitar into hip hop in 1986 with their remake of Aerosmith's "Walk This Way," and Tōne Lōc had a huge hit in 1989 with "Wild Thing," a rap song built around guitar and drum licks digitally sampled from a song on Van Halen's first album. Pop stars frequently used metal guitar sounds to construct affective intensity and control, as in Robert Palmer's "Simply Irresistible." By the middle of the decade, metal sounds had begun appearing often in advertising jingles. Even ads for the U.S. Army ("Be All That You Can Be") featured metal guitar in a kind of subliminal seduction: military service was semiotically presented as an exciting, oppositional, youth-oriented adventure. Rebel, escape, become powerful: join the army!

Like the boundaries of the genre, the history of heavy metal is widely contested. In October 1988, MTV conducted a survey of its viewers, asking the question "What was the first metal band?" The bands most often named were Led Zeppelin, Kiss, Alice Cooper, Black Sabbath, and Metallica. The first of these is not a surprising choice; the others perhaps are. But Kiss and Alice Cooper did found that type of heavy metal that is heavily dependent on spectacle, while Black Sabbath initiated dark metal, oriented toward the occult. Even the choice of Metallica can be understood, as it was that band that brought speed metal to the attention of a wide audience.

The ancestors chosen by fans and musicians reflect the characteristics of metal they valorize. Some want to connect metal closely to the history of rock music, while others emphasize that metal is something new and original. Heavy metal vocalist Dee Snider stresses connections to rock's roots and an "authenticity" grounded in protest: "Heavy metal is the only form of music that still retains the rebellious qualities of '50s rock and roll."[44] Responding to the common perception of technological mediation as artifice and commercial mediation as ideological compromise, critics sometimes minimize metal's musical and technical complexity:

While modern musical technology continued to gather praise from the elite caught up in its spell, a special breed of musicians remained true to "the roots." Instead of layering their sound with electronics, they chose to TURN IT UP! Rock and Roll, they said, was raw and gritty; a means of escape; an uncomplicated element whose purpose was to entertain. Those groups, the survivors, upheld "the roots" in their original form, delivered at blistering volume, filled with urgency and fury. They earned the title Heavy Metal.[45]

Here metal fans are hailed as hardheaded realists, members of a grass-roots community unswayed by the false hype that has lured "the elite" away from the clear purpose and simple means of early rock. Yet such explanations obscure aspects of metal that are equally important and collapse tensions that are mediated by metal, for much heavy metal places a great premium on virtuosity and innovation, on spectacle, on effects that can be created only with the help of very sophisticated technology. Heavy metal history, its genre distinctions, and the interpretation of its texts and practices all depend upon the ways in which metal is used and made meaningful by fans.

Headbangers

I Metallari di Salerno Salutano i Metallari di Firenze —Graffito scrawled
on the Uffizi Museum in Florence, July 1989.[46]

Who is the audience for heavy metal? As recently as 1985, *Billboard* asserted that heavy metal fans were still most concentrated in "the blue-collar industrial cities of the continental U.S."[47] A different marketing study, conducted at about the same time, concluded that the metal audience lived in "upscale family suburbs."[48] Probably both are correct; class background correlates, to some extent, with preferences for different kinds of metal, but heavy metal in the 1980s claimed a huge audience that overruns these categories. And they are an active audience; the fans I surveyed claimed, on the average, to buy a new metal recording every week, even though many of them have little money.[49] Heavy metal fans are loyal concertgoers, too; many metal bands, long denied radio airplay, have built their audiences through touring, and according to *Billboard*, metal "attracts a greater proportion of live audiences than any other contemporary music form."[50]

Fans of heavy metal are also, overwhelmingly, white. Neither the lyrics nor the fans are noticeably more racist than is normal in the United States; in fact, the enthusiasm of many fans for black or racially mixed bands, like Living Colour and King's X, and their reverence for Jimi Hendrix suggest the opposite. If few African-Americans have been attracted to heavy metal, it is probably due in part to the genre's history. For heavy metal began as a white remake of urban blues that often ripped off black artists and their songs shamelessly. If the motive for much white music making has been the imperative of reproducing black culture without the black people in it, no comparable reason exists to draw black musicians and fans into traditionally white genres. Heavy metal has remained a white-dominated discourse, apparently offering little to those who have been comfortable with African-American musical traditions. Moreover, it has been transformed into something quite different from its blues origins. Metal's relatively rigid sense of the body and concern with dominance reflect European-American transformation of African-American musical materials and cultural values. At the end of the 1980s, though, musical interactions among metal, rap, rock, and funk became increasingly popular, perhaps presaging at least a partial breakdown of the racial lines that often separate music audiences (hip hop has already accomplished this to a considerable extent).

To begin assembling some information about metal fans and to make contacts for later interviews, I distributed questionnaires to fans at several concerts and through a record store.[51] The fans I surveyed ranged in age from eleven to thirty-one years, with an average age of nineteen. This reflects the specific demographics of concert audiences, rather than magazine readers or record buyers, for example; a survey done in 1984 found that two thirds of heavy metal fans were between the ages of sixteen and twenty-four; one fifth were under fifteen.[52] My sample, like the actual crowds I saw, was almost evenly balanced in gender. Their occupations ranged from car wash attendant to law school student, from computer programmer to construction worker. Their parents' occupations covered the whole gamut of working- and middle-class jobs, with the exception of one sample, collected in a bar in Detroit, which was entirely industrial working class.

The questionnaire began with items intended to pique the curiosity of the fans, such as queries about how long they have listened to heavy metal and how many hours each day, on the average, they hear metal. Further questions concerned subcultural activities, such as watching MTV's "Headbanger's Ball" or reading fan magazines. Eventually, I asked more personal questions about age, occupation, gender, and parents' occupations. At the very end of the form, most fans indicated that they were willing to be interviewed and provided their names and phone numbers.

I am making no claims for the statistical precision of my sample— I used it as a source of guidance and contacts with fans—but I will summarize the responses I found clear and useful. Nearly all of the fans said that most of their friends were also metal fans, an indication of the centrality of heavy metal to fans' social lives. More listen to metal from recordings than from radio programming, confirming the importance of the fan activities of owning, collecting, and being knowledgeable about the music (and the paucity of metal programming on the radio). Nearly all fans sing along with heavy metal lyrics, suggesting that, however unintelligible they may sound to outsiders, lyrics are comprehended by fans. Although this contradicts some academic studies, it agrees with Iron Maiden guitarist Steve Harris's observation that in the United States, "about 90% of the fans know the words to every song." [53]

There were substantial differences among the audiences I surveyed. Compared to the fans at a Poison concert, for example, Judas Priest fans were somewhat older and more likely to be male. While quite a few of the Poison crowd indicated that they play musical instruments, a clear majority of the Judas Priest sample played instruments and owned musical equipment. The Poison fans called "Top 40" their second favorite style of music, while Priest's fans chose classical music as the runner-up to metal. One section of the questionnaire (which many fans told me was their favorite part) invited fans to indicate whether or not they considered various bands to be "heavy metal." Judas Priest fans clustered around other hard metal bands, like Iron Maiden and Metallica, while Poison's fans extended the genre label to Bon Jovi and Mötley Crüe as well.

There was much overall agreement about why heavy metal was important. To avoid asking fans to compose brief explanations of complex feelings at the drop of a hat, I developed a list of plausible statements about metal from my study of fans, magazines, and music. I included a wide range of possibilities, including some that were mutually contradictory; fans were asked to check those with which they most agreed:

——It's the most powerful kind of music; it makes me feel powerful.
——It's intense; it helps me work off my frustrations.
——The guitar solos are amazing; it takes a great musician to play metal.
——I can relate to the lyrics.
——It's music for people like me; I fit in with a heavy metal crowd.
——It's pissed-off music, and I'm pissed off.
——It deals with things nobody else will talk about.
——It's imaginative music; I would never have thought of some of those things.
——It's true to life; it's music about real important issues.
——It's not true to life; it's fantasy, better than life.

There was solid concurrence that the intensity and power of the music, its impressive guitar solos, the relevance of its lyrics, and its truth value were crucial. Surprisingly, fans overwhelmingly rejected the categories of the pissed-off and the fantastic. The most common grounds for dismissal of heavy metal—that it embodies nothing more than adolescent rebellion and escapism—were the qualities least often chosen by fans as representative of their feelings.[54] Megadeth's video for "Peace Sells . . . But Who's Buying?" makes this point explicitly. A young headbanger is watching metal videos when his father interrupts: "What is this garbage you're watching? I want to watch the news." The dad brusquely changes the channel but his son switches it back, explaining: "This *is* the news."

While the responses to my questionnaire cannot be taken as transparent explanations of heavy metal's social functions, they are revealing of the ways in which fans make sense of their own responses, as are the collective understandings developed by fans through their involvement with magazines, friendships, and fan clubs. Besides the separate fan clubs surrounding each band (which are usually not clubs as much as marketing lists) there exist social clubs for particular groups of metal fans, from the Gay Metal Society in Chicago to the Headbanger Special Interest Group of American Mensa. Clubs usually publish their own newsletters (GMA puts out *The Headbanger*, and the Mensa group calls theirs *Vox Metallum*); they also sponsor social events and promote discussion of metal and related issues. Such internal analyses of heavy metal culture contrast sharply with most discussions by outsiders.

"Nasty, Brutish, and Short"? Rock Critics and Academics Evaluate Metal

Heavy metal: pimply, prole, putrid, unchic, unsophisticated, antiintellectual
(but impossibly pretentious), dismal, abysmal, terrible, horrible, and
stupid music, barely music at all. . . music made *by* slack-jawed, alpaca-haired,
bulbous-inseamed imbeciles in jackboots and leather and chrome *for* slack-
jawed, alpaca-haired, downy-mustachioed imbeciles in cheap, too-large
T-shirts with pictures of comic-book Armageddon ironed on the front. . . .
Heavy metal, mon amour, where do I start?   —Robert Duncan [55]

Heavy metal has rarely been taken seriously, either as music or as cultural activity of any complexity or importance. At best it is controversial;
the enthusiasm of metal fan magazines is paralleled by the hysterical denunciation of the mainstream press and smug dismissals of most rock
journalism. And like country music, metal is a genre that rarely inspires
uncertainty in its critics; though few commentators lay claim to much
knowledge or understanding of the music or its fans, such ignorance
is seldom allowed to hinder confident judgment of both as simple and
brutal. Even critics and academics who are scrupulous in distinguishing
among the details of other genres display unabashed prejudice when it
comes to heavy metal.

For example, the only reference to metal in a recent book on the rock
music industry is this casual summation: "Today's 'hot' rock is heavy
metal, this generation's disco, an apolitical sound more concerned with
the conquest of women than the triumph of the spirit." [56] Another new
book on rock music offers nothing but heavy metal's bottom line, apparently so obvious as to require neither evidence nor even argument:
"This is not a music of hope, and in no way is it a music of real freedom,
because it firmly rejects the possibility of actual change. . . . the rules
of the form have been established . . . they cannot be violated." Moreover, the author assumes that the credibility of this judgment will be
unaffected by his nonchalant admission: "I don't know anything about
heavy metal." [57] Articles on heavy metal in news magazines, like the infamous *Newsweek* conflation of metal and rap as "the culture of attitude,"
usually replicate the same combination of derogatory stereotypes and
blithe ignorance. In an advertisement for their special issue on teenagers,
Newsweek located them in "the age of AIDS, crack, and heavy metal." [58]

Those rock critics who actually do know the music have rarely written
anything about it that its enemies haven't already said. Robert Duncan's vivid description of heavy metal, quoted above, defiantly celebrates
an outsider's fearful view of metal. But his defense is superficial, never
really taking the metal seriously as music or politics; he ends up mutter-

ing about "draining of hope," "deadening of passion," metal as "anaesthetic."[59] Chuck Eddy's guide to the five hundred best metal albums is filled with virtuosic style analysis; ultimately, though, Eddy seems envious of a nihilism he thinks he sees in heavy metal but that he could never quite dare to embrace.[60] Charles M. Young says fondly: "Heavy metal is transitional music, infusing dirtbags and worthless puds with the courage to grow up and be a dickhead."[61] Young makes some good comments about how metal creates feelings of equality and worth, but lacking analysis of musical and social tensions, his article is much better at asking questions than answering them. Other than Philip Bashe's useful history and some fine analytical and historical articles in guitar players' magazines, rock journalists have published relatively few insights about heavy metal.[62]

Academics have achieved much less. The academic study of popular music is in transition; scholarship of recent popular music has until recently been dominated by sociological approaches that totally neglect the music of popular music, reducing the meaning of a song to the literal meaning of its lyrics. This is called "content" analysis, and it assumes that an outside reader will interpret lyrics just as an insider would; it also assumes a linear communication model, where artists encode meanings that are transmitted to listeners, who then decipher them, rather than a dialectical environment in which meanings are multiple, fluid, and negotiated. Parallel to this, it presumes a Parsonian view of society, wherein social systems tend toward a natural equilibrium, instead of seeing society in permanent flux, as various groups strive for equality or dominance. Most writing about popular music also suffers from a lack of history; with little sense of how music has functioned in other times and places, writers often mistake transformations of ongoing features of popular music for unprecedented signs of innovation or decay. Also, most sociological studies offer no integration of ethnographic and textual analytic strategies. Mass mediation is typically assumed to be a barrier, standing between artist and audience with the power to corrupt both. But while it is crucial to acknowledge that mass mediation functions to disrupt a sense of history and community, it is just as important to see how it can make available the resources with which new communities are built.[63]

Quite a few "content analyses" of heavy metal lyrics have been published. Usually, the researchers who conduct such studies evince an obliviousness to power relationships, which they regard as "objectivity." They may interview fans at school, with no thought to the constraints on articulation that are already in place in that setting. Students have little motivation to admit to knowledge of lyrics of which their teachers or parents would not approve, and researchers are too willing to see teen-agers as inarticulate. For example, Prinsky and Rosenbaum concluded that recent efforts at censorship of rock lyrics are misguided because fans are too dumb to know what the lyrics mean.[64] Their study not only ignored the constraints imposed by the classroom environment and the estrangement caused by the researchers' own "objectivity"; it also im-plicitly assumed that adults would do better, without considering that classical music audiences, for example, would probably be even less likely to be able to summarize song texts to their satisfaction. Many opera fans prefer not to know what the lyrics are, and the hermeneutic frame-work promoted by schools and concert halls emphasizes appreciation of sensuous beauty over understanding of meanings.

In another study, Hansen and Hansen assumed that the "themes" of heavy metal (sex, suicide, violence, and the occult, as they saw them) were obvious at the beginning of the experiment. Thus they chose songs they thought fit each category and had four undergraduate research as-sistants grade heavy metal fans' understanding of the lyrics. For example, after reading two lines from Ozzy Osbourne's "Suicide Solution"—"Evil thoughts and evil doings / Cold, alone you hang in ruins"—fans were asked "What does 'hang in ruins' mean?" The correct answer was "His life is a mess; every aspect of his world is in shambles." Thus Hansen and Hansen reduced a haunting image to a platitude, made it sexist by inserting a male pronoun, and went on to generate an aston-ishing array of tables of data. Their study is framed by the assumptions that the music of heavy metal is irrelevant (they refer to "distractive influences produced by the music itself"); that images can be reduced to singular, literal meanings; that such meanings exist apart from the contexts of their reception; that sociologists and college students under-stand heavy metal better than metal fans do; that "correct comprehen-sion" of lyrics is a measure of the seriousness and worth of a musical genre or a cultural activity. Hansen and Hansen were arrogantly "ob-jective"; their study tells us nothing about heavy metal because their premises produced their results.[65]

The growing impact of British cultural studies and new approaches to musicology has so far had disappointingly little effect on the study of rock music, despite the appearance of several pieces on heavy metal that claim that influence. In one of the earliest academic articles about heavy metal, Will Straw argued in 1984 that metal fans do not comprise a subculture because fans don't engage in subcultural activities, such as record collecting and magazine reading, and because there are no intermediate strata between fans and stars, which indicated little chance for participation. All of these assertions are contradicted by my research, although it is possible that Straw's assessment may have been partially true of heavy metal at an earlier moment. It is difficult to know how much credence to give to his arguments, however, since Straw gives no evidence of ever having read a fan magazine, talked with a fan, attended a concert, or even listened to a record. The first published version of his paper "explained" heavy metal as an epiphenomenon of record industry shifts, thus removing politics and agency from the activities of everyone except record industry executives.[66]

Marcus Breen has offered an explanation of heavy metal that combines the worst characteristics of postmodern theorizing. For Breen, metal celebrates numbness and oblivion; it is "a joyride into the spirit of post-industrial alienation."[67] Such conclusions are possible because Breen's analysis is equally unhampered by musical analysis and ethnography. In an amazing flight of fancy, he imagines that when Axl Rose sang, "I want to see you bleed" (in "Welcome to the Jungle"), he might have been referring to menstruation. Lacking any understanding of how heavy metal could be a vehicle for meaning, he concludes that its popularity is due to the "modern marketing and selling methods" of a show business cabal.

Late in 1991, the first book-length academic study of heavy metal was published, Deena Weinstein's *Heavy Metal*.[68] Weinstein is a sociologist, and her book has all of the virtues and faults of most strictly sociological studies of popular culture. It carefully summarizes the details of concert behavior, describing the icons and activities of metal fans and musicians. But Weinstein has nothing useful to say about the music of heavy metal, and her perspective is a familiar Parsonian one, grounded in "taste publics" and structural positions. "Music is the master emblem of the heavy metal subculture," she asserts, a tribute that makes the latter static and trivializes the former. In fact, Weinstein regards the music as but a distraction from analysis; when she teaches about heavy metal, she no longer makes tapes available, giving her students only lyrics to work with.[69]

Though her book is nothing if not an impassioned defense of heavy metal, Weinstein, as a sociologist, must aspire to "objectivity," and she even disingenuously claims not to be joining in debates over whether metal is good or bad.[70] Weinstein's attempt to efface her own participation in heavy metal (she has long been a fan) results in a particularly strange gap in the book's coverage, for she virtually ignores women's responses to heavy metal. Moreover, her objectivity fosters a peculiar sort of arrogance: she brags of having browbeaten one fan into admitting that his understanding of some metal lyrics was inadequate.[71] Her stance hampers her social analysis seriously, for she rarely moves beyond descriptions of the pleasures of metal—musical ecstasy, pride in subcultural allegiance, male bonding—toward placing the activities of fans in the political contexts that make such pleasures possible.

It is not suprising that academics have ignored or misconstrued heavy metal, although it seems curious that few professional rock critics have found anything interesting to say about what was, in the 1980s, the most popular genre of rock music. For many academics, denigration of metal is a necessary part of the defense of "high" culture, while for rock critics it is as an easy route to hipness: their scorn is displayed as a badge of their superiority to the musicians and audiences of heavy metal. All see metal as a travesty of various dearly held myths: about authenticity, beauty, and culture, on the one hand, and authenticity, rebellion, and political critique on the other. If neither academics nor rock critics have had much impact on metal's popularity with its fans, they have helped to shape the dominant stereotype of heavy metal as brutishly simple, debilitatingly negative and violent, and artistically monotonous and impoverished. Thus it is necessary to examine their views criticially in order to clear space for a different sort of account of heavy metal.

For both careless condemnations and flip celebrations can have serious effects: especially since the mid-1980s, heavy metal has been at the center of debates over censorship. Rock critics and academics have the power to sway public opinion on issues of real consequence, for their access to effective and prestigious channels of mass mediation makes their opinions more influential than the writings of fans and musicians. It is clear from the ongoing public furor that attends metal that this music matters: around it coalesce cultural crises in authority, threats of breakdowns in the reproduction of social relations and identities.[72] Besides the sociological significance of heavy metal as a phenomenon that absorbs the time, energy, thoughts, and cash of millions of people, it is a site of explicit social contestation that can tell us much about contemporary American society. As with country music, such critical dismissals as I have cited are the product of a prejudicial view of metal as something monolithic and crude; many casual condemnations of heavy metal depend upon misunderstanding its complex status as a genre. But the significance of heavy metal, including the opportunities it creates for important debates over social values and policies, makes it imperative to sort out the social and commercial tensions negotiated by heavy metal musicians and fans.

Several recent attacks on heavy metal have made the import of these issues very clear; they will be discussed in greater detail in chapter 5, where I critique several influential denunciations of heavy metal—by Tipper Gore, Joe Stuessy, and others—and propose what I consider more sophisticated explanations of the violent aspects of some metal. My task throughout this book has been to work toward such explanations, and my method is to examine carefully the sounds and images of heavy metal, take seriously fans' statements and activities, and situate metal as an integral part of a social context that is complex, conflicted, and inequitable. This chapter has explored the interests and tensions that have defined "heavy metal" as a genre with a history. In it, I have taken a functional approach to the study of metal, stressing the ways that genres are constituted through social contestation and transformation. The following chapter takes a more structural tack, investigating the specific musical characteristics that underpin heavy metal as a discourse.

CHAPTER TWO

Beyond the Vocals
Toward the Analysis of Popular Musical Discourses

✳

Beyond the vocals, it's the way a guitar makes you feel when
someone hits a particular chord, the way a snare drum is cracked.
—Rob Halford of Judas Priest.[1]

When asked if he thought his mother would approve of his band's lyrics, guitarist Eddie Van Halen replied that he had no idea of what the lyrics were.[2] Many people talk about the "meaning" of a song when what they are really discussing is only the song's lyrics. But verbal meanings are only a fraction of whatever it is that makes musicians and fans respond to and care about popular music. This chapter is a prelude to the musical aspects of the chapters that follow, where heavy metal songs will be analyzed within the context of social practices and ideologies. It is also meant as a contribution to an underdeveloped strain in academic work on popular culture: analysis of the *music* of popular music, in which discussion is grounded in the history and significance of actual musical details and structures, "beyond the vocals." Specifically, it sketches a view of metal as a discourse by analyzing the signifying practices that constitute heavy metal music. But first a more general argument must be advanced: that musical details can be evaluated in relation to interlocked systems of changing practices and that shifting codes constitute the musical discourses that underpin genres.

This chapter has three parts: It begins with discussion of some theoretical bases for the analysis of musical meaning in popular music; then it proceeds to analyze certain generic features of heavy metal and related musical styles, with reference to a single example, a song by Van Halen; finally, a more integrated analysis of that same piece of music appears, as a way of connecting musical details with generically organized social experience.

Genre and Discourse

Nowhere are genre boundaries more fluid than in popular music. Just as it is impossible to point to a perfectly exemplary Haydn symphony, one that fulfills the "norms" in every respect, pieces within a popular genre rarely correspond slavishly to generic criteria. Moreover, musicians are ceaselessly creating new fusions and extensions of popular genres. Yet musical structures and experiences are intelligible only with respect to these historically developing discursive systems. As Fredric Jameson argues,

> *pure* textual exemplifications of a single genre do not exist; and this, not merely because pure manifestations of anything are rare, but . . . because texts always come into being at the intersection of several genres and emerge from the tensions in the latter's multiple force fields. This discovery does not, however, mean the collapse of genre criticism but rather its renewal: we need the specification of the individual "genres" today more than ever, not in order to drop specimens into the box bearing those labels, but rather to map our coordinates on the basis of those fixed stars and to triangulate this specific given textual moment.[3]

Jameson reminds us that genre categories are fluid and that individual texts are never static fulfillments of conventional norms but rather are understood with reference to other texts.

Yet Jameson's concept of genre seems to operate only at the level of texts. We can profitably add to his model Bakhtin's idea of genre as a "horizon of expectations" brought to bear on texts by historically situated readers. Genres are never sui generis; they are developed, sustained, and reformed by people, who bring a variety of histories and interests to their encounters with generic texts. The texts themselves, as they are produced by such historically specific individuals, come to reflect the multiplicities of social existence: in Bakhtin's view, language is irreducibly "heteroglot," and dialogue takes place not only between genres, as Jameson points out, but also within them. Bakhtin contrasts formalistic genre categories with what he calls "speech genres," relatively stable types of utterance. "Each utterance is filled with echoes and reverberations of other utterances to which it is related by the communality of the sphere of speech communication."[4] Thus, we might say that a C major chord has no intrinsic meaning; rather, it can signify in different ways in different discourses, where it is contextualized by other signifiers, its own history as a signifier, and the social activities in which the discourse participates.

Simon Frith has recently called for renewed genre analysis of popular music, at the same time that he has asserted that "we still do not know nearly enough about the musical language of pop and rock: rock critics still avoid technical analysis, while sympathetic musicologists, like Wilfrid Mellers, use tools that can only cope with pop's nonintentional (and thus least significant) qualities."[5] These two needs are connected, for delineating musical parameters may be the best way to distinguish genres, and genre conventions, in turn, can help us to place the significance of musical details. The challenge is to analyze signification dialectically, working between the levels of specific details and generic categories toward social meanings.

Heavy metal seems particularly appropriate terrain for such methods. As it has gained in popularity, metal has grown in stylistic innovation and pluralism. The term "heavy metal" is now used to designate a great variety of musical practices and ideological stances. Moreover, metal has contributed to the development of many discursive "fusions": metal-influenced pop, rock, rap, funk, and so on. But as Jameson argues, the proliferation of styles within a genre and the concomitant lessened capacity of the norms to explain divergent practices do not mean that genre is no longer a fruitful analytical category. On the contrary, the recent expansion and diversification of heavy metal musical practices and their audiences make it all the more imperative to map the norms that make such fusions and transformations intelligible.[6]

The analytical notion of discourse enables us to pursue an integrated investigation of musical and social aspects of popular music.[7] By approaching musical genres as discourses, it is possible to specify not only certain formal characteristics of genres but also a range of understandings shared among musicians and fans concerning the interpretation of those characteristics. The concept of discourse enables us to theorize beyond the artificial division of "material reality" and consciousness. Discourses are constituted by conventions of practice and interpretation, and, as John Fiske puts it, "Conventions are the structural elements of genre that are shared between producers and audiences. They embody the crucial ideological concerns of the time in which they are popular and are central to the pleasures a genre offers its audience." Genre, then, is "a means of constructing both the audience and the reading subject: its work in the economic domain is paralleled by its work in the domain of culture; that is, its work in influencing which meanings . . . are preferred by, or proffered to, which audiences."[8]

Traditionally, only language has been thought to be discursive. But recent usage has opened up the concept of discourse to refer to any socially produced way of thinking or communicating. The literary critic Tzvetan Todorov has analyzed the relationship of genre and discourse in a way that helps clarify the relevance of these terms to music.[9] Building on Bakhtin's theory of speech genres, Todorov argues that discourses are made up not of sentences but of utterances. That is, they are constituted not of abstract rules or patterns but of the concrete deployment of such abstractions in real social contexts. Sentences are transformed into utterances by being articulated among themselves in a given sociocultural context. For music, this implies that any formal or syntactical patterns an analyst may recognize must be interpreted as abstractions from utterances or speech acts that can only be said to have meaning in particular, socially grounded ways.

Genres, according to Todorov, arise from metadiscursive discourse. The discussion in chapter 1 of the competing definitions and understandings of heavy metal promoted by fans, business interests, critics, and others was meant to demonstrate precisely this point. It is from the discourse about discourses that concepts of genre are formed, transformed, and defended. Genres then come to function as horizons of expectation for readers (or listeners) and as models of composition for authors (or musicians). Most important, Todorov argues that genres exist because societies collectively choose and codify the acts that correspond most closely to their ideologies. A society's discourses depend upon its linguistic (or musical) raw materials and upon its historically circumscribed ideologies. Discourses are formed, maintained, and transformed through dialogue; speakers learn from and respond to others, and the meanings of their utterances are never permanently fixed, cannot be found in a dictionary. Thus, the details of a genre and its very presence or absence among various social groups can reveal much about the constitutive features of a society.

Like genres and discourses, musical meanings are contingent but never arbitrary. There is never any *essential* correspondence between particular musical signs or processes and specific social meanings, yet such signs and processes would never circulate if they did not produce such meanings. Musical meanings are always grounded socially and historically, and they operate on an ideological field of conflicting interests, institutions, and memories. If this makes them extremely difficult to analyze, it does so by forcing analysis to confront the complexity and antagonism of culture. This is a poststructural view of music in that it sees all signification as provisional, and it seeks for no essential truths inherent in structures, regarding all meanings as produced through the interaction of texts and readers. It goes further in suggesting that subjectivity is constituted not only through language, as Lacan and others have argued, but through musical discourses as well. Musical details and structures are intelligible only as traces, provocations, and enactments of power relationships. They articulate meanings in their dialogue with other discourses past and present and in their engagement with the hopes, fears, values, and memories of social groups and individuals. Musical analysis is itself the representation of one discourse in terms of another, the point being to illuminate the social contexts in which both circulate.

Many critics and historians of rock music have been dismissive of any sort of musical analysis. Peter Wicke, for example, claims: "Rock songs are not art songs, whose hidden meaning should be sought in their form and structure."[10] Wicke is right to be dubious of the sort of reductive musicological analysis that simply abstracts and labels technical features, but he is wrong to assume that the specific details of rock music are insignificant. He accepts uncritically a highly problematic dichotomy when he argues, "Rock is not received through the critical apparatus of contemplation, of consideration by visual and aural means; its reception is an active process, connected in a practical way with everyday life."[11] To argue that critical scrutiny of the details of rock music is inappropriate because people don't hear that way is like arguing that we can't analyze the syntax of language because people don't know that they're using gerunds and participles. But more important, reception of *all* music is "connected in a practical way with everyday life," however hard some people may work to hide the social meanings of their music. The danger of musical analysis is always that social meanings and power struggles become the forest that is lost for the trees of notes and chords. The necessity of musical analysis is that those notes and chords represent the differences that make some songs seem highly meaningful and powerful and others boring, inept, or irrelevant.[12]

The split between academic contemplation and popular understanding is not a function of repertoires but rather of interpretive ideologies. As recent musicological colonizations of jazz and even rock have shown, any cultural text can be made over into a monument of neutralized order. But too many analysts of popular music are unaware of the extent to which this process has already remade what is now "classical" music. They assume that traditional musicological methods are simply appropriate for the traditional musicological repertoire and that popular musics do not warrant such analysis. Yet much recent work in musicology has been directed toward undoing the formalist depoliticization of classical music. The problem is not with musical analysis per se but with the implicit or explicit ideological context within which such analysis is conducted. Rock songs, like all discourse, do have meanings that can be discovered through analysis of their form and structure, but such analysis is useful only if it is grounded culturally and historically and if it acknowledges its interests forthrightly.

This is where I differ from most semioticians of music. Jean-Jacques Nattiez, for example, might agree with much of what I have asserted thus far, but there are two important divergences.[13] First, his concern is primarily metadiscursive; he seems more interested in debating definitions and concepts than in analyzing actual music and musical activities. Second, while Nattiez recognizes the conventional basis of semiological meanings, he seems to want to retain some sort of absolute notion of truth, against which interpretations can be measured. That is, he stops short of recognizing the conventional basis of semiology itself; he is unwilling to acknowledge the ultimate grounding of analytical credibility in nothing more absolute or less complex than social contestation, institutional prestige, and power. But there can be no meaningful semiology apart from ethnographic inquiry, historical analysis, and argumentation about culture. There is no way to decide what something means without making a political statement. Underpinning all semiotic analysis is, recognized or not, a set of assumptions about cultural practice, for ultimately music doesn't have meanings; people do. There is no essential, foundational way to ground musical meaning beyond the flux of social existence. Ultimately, musical analysis can be considered credible only if it helps explain the significance of musical activities in particular social contexts.

Some semioticians and philosophers of language, such as David Lidov and Mark Johnson, have worked to ground discursive meanings somatically, in terms of (socially constructed) bodily gestures, tensions, and postures.[14] In *The Body in the Mind*, philosopher Mark Johnson argues that meanings of all sorts, even the ones that seem most abstract and mental, are grounded in bodily experience. While Johnson's own analyses of artworks are rather simplistic, his epistemological challenge to the Western mind/body split is important. Human experiences of meaningfulness, Johnson argues, are grounded at the level of prelinguistic structures which organize our experience and comprehension, which he calls "image schemata." These schemata are not concepts; they are patterns of *activity*, fundamental mechanisms of meaning production that inform the more abstract operations of language and conceptual thinking. Johnson argues that metaphor links these bodily image schemata to language. Metaphor, in this view, occupies a central place in the production of human meaning. It is not merely a kind of poetic expression or a literary figure of speech; rather, metaphor is a crucial process for generating meaning, whereby we come to understand one area of experience in terms of another.[15] It is by means of metaphor that image-schematic structures are extended, transformed, and elaborated into domains of meaning that may seem less directly tied to the body, including language, abstract reasoning, and, I would argue, music.

Attempts to explain "music as metaphor" have appeared with some regularity, but metaphorical interpretations appear to many scholars to be arbitrary: the images you describe in response to a piece of music may be wholly unlike those I would use, and a positivistic orientation would then declare meaning, in this sense, subjective and out of bounds. In rebuttal to what he calls the Objectivist rejection of metaphor, Johnson stresses that meanings at the level of image schemata and metaphor are grounded in physical and social experience that is *shared*. He argues that image schemata *"can have a public, objective* character . . . , because they are recurring structures of embodied human understanding."[16] Johnson presents his theory of image schemata and metaphoric links as a solution to what he sees as the false dichotomy between objectivist absolutism and "anything goes" relativism. That is, meanings are neither objectively inherent nor subjectively arbitrary; they arise out of human experiences of social interaction with a material world.

As Johnson acknowledges, experiences of the body differ with place, time, and culture; musical meaning can be situated in bodily experience not in any essentialist way, then, but as a reciprocal element in a "web of culture" in which real human bodies are ensnared and supported. Yet even such theorizing cannot ground meaning "below" the level of discourse, for the body and the physical world cannot be experienced or thought outside of discourse. If musical gestures are experienced as physical or emotional gestures, these experiences are dependent on the discursive operation of the concepts and metaphors that make all of these terms meaningful.

In an important intervention in the field of the cognitive psychology of music, John A. Sloboda argues that while some responses to music seem to be consistent across cultures—fast and loud is perceived as arousing, slow and soft as soothing—listeners within a culture can generally agree upon finer readings of the "emotional character" even of pieces they have never heard before. Thus, musical meanings are neither a matter of "conditioning" through nonmusical associations nor of aggregative perception of atomized sound events—both influential formulations in the field. Rather, Sloboda's arguments point toward the utility of discourse as a way of conceiving of the musical production of meaning.[17]

Even while they try to map the terms of a discourse, analysts must keep in mind that a variety of interpretations of musical texts is always possible, for popularity among various audiences arises both from the polysemy of texts and conventions—their potential to mean different things to different people—and from what Bakhtin calls their heteroglossia: their reproduction of multiple discourses and social voices. That is, signs are always susceptible to various interpretations because meanings can never be absolutely fixed. But because the social world is not monolithic, discourses inevitably structure in plural and contradictory meanings; many meanings are contained within any text. And the more popular a text is, the more likely it is to be found relevant in different ways. As Dee Snider of Twisted Sister says of the song "We're Not Gonna Take It," "It's very general—we weren't specific about just what it is we aren't taking—work, school, whatever—so you can apply it to anything you want."[18] And in fact the song has found unexpected utility as the theme song of several workers' strikes.[19]

However, the fact that ideas can be fairly consistently communicated, regardless of the nuances of individual response, is what points to the importance of musical discourses as coherent systems of signification. The range of possible interpretations may be theoretically infinite, but in fact certain preferred meanings tend to be supported by those involved with a genre, and related variant meanings are commonly negotiated. As Fiske says, the text "establishes the boundaries of the arena within which the struggle for meaning can occur."[20] So while meanings are negotiated, discourse constructs the terms of the negotiation. Genres such as heavy metal are sites where seemingly stable discourses temporarily organize the exchange of meanings. In practice, subcultural and other social alignments play a large role in channeling the reception of popular music. For music is not just a symbolic register for what really happens elsewhere; it is itself a material, social practice, wherein subject positions are constructed and negotiated, social relations are enacted and transgressed, and ideologies are developed and interrogated.[21]

Musical discourses constantly cross national boundaries and revise cultural boundaries, but they signify variously in different contexts. For example, a friend gave me a tape of Pokolgep, a Hungarian heavy metal band, and I discovered that their music is very different from that of the bands that are popular in the United States. It sounds oppressive, lacking what I've called the heavy metal dialectic; the guitar solos, which are fewer than is normal in U.S. and British metal, offer no escape, no transcendence. The guitars don't contribute transgressive fills (harmonics, bent notes, etc.), and the mood is very controlled and mechanical. No harmonic momentum is ever built up; progressions are heavily grounded by dominant chords, which are rare in Western metal. The lyrics, which my friend translated for me, are poignant and desperate, speaking eloquently of a state of alienation where there is no future, no past, no freedom, no security, and also no hope, no fantastic transcendence, no dreams of anything better. The lyrics recount youthful and historical pain but, along with the music, suggest no youthful exuberance, no energetic defiance. I don't know the context well enough to assert that the implications of this reading are correct; what seems clear is that the international conventions of heavy metal have been strongly inflected by the particular ideological needs of a local community.

Musical meaning, then, has more or less broad social bases and constituencies upon which interpretation is dependent, as well as its associated political economies, the commercial contexts that organize all stages of production and consumption. The latter field has been extensively analyzed by scholars of popular music;[22] what has been relatively neglected is the problem of just how popular musical texts produce meaning and how such meanings operate not only within the contexts of political economies but also within social history and lived experience. Specific musical analysis is important because music is social practice. Music and society are not just related phenomena; music is a type of social activity and a register of such experience. John Blacking remarked that it has long been a commonplace of ethnomusicological analysis that, while music is socially grounded, it cannot articulate any new meanings, express anything not already in the mind of the listener.[23] But music can enact relationships and narratives that have not previously been imagined or valued. Its potential to create new meanings for listeners is particularly great in mass media cultures, where music is mobile, sometimes the only means of contact among different ways of life. Thus, musical analysis of popular music can help us make sense of the seemingly fragmented modern world; it can help us understand the thoughts and desires of many whose only politics are cultural politics.

Musicological Analysis

In this section, I want to discuss a few select approaches to musical analysis in order to situate more clearly my own methods and goals. This is in no way a comprehensive or balanced survey; its purpose is illustrative.[24] One of the central issues concerns the disabling methodological split between aesthetic and sociological analysis. The continuing prestige and influence of eighteenth- and nineteenth-century European aesthetics, which relied upon claims of disinterestedness to mask the ideological agendas of its culture, have obscured the fact that this is not typical of how most people have understood the operation of culture throughout history.[25]

In the twentieth century, Theodor W. Adorno has been the foremost musicologist to challenge the Kantian orthodoxy that has ruled musicology.[26] Adorno's musical analysis posited a homological relationship between dynamic processes in music and those most central to society at the time. For him, musical and social structures were metaphorically linked, and musical and social criticism were thus inseparable. Adorno's work has been of major importance for cultural criticism and mass media scholarship, but more as obstacle than inspiration. Although Adorno did attempt to analyze popular music as well as art music, he did so only in order to prove the former's depravity and to underscore its role in perpetuating what he saw as modern capitalism's fascistic control of the masses. Adorno neglected to admit that his illuminating analyses of the German canon were dependent on his encyclopedic knowledge of and ideological commitment to that repertoire. His few analyses of popular music are so vague, vitriolic, and transparently racist that one wishes he had limited the scope of his analytical attentions even more than he did. So for those working in the area of popular music, the need to recoup that music from Adorno's damning criticism has taken precedence over the possibilities of adapting his methods to other ends.[27] This imperative has obscured the potential value of Adorno's methods as a model for analysts who want to understand musical details as socially significant. But Adorno's analyses of classical music ought to be counted important precedents for any project of musical-cultural criticism.

Other approaches pertinent to socially grounded analysis of popular music have emerged from the field of ethnomusicology. One of the most impressive collections of data was developed by Alan Lomax. After an exhaustive, computerized comparison of the "folk songs" of the whole world, Lomax felt able to specify some correlations between the social organization of communities and the musical characteristics of their songs. "In general, a culture's song performance style seemed to represent generalized aspects of its social and communications systems."[28] Lomax described not only homological links within sociomusical systems, but he also posited broader parallels across cultures; for example, he noted correlations between restrictive sexual mores and vocal tension. The range of observed manners of musical organization (e.g., choral singing vs. solo singing, homophony vs. polyphony) was matched with observed social organization, with results that suggest that some sort of connection exists among these practices. Lomax tried to avoid implying anything about the nature of that link; he simply insisted that it was there.

Lomax's refusal to theorize this link greatly reduces the value of his work for cultural studies and for ethnomusicology as well. Lomax and his research team produced a triumph for the positivistic analysis of human behavior: Lomax tried to give the impression that his work proceeded in total objectivity, without *any* informing theoretical bent. But in the end, the data Lomax collected imply that music is simply determined by social structure. In his refusal of theory, he arrived at one of the most unsophisticated of cultural models: he was unwittingly a "vulgar Marxist," for whom base simply determines superstructure. In applying social science methods across cultures and by not questioning the romantic assumption that cultures are naturally pure until corrupted by outsiders, Lomax was drawn into a refusal to supplement "objective" observation with any of the many methods anthropologists have used to make sense of what they see and to learn how others make sense of what they do.[29] By ignoring the ideological basis of meaning, Lomax diluted the richness and complexity of cultural interaction. Lomax discerned a variety of provocative correlations between music and society, but his implicit theoretical model is too simplistic to be of much use in understanding them.

This "scientific" approach to the study of culture continues to have great influence on ethnomusicology and on popular music study as well. The 1970s were the heyday of ethnomusicology's involvement with linguistics. Adopting the Saussurean assumption that symbols are arbitrary, musical scholars reasoned that (as Bruno Nettl summarized this position) "If all music is a system of symbols, one ought to be able to analyze it in a way similar to or derived from the accepted analysis of the intellectual grandfather of symbol systems, human language."[30] Spurred especially by interdisciplinary acclaim for Levi-Strauss's structuralist anthropology, musicologists and ethnomusicologists leapt at analytical models from linguistics and semiotics, adapting them for the study of musical structures, musical grammars, and musics as symbolic systems. The results, for the most part, included disappointingly few useful insights, in spite of a great many breathtakingly intricate charts and thrilling, cryptic abbreviations. As Steven Feld pointed out in 1974, during the midst of the linguistics craze, there was little real theorizing going on as to the *relevance* of linguistic models for the study of music.[31]

Scholars were attracted by the promise and appearance of scientific rigor and precision, but they gave little thought to the price they paid, which was the customary one for formalist prestige—abstraction; that is, abstraction of musical structures out of the richness and social complexity of musical practices. Feld, himself trained in linguistics, asserted that most of this work was little more than trendy dabbling, yielding only fancy new ways to describe musical sound, not explain it. Despite the later development of structuralist thought in anthropology, then, this work seemed to run counter to ethnomusicology's fundamental commitment to an anthropological interest in musical culture, to studying musical activities as well as musical structures.

But ethnomusicology has also fostered a number of sophisticated, sensitive analyses of musical meaning in social contexts; among the best are those by John Blacking and John Miller Chernoff. The latter sometimes presents conclusions very like those Lomax produced; for instance, he argues that "African affinity for polymetric musical forms indicates that, in the most fundamental sense, the African sensibility is pluralistic."[32] But Chernoff's insights are not distanced, "objective" correlations; they result from an extensive and intense engagement with African music and social life. Similarly, Blacking's fieldwork leads him to conclude: "It is not enough to identify a characteristic musical style in its own terms and view it in relation to its society. . . . We must recognize that no musical style has 'its own terms:' its terms are the terms of its society and culture, and of the bodies of the human beings who listen to it, and create and perform it."[33]

Some more recent ethnomusicological work, such as Feld's study of Kaluli aesthetics, further explores homological and complex metaphorical relationships among musical and other cultural practices.[34] And Judith and Alton Becker have written about Javanese music in a way that supports the idea that musical discourses are systems of coherence that differ among cultures and change over time. "We call iconicity the non-arbitrariness of any metaphor. Metaphors gain power—and even cease being taken as metaphors—as they gain iconicity or 'naturalness.'"[35] Becker and Becker argue that scholars must discover what makes a music powerful and relate its iconicity to epistemology, to the understandings and desires that make that music meaningful to a particular group of people. In the Javanese gamelon music they study, for example, cyclicity and coincidence establish the coherence that organizes meaning, in contrast to the way that tonality organizes the production of meaning in Western classical music. This suggests that heavy metal, too, should have its own mechanisms and metaphors, its own terms of discourse. Although few ethnomusicologists have produced studies of popular music, their field provides important models for such work.

The discipline of musicology, with its long history of positivism and ideological commitment to a canon of European "classical" music, has much less to offer scholars of popular music. Many musicologists remain unconvinced that any music outside their canon could be worth studying, and, as Simon Frith complains, the few who have addressed popular music have largely missed the point. More promising is the fact that a few musicologists, influenced by anthropology, feminism, and literary theory and building on the syntactical and affective insights of Theodor Adorno, Leonard Meyer, and others, have begun to produce detailed analyses of the Western musical canon in its social and political contexts.[36] Such sophisticated engagements with classical music are of great value for the study of popular music, both for the deconstructive, demystifying task they perform, which allows the investigation of popular music to proceed without an inferiority complex, and for their specific contributions to our understanding of musical texts and their cultural operation.

A singular exception to the predominant tendency to ignore music itself when studying popular music is found in the work of Philip Tagg.[37] Yet Tagg's work has had much less impact on the study of popular music than such distinction would seem to merit because of what many see as the excessive complexity and artificiality of his analyses. Tagg has created an elaborate taxonomy of the analytical process, built up through interrelationships of acronymic abstractions reminiscent of structuralist linguistics or of the formalist music analysis Tagg himself rejects. Tagg admits that his methodology is "cumbersome," but he sees no alternatives, for if "sterile formalism" is unproductive, "unbridled application" of hermeneutics is no better.[38] Tagg's results command a certain amount of respect: he is almost alone in having produced compelling explanations of the meanings of musical details in popular music. Moreover, Tagg's analysis of the historical factors that have led to musicology's denial of semiotic meaning are acute, and his rigor and caution are understandable given this context. As he well knows, to try to make the case that a particular musical configuration sounds mournful (something that may be obvious to virtually all listeners), in the face of dominant ideological commitments to formalism and the ineffability of artistic meaning, is to have to invent a philosophical argument for meaning in music and to try to reconstruct long-forgotten or suppressed codes.

Tagg's skill at unpacking the significance of musical gestures and structures is impressive, but he too often ignores or marginalizes both the political economy of popular music and its actual operations in social contestation. The features of his method that provoke resistance among scholars of popular music are mostly the product of methodological assumptions Tagg accepts from formalist musical and linguistic analysis. For example, the scientific rigor for which he assumes it is necessary to strive and the objectivity that is supposed to guarantee accurate delineation of meaning actually inhibit the kind of social explanations Tagg seeks. The problem is that there are no people in Tagg's analytical world save anonymous "respondents" who help the researcher establish "a bank of IOCM" (interobjective comparison material). There are no voices but Tagg's own; musicians and fans are dehumanized into "Emitters" and "Receivers," perpetuating the flawed model of art as a pipeline for delivering meaning, rather than as a social field for constructing, negotiating, and contesting it.[39] Tagg accepts too many of the premises of the people with whom he is arguing: you have the problem of connecting art and society only if you accept the assumptions that separate them; if you don't, then you work at explaining how meanings and relationships are created through artistic activities. Ultimately, Tagg is able to pay little attention to how popular music circulates socially, how it functions in articulating complex senses of identity, why people care about it.

Writing about Music

As Rob Halford and Eddie Van Halen remind us, musicians and fans alike tend to respond primarily and most strongly to musical meanings.[40] Analysts and critics, on the other hand, are trained in ways that privilege literate over oral modes of communication. A fundamental problem in accounting for musical meaning has always been the conflicting modalities of print and sound. Both music and language are meaningful to us, but they seem to be fundamentally different sorts of discourse. We can use language to describe musical processes or effects, but we usually find that propositional statements about music are clumsy compared to the efficiency of the music itself, and the feeling persists that much remains unaccounted for, no matter how lengthy the explanation. It seems to me that the uneasy fit of musical practices and linguistic theory is the result of epistemological tensions: on the one hand, the often very satisfying intuitions we gain from ethnography, listening to music, and performing it; and on the other, the understanding of all meaning as abstract and propositional that we inherit from the dominant philosophical tradition of the West. When we talk about music, we must use propositional language, but our mode of description is not the same as what we describe. Moreover, as Mark Johnson argues, propositional meaning in language, as well as musical meaning, is itself dependent on nonpropositional experience. Propositional statements cannot account fully for any kind of meaning.

The problem is not only that of representing musical experiences in words but more fundamentally one of analyzing musical meaning in terms of literate conceptions. Fiske and Hartley compare oral and literate modes of communication by means of a list of differences:[41]

Oral Modes	Literate Modes
dramatic	narrative
episodic	sequential
mosaic	linear
dynamic	static
active	artifact
concrete	abstract
ephemeral	permanent
social	individual
metaphorical	metonymic
rhetorical	logical
dialectical	univocal/"consistent"

The correspondence of music as discursive sound to the first column, and music's lyrics, scores, and criticism to the second is striking. Music enacts through patterns and gestures of sound a dramatic, episodic, dynamic experience, at once concrete and ephemeral. It is a social practice, rhetorically powerful and dialectically active. Writing about music, on the other hand, tends to treat music as an artifact, as it attempts to pin down the concrete realities of sound into static, abstract words in a logical, linear order. Musical scores and song lyrics, as literate modes of communication, are both closer in character to writing about music than to music itself. This discursive affinity is itself in part responsible for the historical neglect of musical meaning in popular music, in favor of concentration on either lyrics or static score-based musicological analysis.[42]

The argument is not that true meaning resides in the music, that popular music should be analyzed only in terms of sounds, removed from their distracting visual and verbal contexts. But lyrics have been granted disproportionate significance. Class and race prejudices have long inhibited the study of popular music by musicologists, and a long tradition of literate-mode analysis—of lyrics, interviews, etc.—has disguised the fact that we don't know nearly enough about how popular music constructs meanings musically. But I would argue that musical codes are the primary bearers of meaning; lyrics, like costumes and performers' physical motions, help direct and inflect the interpretation of the meanings that are most powerfully delivered, those suggested by the music. The most pressing task for the study of popular music is to begin to analyze the musical production of meaning within a discursive framework that is sensitive to many kinds of social experience even as it focuses on specifically musical practices.

I will turn now to a series of discursive parameters, discussing each in turn as it relates specifically to the musical practices of heavy metal. After introducing each parameter and tracing its operation in the case of metal rather generally, I will discuss its bearing on the song I have chosen to serve as an illustrative example. That song is "Runnin' with the Devil," written and recorded by Van Halen and released in 1978 as the first cut on their debut album, *Van Halen.* "Runnin' with the Devil" helped to propel the group to both popular success and critical acclaim, and it is still rated by critics and fans as among the best heavy metal songs ever recorded.[43] As we will see, this song is not paradigmatic in every respect; arguably, no text ever is perfectly representative of a genre. But its popularity and influence qualify it as an approximation of a "fixed star," as Jameson calls the hypothetical texts that help define genres. And the ways in which "Runnin' with the Devil" fails to exemplify the norms of heavy metal also are significant. But the main purpose of this section is to outline the qualities that are important in heavy metal and to describe how they signify. The first question is: what makes heavy metal heavy?

Metal as Discourse

TIMBRE: GUITAR DISTORTION

Of all musical parameters, timbre is least often analyzed, but its significance can hardly be overstated. Scan across radio stations, and a fraction of a second will be sufficient time to identify the musical genre of each. Before any lyrics can be comprehended, before harmonic or rhythmic patterns are established, timbre instantly signals genre and affect. Imagine this text being done by AC/DC, with raucous screaming and pounding: "I hear footsteps and there's no one there; I smell blossoms and the trees are bare." Now compare Frank Sinatra crooning it, backed by strings. The musical cues create very different effects: one is the frantic agony of paranoia; the other is the delicious disorientation of bourgeois love.

The most important aural sign of heavy metal is the sound of an extremely distorted electric guitar. Anytime this sound is musically dominant, the song is arguably either metal or hard rock; any performance that lacks it cannot be included in the genre. For people who use any sort of audio equipment, the relationship of distortion to power is familiar:

a small radio turned on full blast, a portable cassette player booming cacophonously, a malfunctioning stereo system. This electronic distortion results when components are overdriven—required to amplify or reproduce a signal beyond their capacity to do so "cleanly." Historically, such distortion has been regarded as undesirable, and generations of audio engineers have joined in the quest for perfect audio fidelity, laboring to eliminate all types of distortion while increasing power-handling capabilities. To the horror of these engineers, in the 1960s they began to receive requests from guitar players to produce devices that would deliberately add electronic distortion (in the late 1950s, guitar players had experimented with distortion by slashing their speaker cones). For despite its previous status as noise, at this historical moment such distortion was becoming a desirable sign in an emerging musical discourse.

Not only electronic circuitry, but also the human body produces aural distortion through excessive power. Human screams and shouts are usually accompanied by vocal distortion, as the capacities of the vocal chords are exceeded. Thus, distortion functions as a sign of extreme power and intense expression by overflowing its channels and materializing the exceptional effort that produces it. This is not to say that distortion always and everywhere functions this way; guitar distortion has become a conventional sign that is open to transformation and multiple meanings. Heavy metal distortion is linked semiotically with other experiences of distortion, but it is only at a particular historical moment that distortion begins to be perceived in terms of power rather than failure, intentional transgression rather than accidental overload—as music rather than noise.

Overdriving an amplifier actually creates two main effects: harmonic distortion and signal compression. The latter translates aurally as sustain; while a note played on an acoustic guitar or a nonoverdriven electric guitar decays quickly, a heavily distorted guitar signal is compressed and fed back so that the note, once struck, can be held indefinitely, with no loss of energy or volume. Since sustaining anything requires effort, the distorted guitar sound signals power, not only through its distorted timbre but also through this temporal display of unflagging capacity for emission. As one successful heavy metal producer puts it, "Distortion gives that feeling of ultimate power. The more distortion you get, the more satisfying it is. There's something slightly superhuman, psychologically speaking, about the sustain, the nearly endless notes."[44]

In Western musical history, the only other instrument capable of indefinite, unarticulated sustain is the organ (and its contemporary descendant, the synthesizer), which shares one other singular attribute with the electric guitar: the capacity to produce power chords. Power chords result from distortion of the chord voicings most often used in metal and hard rock, an open fifth or fourth played on the lower strings. Power chords are manifestly more than these two notes, however, because they produce resultant tones. An effect of both distortion and volume, resultant tones are created by the acoustic combination of two notes.[45] They are most audible at high volume levels, and they are intensified by the type of harmonic distortion used in metal guitar playing. Such resultant tones are also produced by pipe organs, where high volumes and open voicings on very low notes are sometimes employed to similar effect: to display and enact overwhelming power—usually, in that context, for the greater glory of God.

The strongest resultant tone is produced at the frequency that is the difference between the frequencies of the main tones. If, for example, the open A string on the guitar (which vibrates at a frequency of 110 cycles per second, or 110 Hz) and the E above it (165 Hz) are played as a power chord, then the A an octave lower (165 − 110 = 55 Hz) will sound very prominently as a resultant tone. If the A is played with a fourth above instead of a fifth, D (147 Hz), the D two octaves lower (37 Hz) will be produced. These resultant tones are often at frequencies lower than the instrument itself can normally produce; both of these examples result in the production of pitches far below the actual range of the guitar.

Distortion also results in a timbral change toward brightness, toward a more complex waveform, since distorting a signal increases the energy of its higher harmonics. Power chords, on the other hand, produce powerful signals *below* the actual pitches being sent to the amplifier. Thus, the distorted guitar signal is expanded in both directions: the higher harmonics produced by distortion add brilliance and edge (and what guitarists sometimes call "presence") to the sound, and the resultant tones produced by the interval combinations of power chords create additional low frequencies, adding weight to the sound. The power of power chords, the weight of heavy metal, the hardness of hard rock are all constructed and maintained discursively by factors besides timbre, but the sustain, distortion, and resultant tones discussed above are absolutely crucial.

The guitar sound in "Runnin' with the Devil" is famous among guitarists and often celebrated as paradigmatically "hot." Guitarist Eddie Van Halen produced this sound by means of a risky but effective innovation: using a voltage controller to increase the power source to the guitar amplifier from normal wall voltage (110–120 volts) to 140, 160, or more volts. The stronger power source overdrives the amplifier, creating an extremely energized sound, with maximum sustain and distortion (along with frequent destruction of amplifiers through burnout and the risk of electrocution). Van Halen's method was unusual, but it is symptomatic of the fanatical attention to "sound"—qualities of timbre and distortion—that is typical of all metal guitarists.

The quality of heavy metal distortion depends mainly on the amplifier and the pickups of the guitar. The Marshall amps Van Halen uses are overwhelmingly the heavy metal amp of choice, but many companies compete to offer the player the crucial "sound." Their advertisements are useful documents because they establish links between sound quality and the music's desired effects. For example, this description accompanies a picture of an explosion inside a vacuum tube:

> One Word. Tube. Musicians call it *The Sound*. It's what matters in your music; It cannot be measured by watts or metered distortion, only by ear. Yours. The Classic Tube Sound. Overlord has harnessed the sound by using a genuine vacuum tube. It will give your music the power and mystery, color and range of the classic tube sound. Fire over to your music store and hear the sound in your soul. But beware, for Overlord takes no prisoners.[46]

The ad copy employs short, blunt sentences and a menacing tone to evoke a mysterious, powerful aura for what is, actually, a little metal box. Compare this ad for guitar pickups, which relies on the reputation of virtuoso guitarist Yngwie Malmsteen:

> Yngwie's brand of drop dead playing is loaded with darkly mythic themes, classically-inspired solo riffs played at hypersonic speed and brutally precise technique—all executed with the Devil-may-care defiance of a true rock warrior. DiMarzio delivers all the power, tone and deadly accurate performance Yngwie demands. He uses two HS-3 ™ vertical humbuckers in the neck and bridge because he likes their fat, "single-coil" tone, and they give him the smooth sound he needs for playing at blistering volume with no hum or screechiness.[47]

Musicians themselves also testify to the importance of sound in interviews. Judas Priest's Glenn Tipton emphasizes: "If you've got a bad sound or very little sustain, where your guitar is not singing, it's very difficult to play a lead break. . . . If you've got a sound that you're struggling with then you'll never play a lead break properly or with the right amount of feel."[48] Such comments and advertisements are valuable corroboration of the discursive significance of timbre as a means of articulating power and affect.

VOLUME

Timbre is in part dependent on volume, and heavy metal is necessarily loud. The complete electronic control of sound reproduction that characterizes modern music allows metal to be reproduced, theoretically, at any dynamic level. However, the nature of metal and the needs and pleasures it addresses demand that it always be heard loud. Even when it is heard from a distance, or even softly sung to oneself, metal is imagined as loud, for volume is an important contributor to the heaviness of heavy metal. Robert Duncan writes of the "loudestness" of heavy metal, its perceived status as the most sonically powerful of musical discourses.[49]

Heavy metal relies heavily on technology for its effects, not least for this sheer volume of sound, impossible until recent decades. But reverb and echo units, as well as sophisticated overdubbing techniques, have also become important to metal performance and recording. Such processing can expand aural space, making the music's power seem to extend infinitely. This spatiality complements the intense physicality of what is aptly called "heavy metal," a materiality paradoxically created by sound, but sound so loud and compelling as to conflate inner and outer realities for the audience. Both extreme volume and artificially produced aural indicators of space allow the music to transform the actual location of the listener; music affects the experience of space as well as time. Loudness mediates between the power enacted by the music and the listener's experience of power. Intense volume abolishes the boundaries between oneself and such representations; the music is felt within as much as without, and the body is seemingly hailed directly, subjectivity responding to the empowerment of the body rather than the other way around.

VOCAL TIMBRE

The vocal sounds of heavy metal are similar, in some ways, to the guitar sounds. Quite often, vocalists deliberately distort their voices, for many of the same reasons that guitar players distort theirs. Heavy metal vocalists project brightness and power by overdriving their voices (or by seeming to), and they also sing long sustained notes to suggest intensity and power; sometimes heavy vibrato is used for further intensification (Rob Halford of Judas Priest is a prominent example).[50] The tough solo voice, the norm of vocal delivery, is occasionally supplemented by a chorus of backup voices, most often during the chorus section of the song. These additional voices serve to enlarge the statements of the solo vocalist, enacting the approval or participation of the larger social world, or at least a segment of it.

David Lee Roth's vocals on "Runnin' with the Devil" are typically raucous and flamboyant. His lyrics are punctuated by screams and other sounds of physical and emotional intensity. Singing alone on the verses,

Roth is joined by a chorus on the chorus, where the title hook, "Runnin' with the Devil," is confirmed by other voices. Processed to give a sense of great space, these chorus vocals virtually demand that the listener feel included in the collective affirmation of what is presented as an exciting image.

MODE AND HARMONY

A basic component of any song's affect is the set of pitch relationships it establishes, which is often referred to as a musical mode. Scholars seldom examine the operation of mode in popular music, but discussions of mode are common in professional and semiprofessional guitarists' magazines like *Guitar for the Practicing Musician*, *Guitar Player*, and *Guitar World*.[51] Academics usually think of mode as but a technical, descriptive category, while rock journalists are likely to regard any discussion of mode as academic obfuscation. The guitarist/theorists who write for other guitarists, on the other hand, often explicitly discuss the affective meanings of specific modes: "The patented quasi-classical, Gothic sound of the Aeolian mode (natural minor) is found in numerous familiar applications. . . . Another modal sound closely associated with modern metal is the more exotic Phrygian mode."[52]

Mode is, in fact, widely acknowledged by heavy metal musicians as a crucial part of the musical production of meaning; they know their audiences respond differently to each mode, and they find it useful to think and teach in terms of modal theory.[53] On my first day of heavy metal guitar lessons, my teacher, Jeff Loven, gave me a mimeographed handout he had devised called "Those Crazy Modes." It spelled out the seven medieval modes and, more important, gave examples of specific songs and typical chord progressions for each mode.

The terminology for these modes is borrowed from medieval and Renaissance music theory, which had already borrowed from an ancient Greek theoretical system, where scales were named after the musical practices of various ancient ethnic groups: the Dorians, the Aeolians, the Phrygians, and others. While the particular associations that were once attached to each mode vanished long ago, modes continue to produce powerful and specific affective charges. In fact, mode is one of the primary constituents of genre in popular music. Most heavy metal is either Aeolian or Dorian, for example, although speed metal is usually Phrygian or Locrian; most pop songs are either major (Ionian) or Mixolydian.

To say that a piece is in a particular mode is to suggest quite a bit about how that piece works, for a mode is a scale that also implies a set of functional syntactical relationships and affective potentials. The differences are quite easy to hear: imagine (or play) the beginning riff of Deep Purple's "Smoke on the Water" in its original blues-Aeolian form (G–B♭–C, G–B♭–D♭–C); now play it in major/Ionian (G–B–C, G–B–D–C)—it sounds like a Pat Boone cover; give it a Phrygian twist (G–A♭–D, G–A♭–E♭–D), and it sounds like Megadeth.[54] Modes are not merely abstruse theoretical categories; they can serve as a shorthand for referring to sets of meaningful elements of musical discourses.

The pitch relations established by modes provide the framework within which harmonic progressions operate. Wolf Marshall, a prominent teacher of metal guitar theory and technique, summarizes the basics: "By building triads or power chords on root, 7th, and 6th: i, VII, and VI—Am, G, F—the characteristic Aeolian chord progression, absolutely indigenous to modern rock/metal, is generated." Marshall continues with the Phrygian mode, which "produces an immediately recognizable chord sequence by building chords on root, 2nd, and 7th—i, II, and VII—Am, B♭, G."[55] Affectively, the Phrygian mode is distinctive: only this mode has a second degree only a half step away from the tonic instead of a whole step. Phenomenologically, this closeness means that the second degree hangs precariously over the tonic, making the mode seem claustrophobic and unstable. Hedged in by its upper neighbor, even the tonic, normally the point of rest, acquires an uncomfortable inflection in this mode.

Many academics who write about popular music have continued to assume that rock harmony is simple, even "primitive." There are two problems with this view. First, calling something simple does not explain its function, and second, all rock harmony is *not* simple, especially in the 1980s. Consider this excerpt from the "Performance Notes" for a published transcription of a heavy metal guitar solo by Joe Satriani, on his song, "Surfing with the Alien":

"Surfing" . . . literally explodes (using an overdubbed jet plane sample) into the opening rhythm figure based on the G Dorian mode. The melody enters eight bars later and by alternating between phrases using both the major and minor 3rd (B and B♭) a combined modality of Dorian and Mixolydian modes is achieved using a "Pitch Axis" of G. . . . After another jet plane break, we hit hard into the first guitar solo on the "and" of beat 4, launching into a series of trilled sextuplets based on the C♯ Phrygian-Dominant mode (the fifth mode of F♯ harmonic minor).[56]

Not only is heavy metal harmony often quite complex, but the analytical discourse used by teachers and players is often very sophisticated (see chap. 3). Cultural critics can make use of the analytical categories provided by modal theory, and used by many popular musicians themselves, to produce more detailed explanations of musical effects.

"Runnin' with the Devil" makes its Aeolian basis clear immediately. Over a pulsing pedal E in the bass, guitar chords move from C to a suspended D, then finally resolve to the tonic E. This is the ♭VI–♭VII–I harmonic progression discussed by Wolf Marshall; its affective character is discursively coded as aggressive and defiant (in part because of its difference from the tonal syntactical norms that underlie other popular music). But the modal basis of this song is unusually active; it is transformed at the end of every two-measure rhythmic phrase. The opening chords are all power chords, without thirds, and thus the minor implication of the E chord is established by the G in the C power chord. But the resolution from the suspended D to the tonic E is accomplished through a passing full A chord, which resolves to a full E chord with a G♯. I will return to the significance of this modal shift (from Aeolian to Mixolydian) when I discuss the song in a more integrated way later on.

RHYTHM

Rhythm has been particularly neglected in Western theories of musical meaning. This is usually explained in terms of the difficulty of generalizing rhythmic concepts except on the simple metric level. But it is also because it is in rhythm that the relationship of bodily experience to musical gesture is most apparent. Music theorists who are concerned with addressing rhythm have either ignored the body completely or argued that physical involvement with music is perverse or primitive:

Of course one often does hear exciting interpretations that build up so much energy that the overflow is imparted to the audience, which has to respond by immediate clapping; but I wonder whether these performances are not, for that very reason, a bit meretricious. Leo Stein has suggested that music requiring bodily motion on the part of the listener for its complete enjoyment, like much popular dance music, is by that token artistically imperfect.[57]

Denial of the body, related to the common fear of music's "feminizing" effects, is a recurrent anxiety of Western music criticism (and Western culture more generally). It is connected with suspicion of the sensual subversion of reason, and it is often invoked in the context of the reactionary projection of innovative threats onto the most immediate—and therefore dangerous—of others: women.[58] The fact that non-Western and popular cultures have not evinced the same commitment to denying physical meaning and pleasure has historically been construed, circularly, as evidence of their inferiority. In situations where the radical splits of Western culture—mind/body, art/life, individual/social—are not epistemological givens, quite different accounts of the role of the body in making and enjoying music are told.

Although rhythm is generally understood to be an important parameter of musical meaning in popular music, and the importance of the body's physical response is more openly acknowledged there than in "art" music, rhythm remains an elusive aspect to theorize and explain. One study of rhythm in popular music implicitly assumes that rhythmic complexity is equivalent to artistic merit and compares the simple rhythms of much rock with the military march: "The relentless drumbeat of the military band helps to mobilize soldiers for mindless war games, while the oppressive 4/4 beat that characterizes so much commercial rock captures and concentrates young people's energies on less harmful, but equally mindless, activity."[59] But the author misses the point of military marches, which is not to inculcate mindlessness but rather *single*-mindedness. He assumes that rhythmic complexity corresponds to artistic value; but both marches and metal sometimes rely upon an impression of simplicity for their social effectiveness, an impression that in fact may be made possible only by considerable skill and technical mediation and that may serve to help articulate complex social meanings.

Rhythm in heavy metal often seems very simple; it appears only to rouse physical energy and cue collective participation in heavy metal's version of dancing, headbanging. But a dialectic of freedom and control, which I will later trace in terms of ensemble and solo sections, is also inscribed rhythmically. Accents and rhythmic deviations, whether performed by the vocalist, the guitar soloist, or the whole band, are all the more significant for being played against the solid pulse that characterizes metal. Although most metal is in 4/4 time, the rhythmic framework is organized more basically around a pulse than a meter. Ensemble punches and solo or vocal syncopations alike strain against the beat more than the barline. Larger metrical patterns, usually two measures or four, function like harmonic progressions in indicating short-term goals.

The simple rhythmic pulse of "Runnin' with the Devil" is a major contributor to its affective power. Introduced by the bass alone at the beginning, a monolithic, inexorable pulse underlies most of the rest of the song. There is no interplay of polyrhythms, such as John Chernoff relates to the complex social networks articulated through African rhythmic polyphony. Instead, the pulse utterly dominates the rhythmic dimension of the piece; its function is in part to articulate control of time and energy. The control it represents is unitary, not multiple, and insofar as power is strongly gender-coded, it could be called phallic (see chap. 4). Rhythmically, "Runnin' with the Devil" celebrates power and offers to the listener an experience of that power; the pulse lets us feel what we might imagine extreme power feels like. The guitar chords pull away from that control and return to alignment with it, as do the vocals, in order to offer the pleasures of escape and reintegration.

MELODY

Melody is relatively less important in metal than in many other kinds of music, just as timbre is much more significant; discourses implicitly prioritize musical parameters differently. Two typical characteristics of metal melody stand out: first, melodic patterns in heavy metal frequently include long notes at the ends of phrases; these notes are either held out to signify power and intensity, like sustained notes on the guitar, or they are rasped, shrieked, or moaned, to contribute noise and extremity. Second, some singers tend to use a great deal of syncopation in their melodic lines. This can function as a solution to the problems of intelligibility in the face of metal's high instrumental volumes, as the singer places syllables between the beats, or it can have the effect of signifying resistance with respect to the context constructed by the instruments.

The former problem is not present in "Runnin' with the Devil," since it is the guitar that syncopates and since the accompanying instruments reduce their volume during the verses. And vocal syncopation as resistance is inappropriate here because the singer's rebellion is supported by the music rather than opposed to it. Closer attention to melody in "Runnin' with the Devil" would be repaid to some extent. For example, the opening vocal phrase is distinguished by an upward leap from the tonic A to the seventh degree of the mode, which then functions in a 4–3 suspension over the D chord. In the context of the song, the leap contributes to the sense of willfulness and excess that the lead singer projects, and the fact that he leaps to a suspension adds striving to the gesture.

GUITAR SOLOS

The electric guitar is the most important virtuoso instrument of the past three decades. Virtually every heavy metal song features at least one guitar solo; few contain solos by any other instrument (drum solos are special set pieces, often performed once during a concert but almost never recorded, at least in the 1980s). The sustain of the distorted electric guitar, besides being important for the production of power chords, increases its potential as a virtuoso solo instrument.[60]

Eddie Van Halen revolutionized electric guitar playing, as had Jimi Hendrix before him, in the direction of greater virtuosity. Van Halen's solos, featured on nearly every song his band recorded, along with his sensitive, imaginative "comping" behind the singer, inspired a whole generation of young guitar players toward greater technical facility and theoretical sophistication. It is therefore surprising and significant that no real guitar solo appears in "Runnin' with the Devil." Several guitar solos will be analyzed in the next chapter, but to explain their absence in "Runnin' with the Devil" requires a more integrated reading of that song.

"Runnin' with the Devil"

Simultaneous with the release of Van Halen's first album came the release of the band's image. Although all four members of the band were reputed to be wild and party-prone, perhaps the most important gossip concerned David Lee Roth, the lead singer, for the lead singer of a rock band usually "fronts" the band not only on stage but in interviews and in rumor. Roth's notoriety and success grew when it was revealed that he had purchased insurance against paternity suits from Lloyd's of London. Lewd and athletic on stage, Roth also affected exaggeratedly sexy costumes, such as tight leather pants with most of the buttocks cut out.

The cover of the first Van Halen album featured motion-blurred photos of the four band members, each figure accented with colored light against a deep black background. The musicians appear in an abstracted performance scene, and all four are caught in poses that suggest physical intensity: bodies bent and taut, mouths open as though screaming. Roth displays his naked chest and holds his microphone so that it juts from his crotch. The Van Halen logo, bright and metallic, connects the four musicians. On the inner sleeve another set of pictures portrays the band members as though they have just finished playing: exhausted, dripping with sweat, drained yet satisfied. In a live performance, a tremendous apparatus of promotion and production comes into play to help define the event, as well as lighting, special effects, musicians' behavior and banter, and the crowd's own contribution to the dynamic of the performance. But even when a listener encounters only the album, much of the same framing is presented, as the packaging of the album is designed to evoke the excitement of live performance.

The lyrics emphasize that running with the Devil is a trope for having freedom; the music glorifies that image by implying power as well.

> I live my life like there's no tomorrow
> And all I've got, I had to steal
>
> .   .   .   .
>
> I've got no love, no love you'd call real
> Ain't got nobody waiting at home
>
> Runnin' with the Devil . . .

Freedom is presented as a lack of social ties: no love, no law, no responsibility, no delayed gratification. One might feel lonely, but that loneliness can also be a source of pride. Running with the Devil means living in the present, and the music helps us experience the pleasure of the moment. The fantasy is one of escape from all social conventions; it is based on a quite bourgeois concept of the individual, who supposedly has some sort of essence that can be freed from social constrictions. In fact, though, the social boundaries that are felt to contain are also the structure within which these very fantasies are produced.[61]

The verses and choruses are presented from very different perspectives. The verses relate an individual experience; the singer is reflective and confessional as he describes his life-style. Indeed, during the verses, which are presented musically in a different key, the lyrics are inflected with awareness of doubt and guilt. The fantasy is even questioned: the singer admits that running with the Devil is not exactly as he thought it would be, that it has its drawbacks. But the choruses sweep those doubts away in a collective affirmation of the fantasy. It is the backing chorus that is so sure of the fantasy's validity, not the singer, who punctuates the chorus lines with pained/ecstatic screams. This is fundamentally a social fantasy, one believed in much more completely by those who feel constrained than by the lonely individual on the road, who is able to see its contradictions.

That the fantasy is so powerfully articulated, though, is due to the music of the chorus. In particular, the chords move from a typically metallic Aeolian ♭VI–♭VII motion through a surprise transformation to the tonic major. The main gesture is a syncopated suspension of a power chord on ♭VII (D) over the pulsing bass tonic (E); the E serves as a pedal point that clashes with the D, creating desire for resolution while guaranteeing it. But the resolution is simultaneous with a modal shift that occurs every two measures and constructs an affective transcendence. Every two bars we are lifted out of the familiar negative Aeolian terrain into the perfect resolution of the major mode's tonic.

Immediately thereafter, we are plunged again into Aeolian gloom and then carried up out of it once more. This description may seem fanciful in words, but the affective meaning is unmistakably coded discursively.[62]

This two-measure pattern of tension and release, negativity and transcendence, is the most important signifying feature of the song. This modal shift is the song's "hook," and the formal/narrative structure of the song is built around it. After each statement of a verse, there is a tremendous affective charge in moving into this chorus material. In part, this is a switch from an individual, prominently verbal section into a section of collective participation, backed by higher musical energy. Audiences respond to narrative patterns such as this by increasing their physical response and engagement at the beginning of the chorus.

The move into the chorus is propelled not only by shifts in key and mode but also by dynamic, timbral, and rhythmic changes. The verses are quieter, accompanied by syncopated, descending chords (not power chords) in the guitar. All of this is blown away with each entry of the chorus, with its power chords and inexorably pulsing bass. The rhythms of the chorus are not static, though; the two-measure units of the chorus's harmonic progression are also articulated rhythmically. The $\flat$VII power chord suspension begins on the upbeat of beat 1, is held through the bar, and is resolved on the upbeat of beat 2 of the next measure. The attack of the suspension feels jarring, but its resolution anticipates rather than follows a strong beat (beat 3). Thus, the harmonic resolution (and modal shift) precedes the rhythmic resolution, stretching out the moment of transcendence.

"Runnin' with the Devil" has one other formal section that has not yet been discussed: the four-measure guitar solo that comes after the chorus following the second verse (and again when the second verse is repeated). The guitar is featured alone, with its own melodic material, but these four bars are actually very little like most heavy metal guitar solos: too short, too simple, and since the same statement is repeated later in the song, the necessary impression of spontaneity and improvisation is lacking. Most recorded solos are, in fact, composed and practiced ahead of time, but a sense of immediacy is crucial, for metal guitar solos typically take the form of rhetorical outbursts, characterized by fast licks and soaring, amazing virtuosity that can create a sense of perfect freedom and omnipotence; they model escape from social constraints, extravagant individuality (see chap. 3).

Heavy metal revolves around identification with power, intensity of experience, freedom, and community. Musically, a dialectic is often set up between the potentially oppressive power of bass, drums, and rhythm guitar, and the liberating, empowering vehicle of the guitar solo or the resistance of the voice. The feeling of freedom created by the freedom of motion of the guitar solos and fills can be at various times supported, defended, or threatened by the physical power of the bass and the violence of the drums. The latter rigidly organize and control time; the guitar escapes with flashy runs and other arrhythmic gestures. The solo positions the listener: he or she can identify with the controlling power without feeling threatened because the solo can transcend anything.

Why, then, is there no true heavy metal guitar solo in "Runnin' with the Devil," which many have argued is exemplary metal? It is certainly no accident; not only are solos virtually required by the conventions of the genre, but Van Halen's success was largely owing to the phenomenal virtuosity of Eddie Van Halen's guitar playing. The "song" that follows "Runnin' with the Devil" on the album is simply an extended guitar solo, an unaccompanied cadenza called "Eruption." Every other song on the record boasts at least one real guitar solo; why not this one?

"Runnin' with the Devil" is an exception to the norms of the genre because it conflates control and freedom, two core concerns of the genre, in a way that is unusual in metal. The brief guitar fills allow some display of the guitar without the disruption that a real solo would cause. But the transcendent moment usually provided by a guitar solo can be omitted since it is already constructed every two measures through a harmonic/modal shift. The chorus of the song is at once powerfully controlled—stable, regular phrases; an immutable bass pedal point, pulsing absolutely reliably—and free, constantly transcending its modal premises. This is not to say that the guitar solo *had to be* left out but rather to explain how the song could deviate from generic norms and still be effective.[63]

Because the verses and guitar fills are presented in a different key, the modulation back to the chorus reestablishes order (the proper, original key). But since the chorus section begins with a *suspension* in that key, it is not legitimated by any harmonic logic, and the reestablishment of the tonic key is heard at the same time as an arbitrary leap. The usual dialectical tension between the rhythm section's control and the soloist's freedom has been obviated by this unusual fusing of both impulses within the same musical phrase. Much of the pleasure of "Runnin' with the Devil" is a result of this ingenious, compelling reconciliation of these two fundamental desires for freedom and security—ideologically crucial concerns in the world of heavy metal.

Negotiation and Pleasure

Early in this chapter, I asserted that it was important to analyze musical texts in ways that kept them open to the kinds of negotiated receptions they get in real life. Yet my analysis of "Runnin' with the Devil" has, so far, been quite monovocal; I have specified meanings that I identified as discursively produced, as though all metal fans had the same understanding of all metal songs. In fact, my interviews with heavy metal fans and musicians tell me that this is not the case. Both groups come to heavy metal with a wide range of personal histories and needs; they all not only take selectively from the genre but contribute to it. Their conversations with each other—at concerts, through magazine letters columns, and among friends—as well as their consumption choices themselves, constitute a dialogue with the shifting structures and meanings of the genre.[64]

However, the word *negotiations* reminds us that discourses do have the power to organize the exchange of meanings; deviations are resistant or creative. For example, the Christian heavy metal band Stryper demonstrates that the specific musical gestures of heavy metal operate within a code to communicate experiences of power and transcendent freedom because their attempt to appropriate the codes of metal is posited on the suitability of precisely such experiences for evangelism. The power is God's; the transcendent freedom represents the rewards of Christianity; the intensity is that of religious experience. Stryper appropriates and reinterprets the codes of heavy metal, using metal's means to produce different meanings. Metal's noisiness might seem incompatible with a Christian agenda, but Stryper exploits just that subversive aura to make more appealing what would otherwise seem a wholly institutional message. Stryper presents Christianity as an exciting, youth-oriented alternative; they offer their fans a chance to enjoy the pleasures of heavy metal and feel virtuous at the same time.

It is easy to forget that culture exerts the influence it does because it provides us with pleasure. Many analyses of musical works give no hint at all that music is experienced, that it has impact because it is enjoyed. In part this is a result of a long Western tradition of rationalist suspicion of sensuality. Yet in modern times, this problem is in part one that chronically plagues those scholars who are interested in taking popular culture seriously: a desire to find explicit political agendas and intellectual complexity in at least some popular art, and a distrust of those dimensions of art that appeal to the senses, to physical pleasure. But pleasure frequently *is* the politics of music—both the pleasure of affirmation and the pleasure of interference, the pleasure of marginalized people which has evaded channelization.

In the case of popular music, this pleasure is largely experienced in response to the discursively organized signification of the music itself—beyond the vocals. The analytical perspectives and techniques developed in this chapter are meant to be both provocative and enabling of further discussions of musical meaning in popular music. And the readings given here are not intended to be essential or definitive; while these interpretive arguments are grounded in ethnography as well as musical and social history, at a more general level this chapter simply points out that there is ample evidence that music is meaningful, notes that musical meanings are almost never dealt with, and insists that this is an important task for scholars, for it seems the only way to account for the power and pleasure of popular music. Beyond this are the questions to be addressed in the following chapters: Whose pleasure? To what ends? In the service of what interests is pleasure offered and experienced?

At the end of an Iron Maiden concert I attended in 1988, light, happy, Muzak-style music came through the house PA system to accompany the crowd's exit. I didn't recognize the tune, but it was very close to "It's a Small World," the mindlessly cute, cloyingly smug song around which an entire ride was built at Disneyland. This vapid music, so incongruous after Iron Maiden's powerful show, was clearly intended to disperse the energy of the concert, promoting orderly exit and calm reintegration with the world outside. It succeeded remarkably: fifteen thousand screaming, sweating, straining heavy metal fans were transformed into a group as sedate as any homeward-bound symphony orchestra fans. This impressive feat can be credited to the invisible, intangible, affective power of music that seemed quite incidental to the concert experience. The orderliness and affirmativity of the exit music had calming effects that no conceivable verbal utterance could have accomplished. It was effective precisely because it, like much of the concert itself, seemed to come from everywhere and no one, from beyond the vocals.

CHAPTER THREE

Eruptions

Heavy Metal Appropriations
of Classical Virtuosity

*

We have now heard him, the strange wonder, whom the superstition
of past ages, possessed by the delusion that such things could never
be done without the help of the Evil One, would undoubtedly have condemned
to the stake—we have heard him, and seen him too, which, of course,
makes a part of the affair. Just look at the pale, slender youth in his
clothes that signal the nonconformist; the long, sleek, drooping hair . . .
those features so strongly stamped and full of meaning, in this respect
reminding one of Paganini, who, indeed, has been his model of
hitherto undreampt-of virtuosity and technical brilliance from the
very first moment he heard him and was swept away.[1]

In the liner notes for his 1988 album *Odyssey*, heavy metal guitarist Yngwie J. Malmsteen claimed a musical genealogy that confounds
the stability of conventional categorizations of music into classical and
popular spheres. In his list of acknowledgments, along with the usual
cast of agents and producers, suppliers of musical equipment, and rela-
tives and friends, Malmsteen expressed gratitude to J. S. Bach, Nicolo
Paganini, Antonio Vivaldi, Ludwig van Beethoven, Jimi Hendrix, and
Ritchie Blackmore.[2] From the very beginnings of heavy metal in the late
1960s, guitar players had experimented with the musical materials of
eighteenth- and nineteenth-century European composers. But the trend
came to full fruition around the time of Malmsteen's debut in the early
1980s; a writer for the leading professional guitar magazine said flatly
that the single most important development in rock guitar in the 1980s
was "the turn to classical music for inspiration and form."[3]

Heavy metal, like all forms of rock and soul, owes its biggest debt
to African-American blues.[4] The harmonic progressions, vocal lines,
and guitar improvisations of metal all rely heavily on the pentatonic

scales derived from blues music. The moans and screams of metal guitar playing, now performed with whammy bars and overdriven amplifiers, derive from the bottleneck playing of the Delta blues musicians and ultimately from earlier African-American vocal styles. Angus Young, guitarist with AC/DC, recalls, "I started out listening to a lot of early blues people, like B. B. King, Buddy Guy, and Muddy Waters."[5] Such statements are not uncommon, and heavy metal guitarists who did not study the blues directly learned secondhand, from the British cover versions of Eric Clapton and Jimmy Page or from the most conspicuous link between heavy metal and blues and r&b, Jimi Hendrix.

But from the very beginning of heavy metal there has been another important influence: that assemblage of disparate musical styles known in the twentieth century as "classical music." Throughout metal's twenty-year history, its most influential musicians have been guitar players who have also studied classical music. Their appropriation and adaptation of classical models sparked the development of a new kind of guitar virtuosity, changes in the harmonic and melodic language of heavy metal, and new modes of musical pedagogy and analysis.

Classical Prestige and Popular Meanings

The classical influence on heavy metal marks a merger of what are generally regarded as the most and least prestigious musical discourses of our time. This influence thus seems an unlikely one, and we must wonder why metal musicians and fans have found such a discursive fusion useful and compelling. Musicologists have frequently characterized adaptive encounters among musical practices as natural expansions of musical resources, as musicians find in foreign musics new means with which to assert their innovative creativity. Yet such explanations merely reiterate, covertly, a characteristically Western interest in progress, expansion, and colonization. They do little to account for the appearance of specific fusions at particular historical moments or to probe the power relations implicit in all such encounters. We will need more cogent explanations than those with which musicology has traditionally explained classical exoticism, fusions of national styles, and elite dabblings in jazz.

I should emphasize that my discussion of the relationship of heavy metal and classical music is not simply a bid to elevate the former's cultural prestige. Attempts to legitimate popular culture by applying the standards of "high" culture are not uncommon, and they are rightly condemned as wrongheaded and counterproductive by those who see such friends of "low" culture as too willing to cede the high ground.

That is, the assumptions that underpin cultural value judgments are left untouched, and the dice remain loaded against popular culture. An attempt to legitimate heavy metal in terms of the criteria of classical music, like prior treatments of the Beatles' and other rock music, could easily miss the point, for heavy metal is in many ways antithetical to today's classical music. Such a project would disperse the differences between metal and other musics, accomplishing a kind of musicological colonization that musicians, fans, and cultural historians alike would find alienating and pointless.[6]

But in the case of heavy metal, the relationship to classical modes of thought and music making is not merely in the eye of the beholder. To compare it with culturally more prestigious music is entirely appropriate, for the musicians who compose, perform, and teach this music have tapped the modern classical canon for musical techniques and procedures that they have then fused with their blues-based rock sensibility. Their instrumental virtuosity, theoretical self-consciousness, and studious devotion to the works of the classical canon means that their work could be valorized in the more "legitimate" terms of classical excellence. But more important, metal guitarists' appropriations of classical music provide a vital opportunity for examining musical signification in contexts of popular creativity and cultural contestation.

The history of American popular music is replete with examples of appropriation "from below"—popular adaptations of classical music. As I discuss examples drawn from heavy metal, I will be describing a number of ways in which classical music is being used, all of which have antecedents in other twentieth-century popular music. The sorts of value popular appropriators find in classical music might be grouped around these topics: semiotics, virtuosity, theory, and prestige. I will explore each of these aspects in turn as I discuss the work of several of the most influential and successful heavy metal guitarists. But before examining the classical influence upon metal, I must clarify my understanding of the term "classical music," particularly my attribution to it of prestige and semiotic significance.

The prestige of classical music encompasses both its constructed aura of transcendent profundity and its affiliation with powerful social groups. Although the potency of its aura and the usefulness of its class status depend upon the widespread assumption that classical music is somehow timeless and universal, we know that "classical music" is a relatively recent cultural construct. The canon of the music now known as "the great works of the classical tradition" began to form early in the nineteenth century, with revivals of "ancient" music (Bach and Mozart) and series publications of composers' collected works. Lawrence W. Levine has carefully detailed the process of elevation and "sacralization," begun midway through the nineteenth century, whereby European concert music was wrenched away from a variety of popular contexts and made to serve the social agenda of a powerful minority of Americans. Along with the popular plays of Shakespeare, German music was elevated, as an elite attempted to impose a monolithic "moral order," repudiating the plurality of cultural life.[7] By the twentieth century, institutional and interpretive structures came to shape musical reception so completely that what we know today as "classical music" is less a useful label for a historical tradition than a genre of twentieth-century music.

Perhaps the most forceful critique of the institution of modern concert music is that of Christopher Small, who argues that this process of sacralization has almost completely effaced original social and political meanings.[8] Musical works that were created for courts, churches, public concerts, and salons of connoisseurs, and that had modeled and enacted the social relationships important to those specific audiences, have become a set of interchangeable great pieces. All of the vast range of meanings produced by these disparate musics are reduced to singularity in the present. That single meaning, Small maintains, is one of defense—specifically, defense of the social relationships and ideologies that underpin the status quo. Cultural hierarchy is used to legitimate social hierarchy and to marginalize the voices of all musicians who stand outside the canon, representing those who stand at the margins of social power. Small's critique is important because it is essential to realize that classical music is not just "great" music; it is a constructed category that reflects the priorities of a historical moment and that serves certain social interests at the expense of others. Classical music is the sort of thing Eric Hobsbawm calls an "invented tradition," whereby present interests construct a cohesive past to establish or legitimate present-day institutions or social relations.[9] The hodgepodge of the classical canon—aristocratic and bourgeois music; academic, sacred, and secular; music for public concerts, private soirees, and dancing—has one thing in common: its function as the most prestigious culture of the twentieth century.

Once established, though, classical music can be negotiated; it has been both a bulwark of class privilege and a means whereby other social barriers could be overcome. African-American performers and composers have long worked to defeat racist essentialism by proving their ability to write and perform European concert music. The chamber jazz of the Modern Jazz Quartet, with its cool fusions of swing and classical forms, was also a statement of black pride, however conservative it seemed amid the turmoil of the 1960s. Duke Ellington was a crucial figure in the struggle to achieve widespread respect for African-American music, in large measure because his skills as composer, orchestrator, and leader made him, of all jazz musicians, most closely match the prestigious model of the classical composer.

Rock fusions with classical styles are most often associated with the "progressive rock" or "art rock" of the late 1960s. With *Sgt. Pepper's Lonely Hearts Club Band*, the Beatles kicked off an era of self-conscious experimentation with the instrumentation and stylistic features of classical music. Producer George Martin's training as a classical oboist exposed him to many of the peculiarities that appeared on the Beatles' recordings: piccolo trumpet (a modern instrument now associated with Baroque music), classical string quartets, odd metric patterns perhaps inspired by Stravinsky or Bartók (or more directly by the non-Western music that had inspired *them*). The Moody Blues collaborated with the London Festival Orchestra for *Days of Future Passed* in 1968, and groups as different as The Who, Yes, The Kinks, and Emerson, Lake, and Palmer composed classically influenced rock songs, rock concertos, and rock operas. Deep Purple, eventually recognized as one of the founding bands of heavy metal, began to develop in that direction only after guitarist Ritchie Blackmore grew dissatisfied with fusions such as keyboardist Jon Lord's ambitious *Concerto for Group and Orchestra* (1969) and reoriented the band: "I felt that the whole orchestra thing was a bit tame. I mean, you're playing in the Royal Albert Hall, and the audience sits there with folded arms, and you're standing there playing next to a violinist who holds his ears everytime you take a solo. It doesn't make you feel particularly inspired."[10] Blackmore realized that the institutions and audience expectations that frame classical music would always control the reception of any music performed within that context; while he was attracted to classical musical resources, he found that he would have to work with them on his own turf.

Discussions of art rock rarely move beyond sketching influences to address the question of *why* classical music was used by these groups.[11] Certainly one of the most important reasons is prestige. Rock critics' own preoccupation with art rock reflects their acceptance of the premises of the classical model. Performers who haven't composed their own material—"girl groups," Motown, soul singers—have rarely won critical respect comparable to that granted artists who better fit the model of the auteur, the solitary composing genius. Sometimes performers stake their claims to classical prestige explicitly. Emerson, Lake, and Palmer's neoclassical extravaganzas, such as their rendering of Mussorgsky's *Pic-*

tures at an Exhibition (1972), were intended as elevations of public taste and expressions of advanced musicianship. Keith Emerson's attraction to classical resources was unabashedly elitist; he considered ordinary popular music degraded and took on the mission of raising the artistic level of rock. In such art rock, classical references and quotations were intended to be recognized as such; their function was, in large measure, to invoke classical music and to confer some of its prestigious status and seriousness.

Other popular musicians have been attracted to classical resources for reasons of signification beyond prestige. At least since the late 1920s, when classical string sections began to appear on recordings of Tin Pan Alley music, classical means have been used to expand the rhetorical palette—and social meanings—of popular music. In Bing Crosby's Depression-era hit, "Brother, Can You Spare a Dime?" (1932), the strings function to underscore the sincerity of Crosby's voice and magnify the poignancy of his character's plight. The recorders on Led Zeppelin's "Stairway to Heaven" (1971) similarly contribute to the song's musical semiotics. They sound archaic and bittersweet; their tranquil contrapuntal motion is at once soothing and mysterious.

Of all of the stylistic or historical subdivisions of classical music, rock music has borrowed most from the Baroque. Richard Middleton has tried to account for this by arguing that there is a "relatively high syntactic correlation" between Baroque and rock musical codes. Like rock music, Baroque music "generally uses conventional harmonic progressions, melodic patterns and structural frameworks, and operates through imaginative combinations, elaborations and variations of these, rather than developing extended, through-composed forms. It also tends to have a regular, strongly marked beat; indeed, its continuo section could be regarded as analogous to the rhythm section of jazz and rock."[12] Middleton suggests, for example, that Procul Harum's "A Whiter Shade of Pale" (1967), by fusing harmonic and melodic material taken from a Bach cantata with the soul ballad vocal style of Ray Charles and Sam Cooke, presented the counterculture with an image of itself as "sensuously spiritual" and "immanently oppositional."[13]

Here the usefulness of Baroque materials depends on both their aura as "classical" and their present semiotic value, to the extent that these meanings are separable. For although this music was composed long ago, it is still circulating, producing meanings in contemporary culture. Metal musicians generally acquire their knowledge of classical music through intense study, but they owe their initial exposure to the music and their audiences' ability to decode it not to the pickled rituals of the concert hall, but to the pervasive recycling of all available musical discourses by the composers of television and movie music. Classical musics are alive and omnipresent in mass culture, despite the best efforts of proponents of cultural apartheid and in part due to their missionary efforts. Mass mediation ensures that there can be no absolute separation of "high" and "low" culture in the modern world; classically trained composers write film scores that draw upon their conservatory studies but succeed or fail on their intelligibility and meaningfulness for mass audiences. Classical music surely no longer signifies as it did originally, but neither are its meanings ahistorical or arbitrary. It is available to culturally competitive groups who claim and use its history, its prestige, and its signifying powers in different ways.

Heavy metal appropriations of classical music are, in fact, very specific and consistent: Bach, not Mozart; Paganini rather than Liszt; Vivaldi and Albinoni instead of Telemann or Monteverdi. This selectivity is remarkable at a time when the historical and semiotic specificity of classical music, on its own turf, has all but vanished, when the classical canon is defined and marketed as a reliable set of equally great and ineffable collectibles. By finding new uses for old music, recycling the rhetoric of Bach and Vivaldi for their own purposes, metal musicians have reopened issues of signification in classical music. Their appropriation suggests that despite the homogenization of that music in the literatures of "music appreciation" and commercial promotion, many listeners perceive and respond to differences, to the musical specificity that reflects historical and social specificity. Thus, the reasons behind heavy metal's classical turn can reveal a great deal, not only about heavy metal but also about classical music. We must ask: if we don't understand his influence on the music of Ozzy Osbourne or Bon Jovi, do we really understand *Bach* as well as we thought we did?

Ritchie Blackmore and the Classical Roots of Metal

That many rock guitarists of the late 1960s experimented with classical influences in their playing can be seen as part of a widespread interest in musical exploration—itself part of the search for social and conceptual options that characterized the decade. Jimmy Page listened to a great range of music to acquire the means to create the varied moods of Led Zeppelin, which ranged from heavy blues to ethereal ballads, Celtic mysticism, Orientalist fantasies, and folkish ballads. Mountain's Leslie West inflected his heavy blues sensibility with classical and jazz licks, and many other early examples could be cited. But the most important musician of the emerging metal/classical fusion was Ritchie Blackmore. As lead guitarist for Deep Purple, Blackmore was one of the most influential guitarists of the late 1960s and early 1970s. Though he was not the first hard rock guitarist to employ classical features, Blackmore greatly affected other players; for many of them, Blackmore's was the first really impressive, compelling fusion of rock and classical music.

Born in 1945, Ritchie Blackmore began playing at age eleven; six years later he was working as a studio session guitarist in London. Blackmore became impressed by Jimi Hendrix's guitar sound, and like Hendrix, he became a pioneer of flashy virtuosity.[14] While young, Blackmore took classical guitar lessons for a year, which affected his fingering technique: unlike most rock guitarists of his generation, he made full use of the little finger on his left hand. But the classical influence shows up most, Blackmore himself maintained, in the music he wrote: "For example, the chord progression in the 'Highway Star' solo on *Machine Head* . . . is a Bach progression." And the solo is "just arpeggios based on Bach."[15] Recorded in 1971 (released in 1972), *Machine Head* contained not only the hits "Highway Star" and "Space Truckin'" but also the heavy metal anthem "Smoke on the Water." The album came to be regarded by fans as one of the classic albums of heavy metal, and it helped generate great enthusiasm for classical/rock fusions.

"Highway Star" is a relatively long and complex song; it winds its way among several different keys, and both Blackmore and the keyboard player, Jon Lord, take extended solos. The organ solo begins over a descending chromatic bass line, reminiscent of the ground bass patterns favored by seventeenth-century composers such as Henry Purcell. Much of the soloing is made up of series of arpeggios, in the style of Vivaldi (or Bach, after he absorbed Vivaldi's influence). The members of Deep Purple abstracted and adapted a particular set of classical features: repetitious melodic patterns (such as arpeggios), square phrase structures, virtuosic soloing, and characteristic harmonic progressions, such as descending through a tetrachord by half steps or cycling through the circle of fifths. The harmonic progressions, as Blackmore asserted, are typically Baroque, as are the rapid, flashy sixteenth-note patterns organized symmetrically through repetition and balanced phrases. In Deep Purple, guitarist and organist alike drew upon these materials to construct a new and effective style of rock virtuosity.

In his "Highway Star" solo, Blackmore begins with blues-derived licks and brings in the Baroque materials climactically at the end, where he overdubs a matching harmony part in thirds, with figuration that recalls Vivaldi's energetic articulation of harmonic progressions in his

Example 1. Deep Purple (1972), "Highway Star," excerpt from Ritchie Blackmore's solo (author's transcription).

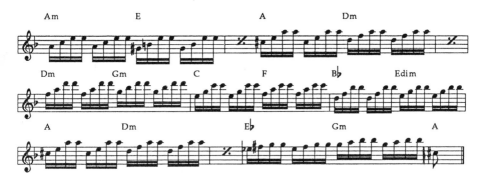

Example 2. Antonio Vivaldi, Violin Concerto in D Minor (F. 1, No. 21 in the *Collected Works,* ed. Malipiero, Edizioni Ricordi, 1949), first movement, mm. 87–97.

violin concerti (see examples 1 and 2). As in Vivaldi, a regular and predictable (though dynamic) harmonic sequence provides the backdrop for exhilarating figuration. The harmonic cycles set up rational articulation of time and direction, enabling us to predict what will come next, and the guitar solo energizes these patterns with virtuosic exhibitionism. As in the concerto grosso, the soloist provides the dynamic individual element, in contrast to the stable collectivity of the rhythm section.[16] Vivaldi's social model transfers well to the context of the guitar hero.

Throughout the 1970s, guitarists continued their experimentation with fusions of rock and classical music. Just as jazz musicians had done in the late 1940s, some rock guitarists turned to classical music theory for new musical resources. The *Thesaurus of Scales and Melodic Patterns* by musicologist Nicolas Slonimsky introduced both jazz and rock musicians to harmonic and melodic possibilities such as harmonic minor scales, modal scales, and diminished arpeggios.[17] Ulrich Roth of the German band Scorpions advanced virtuosic standards with his fast scales and dramatic diminished chords. Jazz/rock fusion guitarist Al DiMeola had an important influence on some rock guitarists; his music was by no means heavy metal, but he used a similar distorted, highly sustained guitar tone, and his melodic and harmonic language was close enough to that of metal that his modal explorations influenced heavy metal musicians.

Other major metal guitarists of this period did not pursue the classical influence directly. Michael Schenker, who was perhaps the most influential metal guitarist of continental Europe during the 1970s, had no formal training and no exposure to academic music theory. He taught himself to play, learning Beatles songs and Clapton solos by ear, and his virtuosity has always been primarily blues-based, grounded in the pentatonicism and timbral nuance of the blues guitar. The musical roots of Angus and Malcolm Young of AC/DC are in early rock and roll and r&b, and they have stuck doggedly to them. Glenn Tipton and K. K. Downing, the guitar players of Judas Priest, also had little formal training, and it was only in the late 1980s that the classical influence became pronounced in their playing. But in spite of these exceptions, appropriations of classical music were increasingly important throughout the history of heavy metal and even helped define the genre.

After leaving Deep Purple to pursue a solo career, Ritchie Blackmore continued his study and adaptation of classical music. The liner notes for his first album with his new band, Rainbow (1975), include the acknowledgment: "Inspiration: J. S. Bach." A few years later Blackmore even took up study of the cello, and Rainbow's 1981 release featured a very direct use of classical music in its title cut, "Difficult to Cure," an instrumental built around the "Ode to Joy" from the last movement of Beethoven's Ninth Symphony. Blackmore begins with a distorted version of Beethoven's instrumental recitative, which he transforms into a sitar-like modal flurry over a pedal; the band then moves into the theme of the "Ode" itself. Initially, Blackmore simply repeats the melody without developing or embellishing it, while the band modulates to different keys to freshen the repetitions. The musicians eventually alter the progression for the solos, which are a blend of a boogie blues rhythmic feel with the Orientalist modality of the beginning. In "Difficult to Cure," classical material is quoted literally so that it is sure to be recognized; in fact, the song is self-consciously parodic. The classical model is spoofed by a bouncy 12/8 beat, an incongruous introduction, and the finishing touch: as the song ends, we hear candid laughter in the recording studio. If Blackmore had drawn on Bach for inspiration, Beethoven was merely quoted, with a funny accent. The major mode of Beethoven's tune is rarely used in heavy metal, and when it is combined with a similarly inappropriate bouncy rhythm, Blackmore's distorted guitar and heavy drums end up sounding frivolous and silly. "Difficult to Cure" is a comic anomaly; it reminds us that heavy metal musicians are in fact very selective in their appropriations of the various styles that are usually lumped together as "classical music," and that fusions signify quite precisely.

In an interview published in 1985, Blackmore was asked about his current musical tastes: "I still listen to a great deal of classical music. . . . That's the type of music that moves me because I find it very dramatic. Singers, violinists and organists are generally the musicians I enjoy listening to most of all. I can't stand guitarists!" [18] Twelve years earlier, Blackmore had recommended to the readers of *Guitar Player* that, above all, they study guitarists. He had complained: "Jimmy Page says he listens to piano solos. But I don't see how that helps, because a pianist can play about ten times the speed of a guitarist." [19] In 1973, such technical limitations had been accepted; Blackmore's change of heart may reflect the fact that in 1978 Edward Van Halen redefined virtuosity on the electric guitar.

Edward Van Halen and the New Virtuosity

Alex and Edward Van Halen were born in the Netherlands (Alex in 1955, Edward in 1957) but moved with their family to California while still in grade school. Their father was a professional musician (saxophone and clarinet) whose gigging included live radio shows; he was "constantly practicing, working and going on the road," according to Alex. [20] Jan Van Halen encouraged his sons to become classical musicians, and both boys started piano lessons while very young, dutifully practicing Mozart until their interests in guitar and drums prevailed. After a brief period during which Edward played drums and Alex guitar, they switched instruments and grew increasingly serious about music, playing in a series of bands that would culminate in their tremendous success with Van Halen. Throughout his teens, Eddie was completely absorbed in the guitar, practicing "all day, every day. I used to cut school to come home and play, I was so into it." [21]

Like most rock guitarists, Van Halen was heavily influenced by the dialogic "question-and-answer" of the blues, which he knew mainly by way of the guitar playing of Eric Clapton. "I started out playing blues,"

Van Halen recalls: "I can play real good blues—that's the feeling I was after. But actually I've turned it into a much more aggressive thing. Blues is a real tasty, feel type of thing; so I copped that in the beginning. But then when I started to use a wang [vibrato] bar, I still used that feeling, but rowdier, more aggressive, more attack. But still, I end a lot of phrasing with a bluesy feeling."[22] But along with the influence of the blues, Van Halen's classical piano training taught him music theory that would later prove useful, and his continuing exposure to classical repertoires helped him to transform the electric guitar and forge a new virtuosity for it. Even after he became a rock star, Van Halen still played piano and violin and continued to listen to classical music, especially Bach and Debussy.

Edward Van Halen's impact on rock guitar playing was enormous. The readership of *Guitar Player* elected him Best New Talent in a 1978 poll, and Van Halen went on to win Best Rock Guitarist for an unprecedented five straight years, 1979–83. Yngwie Malmsteen, who himself won Best New Talent in 1984 and Best Rock Guitarist in 1985, credits Van Halen with revolutionizing rock guitar: "When I heard the first Van Halen album, I couldn't believe how great the guitar playing was. . . . I mean, he totally changed the whole guitar field." And even a decade after Van Halen's debut, Billy Gibbons of ZZ Top asserted that "if you had a guitar poll, I'd put Edward Van Halen in the first five slots and then the next five slots would start opening up."[23]

The solo that transformed rock guitar was called, appropriately enough, "Eruption." Released in 1978 on Van Halen's first album, "Eruption" is one minute and twenty-seven seconds of exuberant and playful virtuosity, a violinist's precise and showy technique inflected by the vocal rhetoric of the blues and rock and roll irreverence. Here and elsewhere, Van Halen's guitar playing displays an unprecedented fluidity, due to his skillful use of string bending, two-handed tapping, and his deft touch on the vibrato (or "whammy") bar.

Van Halen's fluid style and innovative technique depend upon the capabilities of amplification equipment that can produce very high electronic gain and indefinite sustain. The electrification of the guitar, begun in the 1920s, and subsequent developments in equipment and playing techniques, particularly the production of sophisticated distortion circuitry in the 1970s, helped make it possible for Baroque music to be newly relevant to guitar players. The electric guitar acquired the capabilities of the premier virtuosic instruments of the seventeenth and eighteenth centuries: the power and speed of the organ, the flexibility and nuance of the violin. Technological increases in sustain and volume made possible the conceptual and technical shifts that led players to explore Baroque models. Of course, the attraction of guitar players to those models helped spur particular technological developments, as when puzzled engineers reluctantly produced distortion-inducing devices for the first time in the mid 1960s, in response to guitarists' demands. Van Halen himself helped develop the sounds upon which his techniques depend by experimenting with a Variac voltage control that made his amps sound "hotter."[24] Van Halen also built some of his guitars himself, and this knowledge of guitar construction and modification affected his performing, just as his musical imagination drove the technological experiments.

In "Eruption," an initial power chord establishes A as tonal point of departure (see example 3). Van Halen moves the first section from blues-based pentatonic licks in A, through a couple of flashy patterns of less clear provenance, to collapse finally back to a low A, which he "wows" with the whammy bar. The opening sounds startlingly effortless, the easy flow of hammer-ons and pull-offs (articulation with the fretting fingers alone, without picking) interrupted by a few confident pauses and precisely picked harmonics. Three power chords introduce the next phrase, ostensibly moving the tonal center to D, although what follows is still mostly based in the A blues mode. Van Halen quickly moves through some Chuck Berry–inspired bends to an exuberant series of bends and wows in a swung rhythm. This section moves directly into a quotation of the best-known cliché of violin pedagogy, an etude by Rodolphe Kreutzer (see examples 4 and 5).[25] Rather than simply playing it straight, though, Van Halen picks each note three or four times in a tremolo style. He is toying with this primer of classical technique, and after two repetitions he spins down and out of it in the same style, pointedly introducing an F natural—which transforms the mode from Kreutzer's major to a darker Phrygian—on his way to the song's midway resting point.

After a second's silence, the piece is reattacked with a flurry of fast picking and hammering. The initial phrase is repeated, first centered on A, then on E; it is rhythmically very complex but rhetorically clear, the accented interruptions of a line of repeated notes suggesting both resolution and mobility.[26] Each time this motive is played, a disorienting scramble with harmonically remote pitches (deftly played by pulling off to open strings) ends up on a trill of the fifth scale degree, which conventionally requires resolution, thus setting up the repeat. A series of fast trills follows a recapitulation of the entrance on A, leading into the most celebrated section of this solo, the lengthy tapping section with which it culminates.

The audacious virtuosity of the rest of the solo was certainly impressive, but it was the tapping that astonished guitarists and fans. Reaching over to strike against the frets with his right hand, Van Halen hammers and pulls with his left, relying on the enhanced gain of his amplifier to sustain a stream of notes. Although a few other guitarists had used tapping to a limited extent, nothing like this had ever been heard before, and "Eruption" spurred guitarists to hyperbole: "Edward Van Halen practically reinvented the art of electric guitar with his incendiary "Eruption" solo."[27] Rock guitarists hailed tapping as not merely a fad or gimmick but a genuine expansion of the instrument's capabilities, the most important technical innovation since Jimi Hendrix. Their enthusiasm for the potentials of the tapping technique increased throughout the 1980s; since 1988 *Guitar for the Practicing Musician* has published a monthly column by Jennifer Batten, "On Tap," solely devoted to exploring this technique.[28] Edward Van Halen's development of two-handed techniques for the guitar is comparable to J. S. Bach's innovations in keyboard fingering. C. P. E. Bach recalled of his father: "He had devised for himself so convenient a system of fingering that it was not hard for him to conquer the greatest difficulties with the most flowing facility. Before him, the most famous clavier players in Germany and other lands had used the thumb but little."[29] Tapping similarly enabled Van Halen and the players who came after him to deploy more fingers and conquer great difficulties, and it particularly encouraged a "flowing facility."

The final section of "Eruption" is wholly tapped. Here the pitches are formed into arpeggios outlining triads. Van Halen's rhythmic torrent of sextuplets energizes a relatively slow rate of harmonic change, a strategy learned from Vivaldi (see example 6; compare example 3). In "Eruption," C♯ minor is changed to A major by moving one finger up one fret; a diminished triad then pushes through B major to land on E, which is made to feel like a point of arrival. This sense is quickly dispersed, though, when a subtle adjustment transforms the chord to C major. With the help of a couple of passing tones, C moves through D back up to E, in the familiar heavy metal progression of ♭VI–♭VII–I. Chromatic slides confirm E but then sink to establish D and then C in the same way. An abrupt move to B confirms E minor as the new tonic, and increasingly frantic alternation between them (reminiscent of Beethoven's use of similar patterns to increase tension before a final

Example 3. Van Halen (1978), "Eruption" (Music by Edward Van Halen, Alex Van Halen, Michael Anthony and David Lee Roth, Copyright © 1978 Van Halen Music. International Copyright Secured. All Rights Reserved. Reprinted by Permission of Cherry Lane Music Co., Inc. Transcription by Andy Aledort).

Harm.
*T T
Feedback
trem. bar
rit.
(w/echo effect)
Fade out
*Tap open low E at 12 fr, producing harmonic.
Fdbk. pitch: B

Example 4. Rodolphe Kreutzer, "Caprice Study No. #2" for violin, mm. 1–2.

Example 5. Van Halen (1978), "Eruption," excerpt showing transformation of Kreutzer motive.

Example 6. Antonio Vivaldi, Violin Concerto in A Minor, Op. 3, No. 6, third movement, solo violin, mm. 75–91.

cadence; see the end of his Ninth Symphony) leads to a noisy breakdown on E.

Tapping directs musical interest toward harmony, the succession of chords through time. It produces an utterly regular rhythmic pattern to articulate the motion, just as in, for example, J. S. Bach's famous Prelude in C Major, from the *Well Tempered Clavier* (see example 7). As in Bach's prelude and so much of Vivaldi's music, the harmonic progressions of "Eruption" lead the listener along an aural adventure. Van Halen continually sets up implied harmonic goals and then achieves, modifies, extends, or subverts them. At the end of the solo, he increases the harmonic tension to the breaking point with frenetic alternation of tonic and dominant. Finally, he abandons purposeful motion; the piece undergoes a meltdown. It comes to rest finally on the tonic, but echo effects, ringing harmonics, and a gradual fade make this an ambiguous closure. Engaging the listener with the conventions of tonal progress and then willfully manipulating his audience's expectations, Van Halen reiterates Vivaldi's celebration of the rhetoric of the virtuoso.

Though it certainly exists elsewhere, this kind of individual virtuosity is a conceptual model of musical excellence derived from classical music making. The word *virtuoso* is derived from the Italian *virtù*, an important term in the aristocratic courts of northern Italy in the fifteenth and sixteenth centuries. *Virtù* designated a type of individual excellence; as used by Machiavelli, it can denote "talented will," ingenuity, skill, efficacy, strength, power, or virtue. As applied to art, it reflected the relationship of art to power, as larger-than-life images and performances celebrated the wealth and power of an elite.[30] Though it existed earlier in European music, virtuosity came to be especially celebrated in the Renaissance. By the middle of the sixteenth century, a well-developed virtuosic solo repertoire existed, particularly for lutenists. Francesco da Milano, on the lute, and the three ladies of Ferrara, as vocalists, are reported to have astonished and transported listeners with their extraordinary technique and the expressiveness it enabled. Virtuosity attained broader social relevance in the nineteenth century, along with the popularity of public concerts for middle-class audiences. Franz Liszt invented the solo recital in 1839, and the piano—"newly reinforced by metal parts; newly responsive to every impulse of hand, foot, and brain— became music's central vehicle for heroic individualism."[31]

Example 7. J. S. Bach, "Prelude in C Major," from the *Well Tempered Clavier*, Book I, mm. 1–7 (© 1983 by Dover Publications, Inc.).

Virtuosity—ultimately derived from the Latin root *vir* (man)—has always been concerned with demonstrating and enacting a particular kind of power and freedom that might be called "potency." Both words carry gendered meanings, of course; heavy metal shares with most other Western music a patriarchal context wherein power itself is construed as essentially male. At least until the mid-1980s, heavy metal was made almost exclusively by male musicians for male fans, and "Eruption" is a metaphorical ejaculation—a demonstration of physical and rhetorical potency. But it can also signify a more general sort of social capability. It is for this reason that some women are able to identify with even the most macho culture (Judas Priest, Beethoven), mapping its experiences of transcendence and empowerment onto their own social positions and needs. Like all musical techniques, virtuosity functions socially. Some might find virtuosity inherently distancing or elitist, since it is a sensational display of exceptional individual power. But for many others, virtuosi are the most effective articulators of a variety of social fantasies and musical pleasures.

Classical music certainly does not provide the only model for virtuosity, but the prestige of that repertoire has made its particular model very influential. The virtuoso not only possesses unusual technical facility but through music is able to command extraordinary, almost supernatural rhetorical powers. Robert Schumann reported this of a performance by Liszt:

> The demon began to flex his muscles. He first played along with them [the audience], as if to feel them out, and then gave them a taste of something more substantial until, with his magic, he had ensnared each and every one and could move them this way or that as he chose. It is unlikely that any other artist, excepting only Paganini, has the power to lift, carry and deposit an audience in such high degree. . . . In listening to Liszt are we overwhelmed by an onslaught of sounds and sensations. In a matter of seconds we have been exposed to tenderness, daring, fragrance and madness. . . It simply has to be heard—and seen. If Liszt were to play behind the scenes a considerable portion of the poetry would be lost.[32]

Schumann's account points to the importance of spectacle in virtuosic music and to the mystery that surrounds virtuosic performers. Compare Jay Jay French's account of his experiences performing with the heavy metal band Twisted Sister:

> You walk on stage some nights and you feel more muscular, you just all of a sudden feel like the power is pouring out of you, the tune is just ripping itself through your body, out of the speakers, out of the PA, blowing people away, and you haven't even broken a sweat yet. The night's just beginning and they're already going crazy, and you're just cruisin' in first gear. Then you move it up a notch. . . . And you lay it out, and then put it into third, and then it's one of

those nights, and the audience goes even crazier, and you're just blowing away, and you're just lookin' at yourself and you go "Gee, I am God!" And then you kick it into fourth, and the whole night's amazing.[33]

The first truly virtuosic hard rock guitarist was Jimi Hendrix; Pete Townshend of The Who is usually credited with being the first to exploit power chords and feedback for musical purposes, but it was Hendrix more than anyone else who made these techniques—along with whammy bar dives, pick slides, and a bag of other tricks—part of a virtuoso's vocabulary of extravagance and transgression. As Billy Gibbons, ZZ Top's guitarist, said, Hendrix "took the guitar into Martianland."[34] Virtuosity can signify in many different ways, though. Charles Shaar Murray writes of Jimi Hendrix's famous version of "The Star Spangled Banner":

Hendrix's "out" playing was not necessarily always an expression of pain, rage or grief: the brief exercise in pure crash-and-burn pyrotechnica with which he opened up "Wild Thing" at the climax of his Monterey Pop Festival US début was Hendrix *playing* in the most literal sense of the word. It was playful, mischievous, exuberant, euphoric, extrovert; an ex-underdog's high-spirited slapstick display of hey-look-what-I-can-do. But as the mood of the times darkened, so did Hendrix's music; when he moved into his trick-bag, it was increasingly to express that which simply could not be communicated in any other way.[35]

Murray's explication of Hendrix is illuminating; it highlights the fact that virtuosity can have many different sorts of social meanings. Throughout his book, though, Murray indulges in the sort of gratuitous and unsupported bashing of heavy metal that is fashionable among rock critics: "Eddie Van Halen, by far the most influential hard and heavy guitarist of the eighties, has borrowed the Hendrix vocabulary—tremolo tricks and all—in order to say very little."[36] What Van Halen "said" had much in common with the exuberance and struggle of Hendrix's playing; but he became the most influential player of his generation by achieving a kind of rational control over all of these risky, noisy techniques. The oral virtuosity of the blues, nuanced and dialogic, had become in Hendrix a psychedelic wail of transgression and transcendence. With Van Halen, this virtuosity is differently managed; his precision and consistency became new benchmarks for a rock guitar virtuosity more closely tied to classical ideals. For (as I will discuss below) metal guitarists absorbed not only licks and harmonic progressions but ways of making and valuing music derived from classical music.

Many heavy metal musicians link themselves with the classical model of virtuosity quite explicitly. Wolf Marshall, in an article titled "The Classical Influence" in the leading professional guitarists' magazine (*Guitar for the Practicing Musician*), compares today's metal guitarists to

Liszt and Paganini in their virtuosity, bravura manner, mystique, attractiveness to women, and experimentation with flashy, crowd-pleasing tricks.[37] These parallels seem very apt when we recall that women swooned and threw flowers to Liszt during his performances, that fans followed Frescobaldi's tours through Italy, congregating in crowds as large as thirty thousand for the chance to hear him sing or improvise toccatas on the organ.[38] The contemporary description of Franz Liszt with which I began this chapter could just as well refer to Ritchie Blackmore or Eddie Van Halen ("the strange wonder . . . the pale slender youth in his clothes that signal the nonconformist; the long, sleek, drooping hair . . . undreampt-of virtuosity and technical brilliance.").

As I have suggested, the classical influence on heavy metal is due in part to the early training of many guitarists. Moreover, this concept of virtuosity is easy to reinvent in a culture that glorifies competitive individualism in so many other ways. But beginning in the early 1980s, metal musicians turned increasingly to direct study and emulation of modern and historical classical performers. Not only the musical discourse of metal but its conceptions of musicianship and pedagogy were transformed by increasingly vigorous pursuit of classical models. One of the leading players of this moment, hero to thousands of budding metal neoclassicists, was Randy Rhoads.

Randy Rhoads: Metal Gets Serious

Like Edward Van Halen, Randy Rhoads grew up in a musical household. The son of two music teachers, Rhoads was born in 1956, in Santa Monica, California. He enrolled as a student at his mother's music school at age six, studying guitar, piano, and music theory, and a few years later began classical guitar lessons, which he would continue throughout his career. During the late 1970s, Rhoads built a regional reputation playing with Quiet Riot, but his big break came in 1980, when he landed the guitar chair in a new band fronted by ex–Black Sabbath vocalist Ozzy Osbourne, perhaps the single most durable and successful performer in heavy metal. During his brief tenure with Osbourne's band (ending with his death at age twenty-five in a plane crash), Rhoads became famous as the first guitar player of the 1980s to expand the classical influence, further adapting and integrating a harmonic and melodic vocabulary derived from classical music.

Among his early musical influences, Rhoads cited the dark moods and drama of Alice Cooper, Ritchie Blackmore's fusion of rock and classical music, Van Halen's tapping technique, and his favorite classical composers, Vivaldi and Pachelbel.[39] His musical experiences were unusual in their close focus on hard rock and classical music because Rhoads supported himself, until he joined Osbourne, by teaching rather than playing. Unlike many guitar players, Rhoads wasn't out hustling gigs indiscriminately in order to pay the rent. Instead of playing blues, disco, r&b, country, or any of the multitude of styles with which most working musicians must cope, Rhoads concentrated on his chosen interests and learned by teaching: "The way I started to get a style was by teaching. . . . I taught eight hours a day, six days a week, every half hour a different student. I had little kids, teenagers, and even some older people. . . . When you sit there and play all day long, you're going to develop a lot of speed. . . . I started combining what they wanted to learn with a bit of technique. Every day with every student I'd learn something."[40] Rhoads had a lifelong attraction to the technical challenges, the theoretical rigor, and the dramatic syntax of classical music. According to his friend and collaborator Ozzy Osbourne, "Randy's heart was in the classics, to be honest; he wanted to be a classical guitar player. In fact, with the first record royalties he received, he went out and bought himself a very, very expensive classical guitar. He sat there for days and nights working on his music theories. . . . On days off I'd get in the bar. He wouldn't: he'd practice all day, every day."[41]

The classical influence is pervasive in the music Rhoads recorded with Osbourne. Rhoads adapted the harmonic progression of the famous Pachelbel canon for "Goodbye to Romance" (on *Blizzard of Ozz*, 1981), and many songs rely on the gothic overtones evoked by much Baroque music in the twentieth century. The best example of this, J. S. Bach's Toccata in D Minor for organ (1705), has been recycled in movies, television, and advertising as a highly effective aural signifier of mystery, doom, and gloom. A bit of this toccata was used to introduce Bon Jovi's tremendously successful *Slippery When Wet* album (1987); the power and sustain of the organ are matched only by the electric guitar, and Bach's virtuosic style and rhetorical flair is perfectly suited to heavy metal. On Bon Jovi's recording, reverberation is added to evoke the auratic space of a cathedral, imputing similar mystery and weight to the album that follows. Baroque music is most often employed to these ends by metal musicians, but Osbourne also used the artificial archaism of Carl Orff's *Carmina Burana* to open the show on his 1986 concert tour.

Rhoads and Osbourne's "Mr. Crowley" (1981) also begins with synthesized organ, playing a cyclical harmonic progression modeled on Vivaldi. The minor mode, the ominous organ, and the fateful cyclicism, culminating in a suspension, set up an affect of mystery and doom. The sung verses and first guitar solo of "Mister Crowley" are supported by a metal-inflected Baroque harmonic progression: Dm | B♭ | C | Dm | B♭ | Em7♭5 | Asus4 | A. The move from B♭ back up through C (♭VI–♭VII–I) is uncharacteristic of Baroque music (where ♭VI usually resolves to V), but it frequently occurs in metal, where it normally functions in an aggressive and dark Aeolian mood. The progression that underpins Rhoads's "outro" solo at the end of the song is similar, but it is a more straightforward Vivaldian circle of fifths progression: Dm | Gm7 | C | F | B♭ | Em7♭5 | Asus4 | A. Until classically influenced heavy metal, such cyclical progressions were unusual in rock music, which had been fundamentally blues-based. The classical influence contributed to a greater reliance on the power of harmonic progression to organize desire and narrative. The circle of fifths progression was picked up by metal because it sounds archaic, directional, and thus fateful. Rhoads's first solo in "Mr. Crowley" is a frantic scramble against the inevitability of the harmonic pattern. The second rides the wave of harmonic teleology with more virtuosic aplomb (see example 8); Rhoads uses arpeggios, tremolo picking, trills, and fast scales to keep up with the drive of the progression.

Rhoads displays similar techniques on a live recording of "Suicide Solution" (1987) during the course of a lengthy virtuosic cadenza. The crowd's reactions are clearly audible as counterpoint to Rhoads's phrases, confirming that the purpose of virtuosic technique is to facilitate fantastic rhetoric; the virtuoso strives to manipulate the audience by means of skillfull deployment of shared musical codes of signification. In the seventeenth and early eighteenth centuries, music was theorized in these terms very openly in treatises on the *Affektenlehre*, before the rise of aesthetics led to circumlocutions and mystifications of music's power.[42] Moreover, contemporary accounts show that until late in the nineteenth century the behavior of concert audiences was far from today's "classical" norms of silence and passivity. Musical audiences were tamed around the turn of this century, as part of the cultural segregation of private emotions and public behavior so well analyzed by Lawrence W. Levine. Until the twentieth century, it seems that large audiences for opera and public concerts behaved very much like today's audiences for heavy metal and other popular music. Listeners reacted to musical rhetoric with "spontaneous expressions of pleasure of and disapproval in the form of cheers, yells, gesticulations, hisses, boos, stamping of feet, whistling, crying for encores, and applause."[43]

In the studio recording of "Suicide Solution," which appeared on *Blizzard of Ozz* (1981), there is no guitar solo at all, an unusual departure from the formal norms of heavy metal but an appropriate one, given the song's musical delineation of powerlessness.[44] But in concert, Osbourne used "Suicide Solution" as an opportunity for Rhoads to display his prowess as a soloist. Where the song would normally end, it is suspended inconclusively instead, and Rhoads begins a virtuosic cadenza made up of carefully paced statements and flourishes, divided by charged gaps that seem to demand replies from the audience (see example 9). Rhoads uses speedy patterns and fast runs to build excitement, and he manages the rhythmic impulses of his lines so as to create and then suspend metric expectations. Tried and true harmonic devices, such as diminished arpeggios and chromatic "meltdowns," are borrowed from the semiotic trick bag of classical music to manipulate desire by suggesting, deflecting, achieving, or making ambiguous a variety of tonal goals.

Rhetorically, Rhoads's cadenza follows Baroque models. Susan McClary has written about the narrative organization of desire in J. S. Bach's extraordinary harpsichord cadenza for the first movement of his Brandenburg Concerto No. 5. McClary contrasts the manipulative strategies of this unusually lengthy solo with the pressure of generic norms toward closure (see example 10).

Most cadenzas at the time would have been a very few measures long—a slightly elaborate prolongation and preparation before capitulation to the ritornello and the final resolution. . . . Thus in order to maintain necessary energy the harpsichord part must resort to increasingly deviant strategies—chromatic inflections, faster and faster note values—resulting in what sounds like a willful, flamboyant seventeenth-century toccata: in its opposition to the ensemble's order, it unleashes elements of chaos, irrationality, and noise until finally it blurs almost entirely the sense of key, meter, and form upon which eighteenth-century style depends.[45]

Like Bach's cadenza, Rhoads's invokes the toccata, a virtuoso solo instrumental genre of the late sixteenth through mid eighteenth centuries, mainly performed on fretted and keyboard instruments (guitar, lute, organ, harpsichord). Heavy metal guitarists rely on precisely those musical tactics that characterized the toccata: "quasi-improvisatory disjunct harmonies, sweeping scales, broken-chord figuration, and roulades that often range over the entire instrument. . . . [N]othing is more inappropriate than order and constraint."[46]

The formal plan of Rhoads's cadenza is similar, in some respects, to that of Bach's. In both, an impressive array of virtuosic figuration is explored, until a disorienting harmonic meltdown leads to a long drive toward cadence. In Rhoads's solo, the harmonic confusion precedes a lengthly tapped section, which itself melts down. Initially, the tapped arpeggios circumscribe, with only some ambiguity, the closely related

Ending Guitar Solo "Outro"
Rhy. Fig. 2

*Root note only

Repeat Rhy. Fig. 2

Example 8. Ozzy Osbourne (1981), "Mr. Crowley," solo by Randy Rhoads (Words and Music by Ozzy Osbourne, Randy Rhoads, and Bob Daisley, Copyright © 1981 Blizzard Music Limited, 12 Thayer Street, London W1M 5LD, England. International Copyright Secured. All Rights Reserved. Reprinted by Permission of Cherry Lane Music Co., Inc. Transcription by Wolf Marshall).

harmonic areas of E minor and A minor. But a succession of more distant chords—G | Am | F | F aug. | A | C♯m—leads to a complete breakdown, embellished by whammy bar wows and a wailing high harmonic. After pausing to let the audience voice its approval of his transgressions, Rhoads begins again with a fast-picked figure, which he slides chromatically up the neck with increasing frenzy. This sequence winds up with another high wail and some low growls; at this point, he allows the framing "ritornello" to return, and the band joins in a short reprise of "Suicide Solution."[47]

Not only the classical materials in his music but also Rhoads's study of academic music theory influenced many guitarists in the 1980s. Throughout the decade, years after his death, Rhoads's picture continued to appear on the covers of guitar magazines, advertising articles that discussed his practicing and teaching methods and analyzed his music. The inner sleeve of the *Tribute* album (1987) reproduces a few pages from Rhoads's personal guitar notebook. One sheet is titled "Key of C♯"; on it, for each of the seven modes based on C♯ (Ionian, Dorian, Phrygian, etc.), Rhoads wrote out the diatonic chords for each scale degree, followed by secondary and substitute seventh chords. On another page, he composed exercises based on arpeggiated seventh and ninth chords. Rhoads's interest in music theory was symptomatic of the increasing classical influence on heavy metal, but his success also helped promote classical study among metal guitarists. Winner of *Guitar Player*'s Best New Talent award in 1981, Rhoads brought to heavy metal guitar a new level of discipline and consistency, derived from classical models. Besides his classical allusions and his methods of study and teaching, Rhoads's skill at double-tracking solos (recording them exactly the same way more than once so that they could be layered on the record to add a sense of depth and space) was extremely influential on subsequent production techniques.[48] Rhoads's accomplishments also contributed to the growing tendency among guitarists to regard their virtuosic solos in terms of a division of labor long accepted in classical music, as opportunities for thoughtful composition and skillful execution rather than spontaneous improvisation.

Classically influenced players such as Van Halen and Rhoads helped precipitate a shift among guitar players toward a new kind of professionalism, with theory, analysis, pedagogy, and technical rigor acquiring new importance. *Guitar for the Practicing Musician*, now the most widely read guitarists' magazine, began publication in 1983, attracting readers with transcriptions and analyses of guitar-based popular music. Its professional guitarist-transcribers developed a sophisticated set of

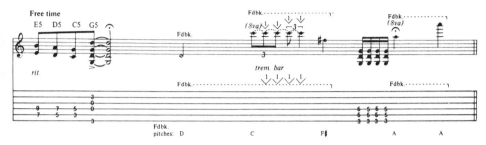

Example 9. Ozzy Osbourne (1981), "Suicide Solution," cadenza by Randy Rhoads (Words and music by John Osbourne, Bob Daisley and Randy Rhoads, Copyright © 1981, 1986, 1987 Essex Music International and TRO Music. Transcription by Wolf Marshall).

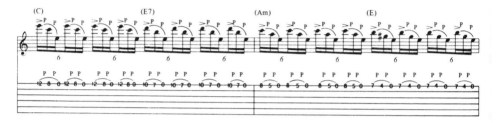

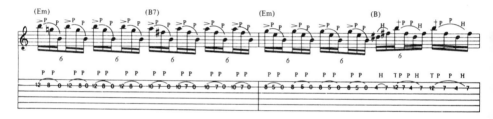

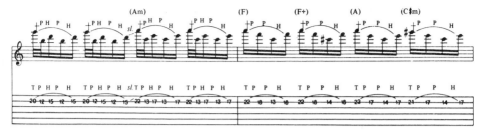

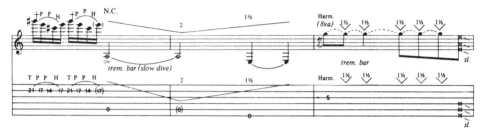

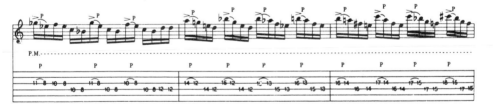

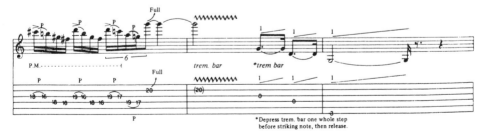

*Depress trem. bar one whole step
before striking note, then release.

Example 10. J. S. Bach, Brandenburg Concerto No. 5, first movement, mm. 199–201

special notations for representing the nuances of performance, rather like the elaborate ornament tables of Baroque music (see example 11). Their transcriptions are usually accompanied by analysis, both modal (e.g., "The next section alternates between the modalities of E♭ Lydian and F Mixolydian") and stylistic, relating new pieces to the history of discursive options available to guitar players.

Other guitar magazines increased their coverage of metal in time with the early 1980s metal boom, not only in order to keep up with musical trends, but also because many of their readers valued technique and heavy metal was the main site of technical innovation and expansion.[49] The magazines became increasingly informed by academic music theory, with columns on modes, harmony, and chord substitution, and analyses of classical music. The first installment of a new column called "Guitar in the 80s" was titled "The Bach Influence."[50] Guitar's columnist discussed two excerpts from J. S. Bach's music for unaccompanied violin, transcribed them into guitar tablature, and suggested playing techniques. The article argued that the point of studying such music is to rise to its technical challenge, to learn from its examples of clear voice-leading, and to understand its relevance to the music of Yngwie Malmsteen and other metal guitarists.

Institutional support for such technical study grew as well. Classical guitar teachers had begun to appear on college faculties around the

TABLATURE EXPLANATION

TABLATURE A six-line staff that graphically represents the guitar fingerboard. By placing a number on the appropriate line, the string and fret of any note can be indicated. For example:

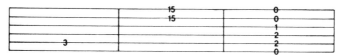

5th string, 3rd fret

1st string, 15th fret,
2nd string, 15th fret,
played together

an open E chord

Definitions for Special Guitar Notation (For both traditional and tablature guitar lines)

BEND: Strike the note and bend up ½ step (one fret).

SLIDE: The first note is struck and then the same finger of the fret hand moves up the string to the location of the second note. The second note is not struck.

TREMOLO PICKING: The note is picked as rapidly and continuously as possible.

BEND: Strike the note and bend up a whole step (two frets)

SLIDE: Same as above, except the second note is struck.

NATURAL HARMONIC: The fret hand lightly touches the string over the fret indicated; then it is struck. A chime-like sound is produced.

LEGATO BEND AND RELEASE: Strike the note. Bend up ½ (or whole) step, then release the bend back to the original note. All three notes are tied; only the first note is struck.

SLIDE: Slide up to the note indicated from a few frets below.

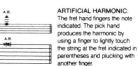
ARTIFICIAL HARMONIC: The fret hand fingers the note indicated. The pick hand produces the harmonic by using a finger to lightly touch the string at the fret indicated in parentheses and plucking with another finger.

GHOST BEND: Bend the note up ½ (or whole) step, then strike it.

SLIDE: Strike the note and slide up an indefinite number of frets, releasing finger pressure at the end of the slide.

ARTIFICIAL "PINCH" HARMONIC: The note is fretted normally and a harmonic is produced by adding the edge of the thumb or the tip of the index finger of the pick hand to the normal pick attack. High volume or distortion will allow for a greater variety of harmonics.

GHOST BEND AND RELEASE: Bend the note up ½ (or whole) step. Strike it and release the bend back to the original note.

PICK SLIDE: The edge of the pick is rubbed down the length of the string. A scratchy sound is produced.

UNISON BEND: The lower note is struck slightly before the higher. It is then bent to the pitch of the higher note. They are on adjacent strings.

HAMMER-ON: Strike the first (lower) note, then sound the higher note with another finger by fretting it without picking.

TREMOLO BAR: The pitch of a note or chord is dropped a specified number of steps, then returned to the original pitch.

VIBRATO: The string is vibrated by rapidly bending and releasing a note with the fret hand or tremolo bar.

PULL-OFF: Both fingers are initially placed on the notes to be sounded. Strike the first (higher) note, then sound the lower note by pulling the finger off the higher note while keeping the lower note fretted.

PALM MUTE (P.M.): The note is partially muted by the pick hand lightly touching the string(s) just before the bridge.

SHAKE OR EXAGGERATED VIBRATO: The pitch is varied to a greater degree by vibrating with the fret hand or tremolo bar.

FRETBOARD TAPPING: Hammer ("tap") onto the fretboard with the index or middle finger of the pick hand and pull off to the note fretted by the fret hand ("T" indicates "tapped" notes).

MUFFLED STRINGS: A percussive sound is produced by laying the fret hand across the strings without depressing them to the fretboard and striking them with the pick hand.

Example 11. "Tablature Explanation and Definitions for Special Guitar Notation" (From *Guitar for the Practicing Musician*, August 1990, p. 33. Copyright © 1992 Cherry Lane Music Co., Inc. International Copyright Secured. All Rights Reserved. Reprinted by Permission of Cherry Lane Music Co. Inc.).

time heavy metal emerged as a genre in the early 1970s. The classical influence owed something to the fact that virtually all of these teachers had started by playing some kind of popular music, turning later to the budding field of classical guitar, which had been almost single-handedly chartered by Andrés Segovia.[51] Other institutions flourished outside the ivory tower, offering their students a much broader professional training. Some of the best-known schools for guitarists have been around since the 1960s, such as the Musicians' Institute in Los Angeles, which incorporates the Guitar Institute of Technology. The recordings of Van Halen and Rhoads, among others, signaled a rise in the technical standards of rock guitar playing that prompted many new players to seek out organized musical study. Music Tech in Minneapolis, founded in 1985, was by 1990 a fully accredited music school with a faculty of 30 and a full-time student body of 195. Their professional programs in guitar, bass, drums, keyboard, and recording engineering include required courses in music theory, history, composition, performance practice, and improvisation in a variety of popular styles. Moreover, all rock guitarists are required to study classical guitar.[52] The success of schools such as GIT and Music Tech demonstrates the incomplete hegemony of classically oriented music schools; since colleges and university music departments have been very slow to broaden their focus to include the musics that matter most in contemporary culture, popular musicians have built their own institutions.

The fluidity of musical discourses enables guitarists to draw upon many influences, and even the guitar magazines cater simultaneously to very different groups of guitarists, contributing to the interchange of styles. Of Def Leppard's guitarists, for example, Steve Clark was classically trained; Clark's father had given him a guitar on the condition that he take lessons, so he learned Bach and Vivaldi along with Led Zeppelin and Thin Lizzy. Phil Collen, on the other hand, studied mostly jazz; Collen says that both influences show up in their music. Dave Mustaine of Megadeth claims as influences the Supremes, Marvin Gaye, and Pink Floyd. Dan Spitz of Anthrax took lessons in jazz while he privately studied the recordings of Iron Maiden, Black Sabbath, Judas Priest, Jimi Hendrix—and lately, rap music. Guitarist Vinnie Vincent was impressed by the speed of classical violinists and attempted to imitate their technical facility with scales and arpeggios, but he also integrated the steel-guitar style he heard his father using in country music.[53]

Guitarists do vary greatly in the degree to which they have adopted the classical model of rigorous practice and theoretical study. Danny Spitz of Anthrax practices guitar five hours each day, more than most classical musicians. Izzy Stradlin' of Guns N' Roses doesn't really practice in the same sense at all; having no technical or theoretical knowledge of music, he "screws around," playing with sounds. Eddie Van Halen seldom practices guitar in any formal way, preferring instead to "play when I feel like it. . . . Sometimes I play it for a minute, sometimes half an hour, and sometimes all day. . . . But I am always thinking music. Some people think I'm spacing off, but really I'm not. I am always thinking of riffs and melodies."[54]

One of the most highly respected heavy metal guitarists of the late 1980s, George Lynch, learned to play entirely without reading music or studying music theory: "What I mean when I refer to myself as being non-technical is that I don't know what I'm doing. It's all up here [points to head]. To be completely honest, I don't even know a major scale. I don't know what one is, if you can believe that. But somehow I get away with it. And sometimes I think I'm afraid to learn because I might spoil a good thing."[55] Lynch is an extraordinary musician, with impeccable technique and awesome rhetorical skills. He certainly does know what he is doing, even if he lacks a technical vocabulary for describing it. Yet he feels keenly the contemporary pressure to theorize, and his fame makes him turn to the new crop of mass mediated private study aids to help him redress this lack: "It's hard to be in the position I'm in and to walk somewhere to get a guitar lesson, so I learn from tapes—home study courses, video tapes. . . . I don't know if I should be admitting any of this."[56]

Such confessions point to the coexistence in heavy metal of completely different ways of understanding musicality and musical creation. But the classical model, stressing rationalization and technical rigor, was ascendant throughout the 1980s. The most influential metal guitarist after Van Halen clarified the issues, expanding the classical influence and also convincing many that the trend toward systemization did not represent unambiguous progress.

Yngwie Malmsteen: Metal Augmented and Diminished

Swedish guitar virtuoso Yngwie J. Malmsteen continued many of the trends explored by Blackmore, Van Halen, and Rhoads and took some of them to unprecedented extremes. Born in 1963, Malmsteen was exposed to classical music from the age of five. But he says, "I played the blues before I played anything."[57] In fact, he relates a pair of musical epiphanies that, taken together, started him on the path to becoming the most influential rock guitarist since Van Halen.

Malmsteen's mother gave him a guitar on his fifth birthday, but he expressed little interest in it at first. She wanted him to be a musician and made sure he received piano lessons, ballet lessons, vocal lessons, flute lessons, trumpet lessons—all in vain. None of it interested him, and he claims to have hated music until "on the 18th of September, 1970, I saw a show on television with Jimi Hendrix, and I said, 'Wow!' I took the guitar off the wall, and I haven't stopped since."[58] Malmsteen's first fruitful encounter with classical music—his exposure to the music of Paganini, the nineteenth-century violin virtuoso—also took place through the mediation of television: "I first heard his music when I was 13 years old. I saw a Russian violinist playing some Paganini stuff on TV, and freaked. . . . Paganini's intensity blew my socks off. He was so clean, dramatic and fast; his vibrato, broken chords and arpeggios were amazing. That's how I wanted to play guitar."[59]

Upon the release of his U.S. debut album in 1984, which won him *Guitar Player*'s Best New Talent award that year and Best Rock Guitarist in 1985, Malmsteen quickly gained a reputation as the foremost of metal's neoclassicists. Malmsteen adapted classical music with more thoroughness and intensity than had any previous guitarist, and he expanded the melodic and harmonic language of metal while setting even higher standards of virtuosic precision: "With the coronation of King Yngwie, there isn't one aspiring guitarist who isn't now familiar with diminished seventh chords, harmonic minor scales and phrygian and lydian modes. His advent has been accepted by guitar teachers as well, because he brought discipline into a world where study used to be considered sacreligious [*sic*]."[60] Not only do Malmsteen's solos recreate the rhetoric of his virtuosic heroes, Bach and Paganini, but he introduced further harmonic resources, advanced such techniques as sweep-picking, and achieved the best impression yet of the nuance and agility of a virtuoso violinist (see his solo on "Black Star," example 12).

Moreover, Malmsteen embraced the premises of classical music more openly than had anyone before him. His fetishization of instrumental technique complemented his move toward "absolute" music. Only two of the songs on his first album have vocals; in the other six, the norms of songwriting are completely subordinated to the imperative of virtuosic display. Melodies are presented by multilayered guitar tracks, interrupted by multiple guitar solos. Later albums, such as *Odyssey* (1988), include more vocals, but it seems clear that Malmsteen regards them as a capitulation to the requirements of commercial success. With titles evoking myth ("Icarus' Dream Suite," *Odyssey*), mysticism ("Crystal Ball," "Deja Vu," "Evil Eye," "As Above, So Below"), and power ("Riot in the

Dungeon," "Bite the Bullet," "Faster Than the Speed of Light," "Far Beyond the Sun"), Malmsteen signals the reliance of his music on the gothic aura of classical music previously exploited by musicians such as Ritchie Blackmore and Randy Rhoads. But these evocations are fleshed out not by means of lyrics so much as through Malmsteen's harmonic progressions and virtuosic rhetoric.

Guitar for the Practicing Musician published a detailed analysis of Malmsteen's "Black Star," from his first U.S. album, *Yngwie J. Malmsteen's Rising Force* (1984). Such analytical pieces are intended as guides to the music of important guitarists, facilitating the study and emulation practiced by the magazine's readers. The following excerpts from Wolf Marshall's commentary can serve both as a summary of some technical features of Malmsteen's music and as a sample of the critical discourse of the writers who theorize and analyze heavy metal in professional guitarists' magazines:

Black Star shows off the many facets of Yngwie's singular style. Whether he is playing subdued acoustic guitar or blazing pyrotechnics, he is unmistakably Yngwie—the newest and perhaps the most striking proponent of the Teutonic-Slavic *Weltsmerz* (as in Bach/Beethoven/Brahms Germanic brooding minor modality) School of Heavy Rock. . . . The opening guitar piece is a classical prelude (as one might expect) to the larger work. It is vaguely reminiscent of Bach's *Bourree* in Em, with its 3/4 rhythm and use of secondary dominant chords. . . . The passage at the close of the guitar's exposition is similar to the effect . . . [of the] spiccato ("bouncing bow") classical violin technique. It is the first of many references to classical violin mannerisms. . . . This is a diminished chord sequence, based on the classical relationship of C diminished: C D♯ F♯ A (chord) to B major in a Harmonic minor mode: E F♯ G A B C D♯. . . . The feeling of this is like some of Paganini's violin passages. . . . While these speedy arpeggio flurries are somewhat reminiscent of Blackmore's frenzied wide raking, they are actually quite measured and exact and require a tremendous amount of hand shifting and stretching as well as precision to accomplish. The concept is more related to virtuoso violin etudes than standard guitar vocabulary. . . . Notice the use of Harmonic minor (Mixolydian mode) in the B major sections and the Baroque Concerto Grosso (Handel/Bach/Vivaldi) style running bass line counterpoint as well.[61]

Marshall's analysis is quite musicological in tone and content; he deliberately compares Malmsteen's recorded performance to classical techniques, contextualizes it through style analysis, and translates certain features into the technical vocabulary of music theory. The style analysis situates "Black Star" with respect to two musical traditions: rock guitar (Blackmore) and classical music (Bach, Paganini, Beethoven, Vivaldi, etc.). Marshall simultaneously presents a detailed description of the music and links it to the classical tradition by employing the language of academic music theory: chords, modes, counterpoint, form.

Example 12. Yngwie Malmsteen's Rising Force (1988), "Black Star," end of exposition and solo by Malmsteen (Words and Music by Yngwie Malmsteen, Copyright © 1985 by Unichappell Music, Inc. and De Novo Music. All Rights Administered by Unichappell Music, Inc. International Copyright Secured. All Rights Reserved. Transcription by Wolf Marshall).

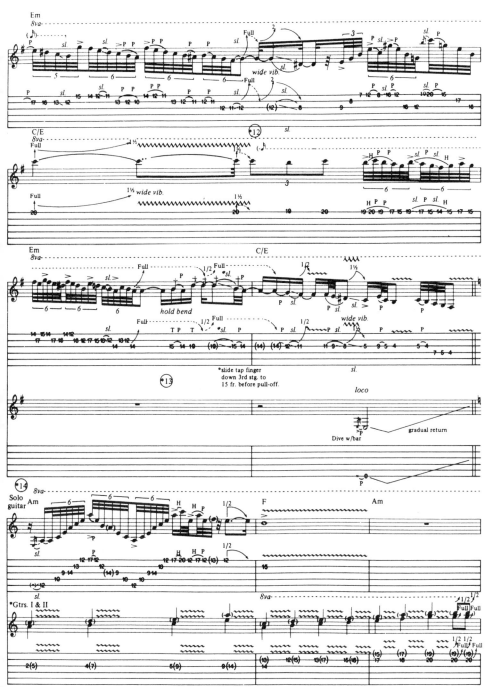

As rock guitarists have become increasingly interested in studying the history and theory of classical music, Marshall can safely assume that his audience is able to follow such analysis. In fact, in my experience, many heavy metal guitarists (most of whom, like Bach and Mozart, never attended college) have a much better grasp of harmonic theory and modal analysis than do most university graduate students in music.

Moreover, Marshall's analysis shows that metal guitarists and their pedagogues have not only adopted the trappings of academic discourse about music, but they have also internalized many of the values that underpin that discourse. Even as he carefully contextualizes Malmsteen's music, Marshall insists on its originality and uniqueness ("Yngwie's singular style," "unmistakably Yngwie"). The commentary emphasizes Malmsteen's precision of execution as well ("measured and exact," "tremendous . . . precision"). Most tellingly, Marshall implicitly accepts the categories and conceptions of academic music analysis, along with its terms.[62] For apart from the comment about "arpeggio flurries," Marshall deals exclusively with pitch and form, the traditional concerns of musicological analysis. And just as the discipline of musicology has drawn fire from within and without for ignoring or marginalizing musical rhythm, timbre, gesture, rhetoric, and other possible categories of analysis, metal guitarists' own theorists and pedagogues could be criticized for the same restricted analytical vision. If they are to become effective musicians, metal guitarists must, in fact, learn to maneuver within musical parameters beyond pitch and form, just as their counterparts within conservatories and music schools must learn much that is not written down. In the academy, such learning is referred to as "musicality," and it is often the focal point of a mystification that covers up classical music's reliance on oral traditions. In both classical music and heavy metal, virtually the same aspects of music are far less theorized, codified, and written; music students must learn by listening, emulating, and watching the rhythm and gesture of bodily motion. Theorists of metal seem no more able than their academic counterparts to deal with musical rhetoric and social meanings; one analysis of Van Halen's "Eruption" merely named the modes employed (E Phrygian, A and E Aeolian) and summed up with the blandness of a music appreciation text: "a well-balanced, thought-out guitar solo, which features a variety of techniques."[63]

Yngwie Malmsteen exemplifies the wholesale importation of classical music into heavy metal, the adoption of not only classical musical style and vocabulary, models of virtuosic rhetoric, and modes of practice, pedagogy, and analysis but also the social values that underpin these activities. These values are a modern mixture of those that accompanied music making of the seventeenth, eighteenth, and nineteenth centuries with more recent cultural imperatives. Along with the model of virtuosity I have described above, the reigning values of metal guitar include a valorization of balance, planning, and originality; a conservatory-style fetishization of technique; and occasionally even a kind of cultural conservatism. Malmsteen bemoans the lack of musicianship in today's popular music and looks back on the "good old days" of the seventeenth century, when, he imagines, standards were much higher.[64]

Malmsteen is particularly noted for his elitism, another value he derives from contemporary classical music and justifies by emphasizing his connections with its greater prestige. In interviews, he constantly insists on his own genius, his links to the geniuses of the classical past, and his distance from virtually all contemporary popular musicians, whose music he regards as simple, trite, and inept. He denounces the genre he is usually thought to inhabit, insisting, "I do NOT play heavy metal!"[65]

While he has been known to claim that, as a genius, he never had to practice, Malmsteen also presents himself as one who has suffered for his art. A joint interview with bassist Billy Sheehan preserves an account of his early devotion to music, and its costs:

> YNGWIE: I was extremely self-critical. I was possessed. For many years I wouldn't do anything else but play the guitar.
> BILLY: I missed a lot of my youth. I missed the whole girl trip. I didn't start driving until I was 25.
> YNGWIE: I also sacrificed a lot of the social thing. I didn't care about my peers. To me, nothing else was even close in importance.[66]

Such statements undoubtedly reflect the tendency toward self-aggrandizement and self-pity that have made Malmsteen unloved by his peers in the guitar world. But they also further reflect his virtually total acceptance of the model of music making promulgated in classical music. Malmsteen, along with many other musicians, sees a need for music to evolve toward greater complexity and "sophistication." The pursuit of virtuosic technique usually requires many thousands of hours of patient, private repetition of exercises. To this end, many young players pursue a fanatical practice regimen, a pursuit of individual excellence that often leaves little room for communal experiences of music making, just as is the case in the training of classical musicians.[67]

Like most classical musicians, rock musicians usually acquire their skills through total dedication during their youth. Jeff Loven, a professional rock guitar player and teacher, explained how he learned to play: "I taught myself, actually. I sat in my room when other guys were playing baseball and stuff and I just sat and learned solos and songs, note for note: Hendrix songs, a lot of Van Halen, and then Ozzy came out with Randy Rhoads."[68] And one of the guitar magazines recently printed this letter from a young metal musician:

I am a 16 year old guitarist who's been playing since I was six years old. I switched from playing country to rock music when I was 10 and decided that one day I would be among the masters. I started pushing myself with eight hours a day, then slowly but steadily it increased. I now usually practice 16 hours daily, all day and sometimes all night. Recently, I was expelled from school due to my continuous absences when I was practicing. I have become a skilled player, but I am losing sleep and my social life is hurting. My philosophy is practice makes perfect, but my friends, my school, and my parents say I have blown my life out of proportion with it. I could cut my practicing down, but with the excellence among today's players, I fear I will not stay in the game.[69]

The extreme extension of this set of ideological values is the complete withdrawal of the musician from his or her public, in pursuit of complexity and private meanings. This strategy, which had earlier been championed by academic composers such as Milton Babbitt, can now be recognized in some virtuosic guitar players. Steve Vai boasts of his most recent album:

What I did with *Passion and Warfare* is the ultimate statement: I *locked* myself into a room and said, "To hell with everything—I'm doing this and it's a complete expression of what I am. I'm not concerned about singles, I'm not concerned about megaplatinum success, I'm not concerned about record companies." It was a real special time. All too often kids and musicians and artists just have to conform to make a living. I'm one of the lucky few and believe me, I don't take it for granted.[70]

Vai is trying to claim "authenticity" here, trying to prove his autonomy as an artist who is free of the corrupting influences of the very social context that makes his artistic statements possible and meaningful. When he goes on to describe his fasting, his visions, his bleeding on the guitar, he presents himself as an updated self-torturing Romantic artist, reaching beyond the known world for inspiration. When he details his compositional process of painstaking and technologically sophisticated multitrack recording, he updates this vision by celebrating modern means of simulating artistic autonomy. This individualism and self-centeredness unite classical music and heavy metal and stand in stark contrast to many other kinds of music. A bit later in the same issue of *Musician*, B. B. King says: "What I'm trying to get over to you is this: . . . when I'm on the stage, I am *trying* to entertain. I'm *not* just trying to amuse B. B. King. I'm trying to entertain the people that came to see me. . . . I think that's one of the things that's kind of kept me out here, trying to keep *pleasing* the audience. I think that's one of the mistakes that's happened in music as a whole: A lot of people forget that they got an audience."[71]

The success of the classical ideologies of complexity, virtuosity, and individuality is most obvious in the recent emergence of "guitar for guitarists" metal. Hypervirtuosic players like Vai, Joe Satriani, Tony MacAlpine, Paul Gilbert, Jason Becker, Greg Howe, The Great Kat, and Vinny Moore record their albums on specialty labels (such as Shrapnel Records) that sell mainly to the legions of semiprofessional and amateur metal guitarists. Their records tend to follow the template of Malmsteen's early work: few (if any) vocals, heavy classical influences, virtuosic speed and rhetoric, and song titles evocative of intensity and transgression. Most of these "mail order" guitarists rarely tour, and little of this music is known outside its devoted circle of fans, although a few players, notably Vai and Satriani, have achieved some amount of popular success. It is a kind of avant-garde, wherein originality, technique, and innovation are highly prized. MacAlpine and Moore, for example, draw upon nineteenth- and twentieth-century classical music for their metallic fusions: Chopin, Brahms, Liszt, Messiaen. Few find these fusions convincing; I would argue that these musical discourses are less compatible (rhetorically and ideologically) with metal than the seventeenth- and eighteenth-century music that comprises the bulk of the classical influence on heavy metal. But classical music, from any period, provides prestigious materials that can be reworked in a demonstration of musical creativity and sophistication. Paul Gilbert of Racer X (1986), for example, quoted Paganini's "Moto Perpetuo" literally and then went on to outdo it in speed and complexity. Gilbert's quotation is meant to be recognized, and it suggests a kind of seriousness, of meeting the technical standards of "high art," in contrast to Van Halen's more irreverent citations.[72]

Although some of these players have developed a virtuosic technique that is, in some respects, beyond the pioneering achievements of Eddie Van Halen, few are able to deploy their skills with comparable rhetorical success. As Van Halen himself remarked, when prodded to comment on the challenge of his imitators, "Maybe they cop the speed because they can't cop my feel. Maybe they shouldn't think so much."[73] Yngwie Malmsteen claims to be aware of the dangers of speedy, purposeless patterns—"You can do a diminished scale up and down till the fuckin' cows come home, but the cows won't come home"—yet it is for precisely this that he has drawn critical fire (and yawns).[74] Many metal guitarists and critics feel that if listening to one Malmsteen song is an amazing experience, listening to a whole album gets a bit tiresome, and each new album sounds like the last one, only more so. Malmsteen's work has convinced some that the classical influence is played out, even as it has been the leading inspiration for the eager experimentation of the avant-garde. He has helped turn many players to a fruitful engagement with the classical tradition, even as he has helped lead them toward the impoverishing regimens of practice and analysis that now dominate that tradition. And Malmsteen's abrasive elitism contrasts with his attempt to forge links with the musical past and reinvigorate reified discourses for mass audiences. His music brings to light contradictions that can add to our understanding of both heavy metal and classical music.

Popular Music as Cultural Dialogue

There are different ways to view the encounter of classical music and heavy metal, in part because there are, as I have suggested above, two different "classical musics": the twentieth-century genre of classical music, which comprises "great" pieces that are marketed and promoted (in part via "music appreciation") as largely interchangeable; and the collection of disparate historical practices—occupying vastly different social positions, employing incompatible musical discourses to varied cultural ends—that now are called by that name. On the one hand, heavy metal and classical music exist in the same social context: they are subject to similar structures of marketing and mediation, and they "belong to" and serve the needs of competing social groups whose power is linked to the prestige of their culture. The immense social and cultural distance that is normally assumed to separate classical music and heavy metal is in fact not a gap of musicality. Since heavy metal and classical music are markers of social difference and enactments of social experience, their intersection affects the complex relations among those who depend on these musics to legitimate their values. Their discursive fusion may well provoke insights about the social interests that are powerfully served by invisible patterns of sound.

On the other hand, there is a sense in which this sort of fusion marks an encounter among different cultures and affords an opportunity for cross-cultural critique. In their influential book, *Anthropology as Cultural Critique*, George E. Marcus and Michael M. J. Fischer called for new critical projects that would simultaneously explore multiple cultural moments. Besides the usual "objective" studies of individual cultural practices, ethnographic work, they argued, can become cultural criticism by reciprocally probing different "ways of knowing," by encouraging defamiliarization and the location of alternatives, and by breaking through patterns of thought that attempt to keep meanings singular and stable in the face of multiplicity and flux.[75] Marcus and Fischer were primarily concerned with encounters between Western and non-Western cultures; we can see an example of such comparison within one culture in the work of John Berger. Through analysis and juxtaposition of the multiple possibilities contained within a single cultural tradition, Berger's *Ways of Seeing* empowered thousands of scholars, students, and critics of culture by giving them a language for discussing the relationships of visual representation to social contestation.[76] But scholars are not the only ones who undertake such critical juxtapositions; heavy metal musicians, by engaging directly with seventeenth-, eighteenth-, and nineteenth-century composers and performers, by claiming them as heroes and forebears despite contemporary boundaries that would keep them separate, have already done something similar.

Historians and critics of popular music have so far failed to take seriously the musical accomplishments of heavy metal musicians. The prevailing stereotype portrays metal guitarists as primitive and noisy; virtuosity, if it is noticed at all, is usually dismissed as "pyrotechnics." One of the standard histories of rock grudgingly admitted that Edward Van Halen was an impressive guitarist but maintained doggedly that "the most popular 1980s heavy metal acts broke little new ground musically."[77] In the academy, heavy metal (along with rap) remains the dark "Other" of classical preserves of sweetness and light.[78]

Nor are metal's musical accomplishments acknowledged in the reports of the general press, where the performances of heavy metal musicians are invariably reduced to spectacle, their musical aspects represented as technically crude and devoid of musical interest. *Life*'s sensationalist dismissal of Judas Priest is typical: "The two lead guitarists do not so much play as attack their instruments."[79] Given the intensity and aggressiveness of Judas Priest's music, the characterization is not unfair; indeed, such a sentence, if printed in *Hit Parader* or *Metal Mania*, would be understood as a complimentary metaphor, praising the musicians' vigor. But in *Life* the image of attack takes the place of understanding; the magazine plays to class and generational prejudices by mocking the musical skills and imagination of the group.

In fact, heavy metal guitarists, like all other innovative musicians, create new sounds by drawing on the power of the old and by fusing together their semiotic resources into compelling new combinations. Heavy metal musicians recognize affinities between their work and the tonal sequences of Vivaldi, the melodic imagination of Bach, the virtuosity of Liszt and Paganini. Metal musicians have revitalized eighteenth- and nineteenth-century music for their mass audience in a striking demonstration of the ingenuity of popular culture. Although their audience's ability to decode such musical referents owes much to the effects of the ongoing appropriations of classical music by TV and movie composers, heavy metal musicians have accomplished their own adaptation of what has become the somber music of America's aristocracy, reworking it to speak for a different group's claims to power and artistry.

In one of his most incisive essays, Theodor Adorno criticized twentieth-century "devotees" of classical music for flattening out the specific signification of that music, making composers such as Bach into "neutralized cultural monuments."[80] In Adorno's view, the prestigious position of Bach in contemporary culture seems to demand that his music be tamed, that it be made to seem to affirm the inevitability of present social power relationships, at the top of which are the sources of the subsidies that sustain classical music. Metal musicians have appropriated the more prestigious discourses of classical music and reworked them into noisy articulations of pride, fear, longing, alienation, aggression, and community. Their adaptations of classical music, though they might be seen as travesties by modern devotees of that music, are close in spirit to the eclectic fusions of J. S. Bach and other idols of that tradition. While a few musicologists have tried to delineate strategies for performing and interpreting Bach's music that reclaim its cultural politics,[81] it may be that only heavy metal musicians have achieved this to a significant degree. To alter slightly the closing of Adorno's essay on Bach, "Perhaps the traditional Bach can indeed no longer be interpreted. If this is true, his heritage has passed on to [heavy metal] composition, which is loyal to him in being disloyal; it calls his music by name in producing it anew."[82]

For we should have learned long ago from Adorno that social relations and struggles are enacted within music itself. This is especially visible when musical discourses that belong to one group, whose history has been told according to that group's interests, are made to serve other social interests. Metal appropriations are rarely parody or pastiche; they are usually a reanimation, a reclamation of signs that can be turned to new uses. Unlike art rock, the point is typically not to refer to a prestigious discourse and thus to bask in reflected glory. Rather, metal musicians adapt classical signs for their own purposes, to signify to their audience, to have real meanings in the present. This is the sort of process to which V. N. Vološinov referred when he wrote that the sign can become an arena of class struggle. Vološinov and the rest of the Bakhtin circle were interested in how signs not only reflect the interests of the social groups that use them but are also "refracted" when the same signs are used by different groups to different ends. Thus, heavy metal musicians and "legitimate" musicians use Bach in drastically different ways. As Vološinov wrote:

> Class does not coincide with the sign community, i.e., with the community which is the totality of users of the same set of signs for ideological communication. Thus various different classes will use one and the same language. As a result, differently oriented accents intersect in every ideological sign. Sign becomes an arena of the class struggle.
>
> This social *multiaccentuality* of the ideological sign is a very crucial aspect. By and large, it is thanks to this intersecting of accents that a sign maintains its vitality and dynamism and the capacity for further development. A sign that has been withdrawn from the pressures of the social struggle—which, so to speak, crosses beyond the pale of the class struggle—inevitably loses force, degenerating into allegory and becoming the object not of live social intellibility but of philological comprehension. The historical memory of mankind is full of such worn out ideological signs incapable of serving as arenas for the clash of live social accents. However, inasmuch as they are remembered by the philologist and the historian, they may be said to retain the last glimmers of life.[83]

The discourse of signs that make up "Baroque music" certainly survives in the present; since its revival in the middle of the nineteenth century, Bach's music has occupied an important place in the concert and Protestant liturgical repertoires. Moreover, as with all classical music, Baroque signs appear in the music of television and film, where visual cues depend upon and reinvest the music with its affective power. While the music of the precanonic Dufay or Philippe de Vitry may have become largely the concern of musicological "philologists," mass mediation has made the musical discourses of all times and places available to contemporary composers, and the semiotic vocabulary and rhetoric of the European classical canon still forms the backbone of Hollywood's prodigious musical output.

Heavy metal musicians, too, draw upon the resources of the past that have been made available to them through mass mediation and their own historical study. But it is precisely such predations that the musical academy is supposed to prevent. Bach's contemporary meanings are produced in tandem by musicologists and the marketing departments of record companies and symphony orchestras, and the interpretation of Bach they construct has little to do with the dramatic, noisy meanings found by metal musicians and fans and everything to do with aesthetics, order, and cultural hegemony. The classical music world polices contemporary readings of the "masterworks"; the adaptations of Randy Rhoads and Bon Jovi are ignored while the acceptability of Stokowski's orchestral transcriptions is debated. Malmsteen's performances fall outside the permissible ideological boundaries that manage to contain Maurice André and Glenn Gould. The drive to enforce preferred ideological meanings is, as Vološinov put it, "nondialogic." It is oppressive, authoritative, and absolute. "The very same thing that makes the ideological sign vital and mutable is also, however, that which makes it a refracting and distorting medium. The ruling class strives to impart a supraclass, eternal character to the ideological sign, to extinguish or drive inward the struggle between social value judgements which occurs in it, to make the sign uniaccentual."[84]

But since the world of language (or music) preexists its inhabitants, and since cultural hegemony is never absolute, such appropriations constantly appear on the field of social contestation we call "popular culture."[85] Such disruptions are rarely even acknowledged by academics. In the histories they write and the syllabi they teach, most musicologists continue to define "music" implicitly in terms of the European concert tradition, ignoring non-Western and popular musics and treating contemporary academic composers such as Milton Babbitt as the heirs to the canon of great classical "masters." But Babbitt's claim to inherit the mantle of Bach is perhaps more tenuous than that of Randy Rhoads, and not only because the latter two utilize, to some extent, a common musical vocabulary. The institutional environment within which Babbitt works (and which he has vigorously championed) rewards abstract complexity and often regards listeners and their reactions with indifference or hostility, whereas both Bach and Rhoads composed and performed for particular audiences, gauging their success by their rhetorical effectiveness. Babbitt's music demonstrates his braininess; Bach's and Rhoads's offer powerful, nuanced experiences of transcendence and communality.

Many heavy metal musicians are acutely aware of their complicated relationship to the prestigious music of the classical past. Theorists like Wolf Marshall necessarily refer to that canon in their efforts to account for the musical choices displayed in particular pieces, and other musicians recurringly articulate the similarities they perceive in the values and practices of these two musics, which are usually assumed to be worlds apart. Vocalist Rob Halford earnestly emphasizes the discipline and skill needed to succeed in either style:

This might sound like a bizarre statement, but I don't think playing heavy metal is that far removed from classical music. To do either, you have to spend many years developing your style and your art; whether you're a violinist or a guitarist, it still takes the same belief in your form of music to achieve and create. It is very much a matter of dedication. . . . You get narrow-minded critics reviewing the shows, and all they think about heavy metal is that it is just total ear-splitting, blood-curdling noise without any definition or point. This is a very, *very* professional style of music. It means a great deal to many millions of people. We treat heavy metal with respect.[86]

Metal musicians' appropriations have already profoundly changed not only their music but their modes of theorization, pedagogy, and conceptualization. Their fusions may even come to affect the reception and performance of classical music as well. We should welcome such revitalization: contrast today's pious, sterile reiterations of the "Pachelbel Canon" with Vinnie Moore's furious soloing over that piece in concert. Compare classical musicians' timid ornamentation of Italian sonatas with Yngwie Malmsteen's free and virtuosic improvisations over the chord progressions of Albinoni, more faithful to the practices of the early eighteenth century despite his nonclassical instrument.

Heavy metal musicians erupted across the Great Divide between "serious" and "popular" music, between "art" and "entertainment," and found that the gap was not as wide as we have been led to believe. As Christopher Small put it, "The barrier between classical and vernacular music is opaque only when viewed from the point of view of the dominant group; when viewed from the other side it is often transparent, and to the vernacular musician there are not two musics but only one. . . . Bach and Beethoven and other 'great composers' are not dead heroes but colleagues, ancestor figures even, who are alive in the present."[87]

It should come as no surprise that such an eruption, propelled by the social desires and tensions of patriarchy and capitalism, reinscribes familiar constructions of masculinity and individuality, even as the new meritocracy of guitar technique opens doors to female and African-American musicians.[88] And we should not be dismayed to find that classically influenced heavy metal can reinterpret the past even as it is itself co-opted into the world of advertising and soundtracks. For that is how popular culture works: through ingenuity and contradiction toward revisions of meaning and prestige. Heavy metal musicians' appropriations from classical music have already changed popular music; they may yet change classical music and perhaps even our understanding of how the cultural labor of popular musicians can blur the distance between the two, defying the division that has been such a crucial determinant of musical life in the twentieth century.

Album cover art from heavy
metal recordings.

Ritchie Blackmore. © Justin Thomas/Relay Photos.

Eddie Van Halen. © Bill Thomas/Photofeatures International.

Randy Rhoads. © Relay Photos/Photofeatures International.

Yngwie Malmsteen. © Joe Giron/Photofeatures International.

Lita Ford. © Annamaria Di Santo/Photofeatures International.

Judas Priest. © Ray Palmer/Photofeatures International.

Poison. © Annamaria Di Santo/Photofeatures International.

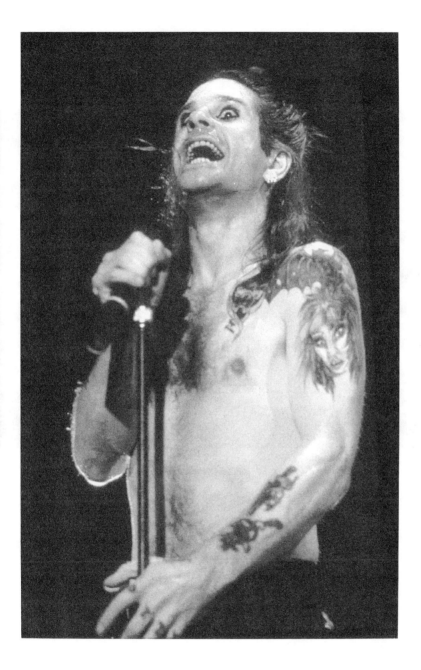

Ozzy Osbourne. © Annamaria Di Santo/Photofeatures International.

Iron Maiden. © Photofeatures International.

Axl Rose. © Gene Ambo/Photofeatures International.

CHAPTER FOUR

Forging Masculinity
Heavy Metal Sounds and Images of Gender

✳

The spectacle is not a collection of images, but a social relation
among people, mediated by images. —Guy Debord[1]

Orpheus, the godlike musician of Greek mythology, was a natural figure
for opera plots, which must reconcile heroics and song; his legend-
ary rhetorical powers made him the most popular subject of early-
seventeenth-century dramatic music, with settings by Monteverdi, Peri,
Caccini, and many other composers. But his story contains a built-in
contradiction: Orpheus must sing in such a way as to demonstrate his
rhetorical mastery of the world, yet such elaborate vocal display threatens to undermine Orpheus's masculine identity. Flamboyant display
of his emotions is required as evidence of his manipulative powers,
but such excess makes him into an object of display himself and suggests a disturbing similarity to the disdained emotional outbursts of
women. Western constructions of masculinity often include conflicting imperatives regarding assertive, spectacular display, and rigid self-
control. Spectacles are problematic in the context of a patriarchal order
that is invested in the stability of signs and that seeks to maintain women
in the position of object of the male gaze.[2]

Today's heavy metal musicians must negotiate the same contradiction. Like the story of Orpheus, heavy metal often stages fantasies of
masculine virtuosity and control. Musically, heavy metal articulates a
dialectic of controlling power and transcendent freedom. Metal songs
usually include impressive technical and rhetorical feats on the electric
guitar, counterposed with an experience of power and control that is
built up through vocal extremes, guitar power chords, distortion, and

sheer volume of bass and drums. Visually, metal musicians typically appear as swaggering males, leaping and strutting about the stage, clad in spandex, scarves, leather, and other visually noisy clothing, punctuating their performances with phallic thrusts of guitars and microphone stands. The performers may use hypermasculinity or androgyny as visual enactments of spectacular transgression. Like opera, heavy metal draws upon many sources of power: mythology, violence, madness, the iconography of horror. But none of these surpasses gender in its potential to inspire anxiety and to ameliorate it.

Heavy metal is, inevitably, a discourse shaped by patriarchy. Circulating in the contexts of Western capitalist and patriarchal societies, for much of its history metal has been appreciated and supported primarily by a teenage male audience. But it is crucial to specify not only age and gender but the corresponding political position of this constituency: it is a group generally lacking in social, physical, and economic power but besieged by cultural messages promoting such forms of power, insisting on them as the vital attributes of an obligatory masculinity. As John Fiske concluded from his study of "masculine" TV shows such as "The A-Team," "our society denies most males adequate means of exercising the power upon which their masculinity apparently depends. Masculinity is thus socially and psychologically insecure; and its insecurity produces the need for its constant reachievement."[3] I would emphasize in Fiske's analysis the words *apparently* and *socially*, for I see sex roles as contradictory, mutable social constructions rather than as normative formations somehow grounded in biology or an ahistorical psychology. Moreover, it is not only masculinity that is insecure; no component of identity is stable or natural. Heavy metal, like all other culture, offers occasions for doing "identity work"—among other things, for "accomplishing gender."[4] That is, notions of gender circulate in the texts, sounds, images, and practices of heavy metal, and fans experience confirmation and alteration of their gendered identities through their involvement with it.

For Fiske, the contradictions built into male sex roles and the insecurity that men feel as a result help explain the episodic and generic aspects of male culture. Television shows such as "The A-Team" are structured as repeated enactments of paradigmatic narratives and representations because their function is to address anxieties that can never be resolved. Fiske's ideas are easily transferable to music and music video, where repetition and genre are also crucial phenomena. The purpose of a genre is to organize the reproduction of a particular ideology, and the generic cohesion of heavy metal until the mid-1980s depended upon the desire of young white male performers and fans to hear and believe in certain stories about the nature of masculinity. But metal's negotiations of the anxieties of gender and power are never conclusive; that is why, as Fiske says, these imaginary resolutions of real anxieties must be reenacted over and over again. That such representations can never be definitive or totally satisfying also means that they are always open to negotiation and transformation. But social circumstances may change so that particular forms of culture are no longer relevant for particular individuals: metal fans tend mostly to be young because much of metal deals with experiences of powerlessness that may be, to some extent, overcome. As they get older, fans may acquire some amount of economic power, or they may beget children who replace them at the bottom of the familial and social ladders, whose physical power and mobility are far less than theirs and who thus assuage some of their culturally produced anxieties.[5]

Such a theoretical perspective cannot be a comprehensive one for the study of gender in heavy metal, though, since there are many female metal fans, for whom such explanations are inadequate. Indeed, since around 1987, concert audiences for metal shows have been roughly gender-balanced. But metal is overwhelmingly concerned with presenting images and confronting anxieties that have been traditionally understood as peculiar to men, through musical means that have been conventionally coded as masculine. Since the language and traditions of heavy metal have been developed by and are still dominated by men, my discussion of gender in metal will initially be an investigation of masculinity; I will return later to issues of the reception of these male spectacles by female fans.

For two decades, heavy metal has offered a variety of compensatory experiences and opportunities for bearing or resolving the contradictions of masculinity as they have been constructed by societies that are aligned by patriarchy, capitalism, and mass mediation. Thus, one of the most important items on the heavy metal agenda has long been to deal with what patriarchy perennially perceives as the "threat" of women. I will be framing my discussion of heavy metal songs and videos in terms of a loose list of strategies concerning gender and power: misogyny, exscription, androgyny, and romance. Heavy metal musicians and fans have developed tactics for modeling male power and control within the context of a patriarchal culture, and metal's enactions of masculinity include varieties of misogyny as well as "exscription" of the feminine—that is, total denial of gender anxieties through the articulation of fantastic worlds without women—supported by male, sometimes homoerotic, bonding. But heavy metal also participates in rock's tradition of rebellion, and some metal achieves much of its transgressiveness through androgynous spectacle. Until the mid 1980s, one of these three strategies—misogyny, exscription, androgyny—tended to dominate each heavy metal band's "aesthetic." A fourth approach, increasingly important in recent years, "softens" metal with songs about romance; this kind of music has drawn legions of female fans to metal.

In spite of the fact that this categorization of metal might look like a menu for sexual abuse, I intend neither to denounce utterly, nor to try to rescue wholesale, heavy metal's politics of gender. To do only the former would be to ignore the politics of critique, particularly the fact that criticism of popular culture never takes place apart from implicit comparisons with more prestigious culture. Like racism, sexism is sustained and naturalized across class lines. Writers who expose racism and sexism in popular culture must take care that their critique does not collude with those who want to identify such barbarisms with an economic and cultural underclass that can thus be more self-righteously condemned and oppressed. Critics of popular music must take care to acknowledge the politics of their work: while it is imperative to be critical, to avoid bland enthusiasm or dispassionate positivism, analyses of popular culture must also be empathetically drawn if they are to register accurately the contradictions and subtleties of popular practices. Otherwise, they too easily serve as mandates for elitist condemnation and oppression. It is beyond dispute that some of the images and ideologies of heavy metal are violent and irresponsible. But of course, the violence and irresponsibility of much so-called high culture and of the economic elite that underwrites its existence is also demonstrable. The politics of prestige work to position "high" culture beyond scrutiny and "low" culture beneath it; in either case the effect is to forestall critical understanding. It is less important simply to denounce or defend cultural representations of gender than to critique them in the context of an explanation of how they work, what social tensions they address, where they come from, and why they are credible to particular audiences.

Gender constructions in heavy metal music and videos are significant not only because they reproduce and inflect patriarchal assumptions and ideologies but, more importantly, because popular music may teach us more than any other cultural form about the conflicts, conversations, and bids for legitimacy and prestige that comprise cultural activity. Heavy metal is, as much as anything else, an arena of gender, where spectacular gladiators compete to register and affect ideas of masculinity, sexuality, and gender relations. The stakes are as high in metal as anywhere, and they are more explicitly acknowledged there, both in visual and musical tropes and in the verbal and written debates of fans. By taking the trouble to distinguish carefully among the varieties of representation within heavy metal, we can gain a better understanding of larger interrelationships of gender and power.

Behind the Screen: Listening to Gender

In her pathbreaking study of music video, *Rocking around the Clock*, E. Ann Kaplan makes two main points about metal videos: that their violence and rebelliousness place them in the "nihilistic" category of her typology of videos and that their reputation for blatant sexism is well deserved.[6] Neither of these might seem particularly bold assertions, but taken together, I think they are contradictory. Sexism is in fact a major ideological constituent of much heavy metal, but sexism is never nihilistic; the intensity and variety of modes of sexist discourse must be understood as indices of the urgency and influence of patriarchal ideals. To call such discourse nihilist is to obscure its real ideological functions.

Kaplan's readings of videos as texts embedded in the contexts of MTV and consumer culture are sometimes acute and illuminating. But two serious methodological shortcomings flaw her comments on heavy metal. First, beyond her observation that metal audiences are made up of "young males," Kaplan's comments appear to be uninformed by any ethnographic or personal contact with the heavy metal musicians and fans whose texts and lives she presumes to explain. While Kaplan's conclusions are based on her analysis of MTV as a spectacular reinforcement of universal decenteredness and passivity, the interviews and questionnaires I have received from heavy metal fans point to a wide range of activities connected to their involvement with the music. "Headbangers' Ball," the weekly three-hour MTV program devoted to heavy metal, is quite popular with the fans I surveyed, but it is hardly the most important aspect of their involvement with metal. Concerts, records, radio, fan magazines, and quite often playing an instrument figure as primary components of metal fans' lives. A significant number of fans (especially male) watch MTV seldom or never, and for many (especially female) the glossy photographs of rampant musicians to be found in the copious fan literature are more important sources of visual pleasure than videos. This is not to argue that metal videos are unimportant but rather to say that they do not operate in a social vacuum: their analysis must be inflected by knowledge of the lives and cultural investments of the viewers.

Second, certainly the most serious shortcoming of Kaplan's book is the almost total neglect of the *music* of music video. Kaplan's few comments addressing musical details of heavy metal songs are hardly helpful: she characterizes heavy metal as "loud and unmelodious," filled with "relatively meaningless screaming sounds."[7] Though musical discourses are invisible, they are nonetheless susceptible to analysis, and musical analysis is crucial for music video analysis because aural texts are indisputably primary: they exist prior to videos and independently of them, and fans' comments make it clear that it is the music of music video that carries the primary affective charge. That is, it is the music that is mostly responsible for invoking the libidinal and corporeal investment that intensifies belief, action, commitment, and experience. The challenge of analyzing music videos is that of interpreting and accounting for *both* musical and visual discourses, simultaneous but differently articulated and assuming a variety of relations.

If the cinema, as Laura Mulvey asserts, "has structures of fascination strong enough to allow temporary loss of ego while simultaneously reinforcing the ego," the same was surely true of music long before cinema was invented.[8] Musical constructions, in metal or elsewhere, are powerful in part because they are made to seem so natural and unconstructed. We experience music's rhetorical pull apart from language, seemingly apart from all social referents, in what is usually thought a pure, personal, subjective way. Yet that impression of naturalness depends on our responding unself-consciously to complex discursive systems that have developed as historically and socially specific practices. It is not only lyrics or visual imagery but the music itself that constructs gendered experiences.[9] The musicians I will discuss have used musical codes to articulate visions of the world that are filled with the pleasures of energy, freedom, power, and a sense of community. Discursively, specific details of rhythm, pitch, and timbre *signify*—some of them through the conventions of heavy metal proper, some as part of a complex, mutable tradition of musical semiotics that stretches back centuries. Such signification always occurs in social contexts structured through political categories such as gender, class, and race; musical meanings are thus inseparable from these fundamental constituents of social reality.

Only with its complex sonic texts and ethnographic contexts disregarded, as in analyses such as Kaplan's, can heavy metal be casually characterized as both sexist and nihilistic or as a monolithic, adolescent deviance. For "heavy metal" is a genre label that, by the late 1980s, included a substantial and growing female audience, a number of distinctive and sophisticated musical discourses, and many different solutions to complex problems of gender relations. As I discuss several heavy metal songs and their videos, I hope to delineate their musical and ideological strategies more precisely than is accomplished by such vague but pervasive terms of dismissal. As I work through the various gender strategies I have identified in heavy metal, I will be arguing, on the one hand, that music videos cannot reasonably be analyzed without the musical component of such texts being examined; and on the other hand, that it is crucial for the cultural critic to develop an understanding of the interests and activities of the communities that find meaning in their encounters with these texts.

No Girls Allowed: Exscription in Heavy Metal

The most distinctive feature of heavy metal videos is that they typically present the spectacle of live performance; bands are shown on stage, performing in synch with the song. Other kinds of pop music videos also frequently feature "live" synched performances, but pop songs are less often "performed" on a stage than mimed in front of fantastic or arty backgrounds or in unlikely locations; often only vocals are synched, as only the singer is visible. In the typical metal video, however, actual concert footage is often used, and when it is not, sets, backdrops, and musicians' posturings usually imitate the spectacle of an arena concert. Bands as different in their styles and constituencies as Guns N' Roses, Poison, and Metallica all rely on scenes of "live" performance for most of their videos. Heavy metal has long had the most loyal touring support of any popular musical genre, and the arena concert experience of collectivity and participation remain the ideal that many videos seek to evoke.

Besides the videos of metal singles to be seen on programs like MTV's "Headbangers' Ball," full-length heavy metal concerts are popular rentals at video stores. Since a favorite performer might come through town once a year at best, and since many younger fans are not allowed by their parents to attend concerts, heavy metal videos make more widely available the singular events that are most highly valued by fans. The video in a concert setting, with or without fans, presents the performers in all their glory, as larger-than-life figures whose presence is validated by feelings of community and power, and evoked by venue and music.

Many such performance videos offer for the pleasure of young males a fantasy not unlike that constructed by "The A-Team," as John Fiske describes it: a world of action, excess, transgression but little real violence, one in which men are the only actors, and in which male bonding among the members of a "hero-team" is the only important social relationship. As Barbara Ehrenreich has pointed out, for young men maturing in a patriarchal world where men dominate the "real" world while women raise kids, growing up means growing away from women.[10] Fiske's analysis of the television show stresses the value of male bonding for creating close social ties while excluding the threat of the feminine: "Feminine intimacy centers on the relationship itself and produces a dependence on the other that threatens masculine independence. . . . Male bonding, on the other hand, allows an interpersonal dependency that is goal-centered, not relationship-centered, and thus serves masculine performance instead of threatening it."[11] Even in many nonperformance metal videos, where narratives and images are placed not on a stage but elsewhere, the point is the same: to represent and reproduce spectacles that depend for their appeal on the exscription of women.

Even exceptions to the metal concert video format emphasize the performative. In Judas Priest's "Heading Out to the Highway," a song from 1981 that was still popular as a video in 1988 and 1989, performance is not literally represented. The band's two guitar players drag race on an empty highway in the middle of nowhere, flagged on by the singer, whose macho stances, gestures, and singing are the only elements of the real performance retained in the fantastic setting. The song and the images are about freedom and adventure, and we don't even need the initial "Hit 'em, boys" to know that we're talking about a specifically male kind of freedom. There are no women to be seen in this video, and what is there to be seen—the cars, the road, the leather, the poses— have long been coded as symbols of male freedom, linked as signs of aggressiveness and refusal to be bound by limits.

The performance enacts this in musical terms as well. The vocals and guitars constantly anticipate the downbeats, punching in ahead of the beat defined by the bass and drums throughout the song. Rob Halford's rough, powerful voice finds support in harmony vocals that sound as menacing as a gang's chant. He sustains triumphant high notes at the end of each chorus, in a display of power that has counterparts in the guitars' solo section and the bass pedal under the verse. Not only his voice but the singer's writhing and posing provide a spectacle of male potency for a male audience, including both the band on-screen and the presumed male viewer of the video.[12]

But images of masculine display are available to be construed in a variety of ways. Gay heavy metal fans sometimes celebrate forthrightly the homoeroticism that is latent in such displays of exclusive masculine bonding. This can be seen, for example, in the activities of the Gay Metal Society, a social club of over one hundred members, based in

Chicago. In addition to sponsoring and organizing parties and nights out on the town for its members, GMS publishes a monthly newsletter that contains commentary on the history, criticism, and discography of heavy metal. The GMS *Headbanger* also functions as a forum for debate of issues involving sexuality and music. Gay fans celebrate metal musicians whom they believe are gay, such as Judas Priest's Rob Halford, and confirm and contest each other's "negotiated" readings of popular texts. They may see metal videos as erotic fantasies, while straight fans resist the homoerotic implications and insist on identification with the power and freedom depicted.[13] Of course, straight fans must negotiate their readings, too. Some of Accept's lyrics are explicitly homosexual if studied closely; despite this, the band is quite popular among heterosexual, often homophobic, men. As with classical music, heterosexual and even homophobic audiences can negotiate their reception and find the constructions of gay composers powerfully meaningful.

Male bonding itself becomes crucial to the reception of metal that depends on masculine display, for it helps produce and sustain consensus about meaning. Exscripting texts do occasionally refer to sexuality, but typically as just another arena for enactments of male power. Mutual erotic pleasure rarely appears in the lyrics of heavy metal, just as it is seldom discussed by men in any other context. Metal shields men from the danger of pleasure—loss of control—but also enables display, sometimes evoking images of armored, metalized male bodies that resemble the Freikorps fantasies analyzed by Klaus Theweleit.[14] The historical context and social location of these fantasies marks them as very different from heavy metal, but the writings and drawings of the German soldiers Theweleit studied evince a similar exscription of women and a concomitant hardening and metallic sheathing of the male body as a defense against culturally produced gender anxieties. Such images from heavy metal lyrics and album cover art could be cited by the hundreds, in a tradition that goes back to one of the founding texts of heavy metal, Black Sabbath's *Paranoid* (1970), which included the song "Iron Man."[15]

The seductive women who sometimes intrude into otherwise exscripting videos signify in several ways. First, these shots function just as they do in advertising: to trigger desire and credit it to the appeal of the main image. But the sexual excitement also serves as a reminder of why exscription is necessary: the greater the seductiveness of the female image, the greater its threat to masculine control. Moreover, the presence of women as sex objects stabilizes the potentially troubling homoeroticism suggested by the male display. I will have more to say about the anxieties produced by homoerotic display in my discussion of androgyny below. There are, however, many videos that attempt to manage gender anxieties more overtly, through direct representations of women.

The Kiss of Death: Misogyny and the Male Victim

Blatant abuse of women is uncommon in metal videos. There are unequivocal exceptions, such as the brutal stage shows of W.A.S.P. or the forthrightly misogynistic lyrics in some of the music of Guns N' Roses and Mötley Crüe. But despite heavy metal's notorious reputation among outsiders, few heavy metal videos have ever approached the degree of narcissistic misogyny routinely displayed by pop star Michael Jackson (e.g., his videos for "Dirty Diana" or "The Way You Make Me Feel"). If the exscripting music of Judas Priest or AC/DC conflates power and eroticism, making pleasure contingent upon dominance, many of heavy metal's critics have similarly confused the issue. Tipper Gore, for example, makes it clear that she considers rape and masturbation equal threats to "morality." And William Graebner has offered an analysis of "the erotic and destructive" in rock music that too often fails to distinguish between the two themes.[16] But articulations of gender relations in contemporary patriarchy are complex, and if constructions of sexuality in popular music are to be understood, their relationship to structures of power and dominance must be delineated, not crudely presumed.

Like heavy metal, sexually explicit films have an undeserved reputation for physical violence, according to a recent historical study of hard-core pornographic films. Building on the observation that sex is more shocking than violence in the United States, Joseph W. Slade explains the rampant violence in "legit" films as a result of prohibitions of representations of eroticism. Violence is often used as a metaphor for passion, Slade maintains, in discourses where explicit depiction of sexual activity is banned. In X-rated films, on the other hand, where representation of sex is not only permissible but primary, power relations are articulated through sexual relations rather than violence. The central purpose of pornography, Slade summarizes, has been "to assuage male anxieties about the sexuality of females."[17] Male authority is characteristically made secure through porn because that authority is represented as being founded in love: women are seen to submit themselves voluntarily and gladly, and force is unnecessary.

While nonviolent fantasies of dominance might be, for some, no less repugnant than blatant misogyny, it is important to recognize that they are different. As is typical of hegemonic constructions, overt force is not only unnecessary in most pornography, but it would be disruptive of a representation that depends on presenting itself as natural and un-coerced. Heavy metal too relies much less on physical violence against women than on a number of more hegemonic representations. Because metal has developed discourses of male victimization, exscription, and androgyny, its power to reproduce or adapt patriarchy is often contingent on the absence of overt violence. Although some of these discourses embody challenges to or transformations of hegemonic ideology, some reproduce rather directly the hegemonic strategies of control and repression of women that permeate Western culture.

For example, there is the strategy of confronting the "threat" head-on: one of the more successful representations of women in metal is the femme fatale. Such images are quite popular, from Mötley Crüe's "Looks That Kill" to Whitesnake's "Still of the Night," but the metal band Dokken could be said to have specialized in such constructions, embedded in narratives of male victimization. Many of their best-known songs enact the same basic story of the male entrapped, betrayed, or destroyed by the female: "Heaven Sent," "Prisoner (Chained by Love)," "Just Got Lucky," "Into the Fire," and "Kiss of Death."[18] Dokken's success with this formula was enabled by two of the band's particular assets: singer Don Dokken's voice and face are clean and soulful, the perfect complement to his tragic, self-pitying lyrics; and guitarist George Lynch is a powerful rhetorician whose solos and fills demonstrate a perhaps unmatched command of the semiotics of frantic but futile struggle.

Dokken's "Heaven Sent" (1987) is reminiscent of nineteenth-century operatic constructions such as Salome and Carmen in the way it locates women at a nexus of pleasure and dread.[19] Dokken sings of a woman who is simultaneously angel and witch, temptress and terror. A slim young woman in the video appears inexplicably, metamorphosed from a much heavier and older woman. She never speaks but walks alone through the night—sometimes in black miniskirt and leather, sometimes in a flowing white gown—holding a candelabra; she is followed by a rushing, tipping camera until she mysteriously dissolves. Jump cuts and shifts in point of view fragment the video, but the decentering and transformations are precisely the point: the boys in the band, first seen playing chess in a bar (in an unlikely portrait of innocence), wind up doing their onstage posturing in a graveyard, to the tune of their own victimization. Of course, the woman in the video never actually does anything threatening; it is enough that she exists. Women are presented as essentially mysterious and dangerous; they harm simply by being, for their attractiveness threatens to disrupt both male self-control and the collective strength of male bonding.

Musically, "Heaven Sent" constructs this victimization through images of constraint and struggle. The song opens with the repetition of a pair of open fifths, a whole step apart. But the fifths are not the usual power chords; they lack sufficient sustain and distortion. Instead, they sound haunting and ominous, and their syncopation and sparseness gives them an anticipatory air, in contrast to the rhythmic control and driving energy of the rest of the song (and of most other metal songs). Once the song gets under way, the rhythm is inexorable and precise, in that articulation of power and control that is one of the primary musical characteristics of heavy metal. In tension with the rhythmic stability, though, are the sudden and unexpected harmonic shifts that articulate "Heaven Sent" formally. Like the jump cuts in the video, these key changes are initially disorienting; but since the song stays in its gloomy Aeolian/Dorian mode throughout, each new section is affectively felt as the same scene, however distant harmonically—just as the various manifestations of "woman" in the video are linked by an aura of mystery and dread.

The guitar solo, often the site of virtuosic transcendence of a metal song's constructions of power and control, is, in "Heaven Sent," a veritable catalog of the musical semiotics of doom. As with "ground bass" patterns in seventeenth-century opera, the harmonic pattern uses cyclicism to suggest fatefulness; as in certain of Bach's keyboard pieces, the virtuoso responds to the threat of breakdown with irrational, frenzied chromatic patterns.[20] The guitar solo is an articulation of frantic terror, made all the more effective by its technical impressiveness and its imitations of vocal sounds such as screams and moans. After the solo, the song's chorus intensifies these images through ellision: seven measures long instead of the normal, balanced eight, the pattern cycles fatalistically, without rest or resolution.

Visual images, narrative, and the music itself combine in this video to represent women as threats to male control and even male survival. The mysteriousness of women confirms them as a dangerous Other, and their allure is an index of the threat.[21] Female fans, who now make up half of the audience for heavy metal (though only a very small fraction of metal musicians are women), are invited to identify with the powerful position that is thus constructed for them. It is a familiar one, since women are encouraged by a variety of cultural means to think of appearance as their natural route to empowerment. Men, on the other hand, are reassured by such representations that patriarchal control is justified and necessary. Such constructions are by no means to be found only in heavy metal, of course; not only do they belong to a long and esteemed tradition of Western cultural history, but their success in the 1980s has been widespread in a political context marked by reactionary governmental policies and a significant backlash against feminism. It is crucial to recognize that heavy metal is not the aberrant Other that many conservatives would have it be. But neither is it simply patriarchal. The sexual politics of heavy metal are, as we will see, a conflicted mixture of confirmation and contradiction of dominant myths about gender.

Living on a Prayer: Romance

Heavy metal changed a great deal in the last half of the 1980s, and one particular album of 1986 is a good register of the shift, as well as a major factor in precipitating it. With *Slippery When Wet*, one of the biggest-selling hard rock albums of all time (over 13 million copies), Bon Jovi managed to combine the power and freedom offered by metal with the constructed "authenticity" of rock, and, most important, the romantic sincerity of a long tradition of pop. Though Bon Jovi offered typical experiences of the heavy metal dialectic of absolute control and transcendent freedom in a performative context of male bonding, lead singer Jon Bon Jovi also projected a kind of sincerity and romantic vulnerability that had enormous appeal for female fans. It is this discursive fusion that enabled the band's mainstream success and helped spark the unprecedented entry of much heavy metal and metal-influenced music into the Top 40 of the late 1980s.

Bon Jovi was certainly not the first to achieve this fusion; bands like Van Halen, Boston, Journey, Foreigner, Loverboy, and others were engaged in similar projects some time before. But Bon Jovi's music was a phenomenal success, and it helped transform what had long been a mostly male subcultural genre into a much more popular style with a gender-balanced audience. The fusion was developed and managed very deliberately: once a standard leather/chains/eyeliner heavy metal band, with lots of tragic, macho songs about running, shooting, and falling down, the band sought to capture a wider audience for *Slippery When Wet*. The most obvious change was in the lyrics: abandoning heavy metal gloom, doom, and creepy mysticism, they began cultivating a positive, upbeat outlook, where the only mystical element was bourgeois love. Writing songs about romantic love and personal relationships, they tempered their heavy metal sound and image and pitched their product to appeal as well to a new, female market.

There is still a lot of metal in Bon Jovi's music, although the question of his inclusion in the genre is vigorously contested among various factions of metal fans. Features of heavy metal are evident in the timbres and phrasing of both instruments and vocals; the emphasis on sustain, intensity, and power; the fascination with the dark side of the daylit respectable world. But by not wearing makeup anymore and by wearing jeans, not leather or spandex, Bon Jovi abandoned much of heavy metal's fantastic dimension in favor of signs of rock "authenticity." Moreover, from pop music the band got its constructed sincerity, just the right degree of prettiness, and a conscious appeal to a female audience. The sustained and intense sounds of heavy metal are channeled behind the romantic sincerity of pop, while smooth, sometimes poignant synthesizer sounds mediate the raw crunch of distorted guitars.

The biggest hit song from *Slippery When Wet* was "Livin' on a Prayer," which invites us to sympathize and identify with Tommy and Gina, a young couple who are good-hearted but down on their luck. Tommy, now out of work, is a union man, working-class tough—but also tender, caring, and musical. He used to make music, that is, until he had to hock his guitar; Tommy's loss of his capacity to make music is a sign of the couple's desperate circumstances. The lyrics of the song fall into three groups, each with a different sort of text and musical affect: the verses of the song tell the story of Tommy and Gina's troubles; the prechoruses are resolutions not to give up, the pair's exhortations to each other about the power of love; and the choruses are Tommy's affirmation that such hope and faith in love is justified, that love really can transcend material problems.[22]

The source of the song's main pleasures is its musical construction of romantic transcendence. As with most pop songs, the transcendent moment is the place in the chorus where the title hook is presented, where the affective charge is highest: it is there, if ever, that we are convinced that Tommy and Gina *will* make it, that love *must* triumph over adverse social conditions, that bourgeois myths *can* survive even the despair of joblessness. Such affirmative stories have led to critical dismissal of Bon Jovi as fatuous rock "perfect for the Reagan era."[23] But such disparagements typically ignore gender as a site of political formation, and critical sneering does little to help us understand the tensions that are mediated by such a vastly popular song.

There are at least three ways of understanding how this sense of transcendence is constructed musically. First, and simplest, it is at this moment that the piece moves out of its minor key and into its relative major. Such a key change accomplishes a tremendous affective change, moving from what is conventionally perceived as the negativity or oppression of the minor key to the release and affirmation of the major.

Experientially, we escape the murk that has contained us since the beginning of the song. Second, this moment in the chorus offers an escape from the C–D–E pattern that has been the only chord progression the song has used until this point and thus has seemed natural and inevitable, however cheerless.[24] "Livin' on a Prayer" breaks out of its gloomy treadmill at this point of transcendence, moving from C to D to *G*, not E. By breaking free of its oppressive minor tonality, and by doing so through a brand-new progression, the song leaps into an exciting new tonal area and constructs a transcended context for Tommy and Gina, and for the song's audience. To clinch it, a background group of voices joins in here to support Tommy's tough solo voice; the rest of the social world seems to join in this affirmation.

Finally, this new progression, C–D–G, has discursive significance. This pattern has been one of the most important formulas for establishing resolution and closure in Western music, from Monteverdi to the "Monster Mash"; it is not, however, a common progression in heavy metal. The C–D–E progression upon which most of "Livin' on a Prayer" is built, on the other hand, is strongly associated with metal. Thus, when "Livin' on a Prayer" reaches its moment of transcendence, the shift in affect is marked by the use of a different harmonic discourse. The transcendence is in part an escape from heavy metal itself, with all of its evocation of gloominess, paranoia, and rebellion. "Livin' on a Prayer" breaks away from the musical discourse of heavy metal at the point where it offers its bottom line: transcendence through romantic love. To offer such a payoff, it *must* break away from metal.

The success of the song depends on the contrast of and tension between two affective states: the Aeolian grunge of the beginning, which sets up the story of Tommy and Gina's hardship, and the transcendent change to G major in the chorus, which symbolically and phenomenologically resolves it. For most of the song, the grunge frames and contains the chorus. It seems more realistic, since it returns as though inevitable whenever Bon Jovi's fervent vocalizing stops. The utopian promise is thus made contingent on the singer's efforts. Only at the end of the song, where the chorus endlessly repeats through the fade-out, does it seem that the transcendence might be maintained—and then only if the singer never ceases. At the same time that the magical power of romantic love, transcending material conditions, is being touted as the solution to what are in fact social problems, the Horatio Alger solution of individual hard work is also suggested. In the end the utopian moment wins out, keeping the realistic grunge at bay and even suggesting that transcendence is more real. But all of this is possible only because Bon Jovi has created these realities: a bleak, resonant social landscape, the power of romantic love to offer transcendence, and a tough but sensitive male to make it work. The patriarchal premises of Bon Jovi's fusion are clear.

Toward the end of the song the transcendent moment is kept fresh through a key change, up a half step. Not only does the pitch rise, creating an overall affective elevation, but it also forces Bon Jovi's voice higher, charging it with even more effortful sincerity and, since he meets the challenge successfully, utopian promise. Moreover, the key change is made to coincide with a dropped beat, so the music jumps forward suddenly, unexpectedly, onto this new, higher harmonic plateau. In the concert footage used in the video of "Livin' on a Prayer," Jon Bon Jovi sails out over the audience on a wire at precisely this moment, tripling the transcendent effect.

The rest of the video seems to have little to do with the song. It consists mostly of grainy black-and-white footage of Jon and the band backstage and in rehearsal, without any visual connection to the song's romantic narrative. Neither is it a typical performance video, like the ones I discussed above, since more camera time is devoted to backstage and rehearsal scenes than to actual or even faked (synched) performance. Yet the video is closely connected to the music; the biggest visual gesture is the sudden switch to color film and a live concert audience, which occurs two thirds of the way through the song, precisely at the climactic moment of transcendence indicated by the song's chorus. The video marginalizes the literal narrative of the lyrics, in accordance with the way that typical heavy metal videos cater to fans' enjoyment of live concerts. The transcendence constructed by the music, originally mapped onto the story of Tommy and Gina, has now become the transcendence available through Bon Jovi: the music, the concert, and even the grainy black-and-white footage that purports to let the fan in on the behind-the-scenes lives of the musicians. What was framed by the lyrics as a moment of transcendence for a romantic, heterosexual couple, made possible by the male narrator, is now a celebration of the band members as objects of desire and of the concert as an experience of collective pleasure. The "Livin' on a Prayer" video is less a romantic story than a spectacle of masculine posturing, and the musically constructed transcendence of the song is linked to patriarchy through both narrative and visual pleasure.

It has been argued that the cinema has only recently begun to present the masculine as spectacle, in something like the way that women have been so presented. This is in contrast to theorizations of earlier cinematographic practice, where women were typically presented as erotic objects of the male gaze, but representations of men functioned as embodiments of a powerful, ideal ego.[25] Such a development is of great interest because the contradictions historically coded into representations of gender result in an almost androgynous glamour being attached to male objects of desire. Bon Jovi's image has been carefully managed so as to simultaneously maintain two different kinds of appeal to male and female fans. For example, the release order of singles from *Slippery When Wet* was carefully balanced between romantic and tougher songs, to sustain interest in the band from both genders.[26] But we will see more serious problems of managing desire in the face of gender blurring in a subgenre of heavy metal distinguished by blatant visual androgyny.

Nothing but a Good Time? Androgyny as a Political Party

Androgyny in heavy metal is the adoption by male performers of the elements of appearance that have been associated with women's function as objects of the male gaze—the visual styles that connote, as Laura Mulvey put it, "to-be-looked-at-ness."[27] The members of bands like Poison or Mötley Crüe wear garish makeup, jewelry, and stereotypically sexy clothes, including fishnet stockings and scarves, and sport long, elaborate, "feminine" hairstyles. Though they are normally included within the genre of heavy metal, such "glam" bands are considered by most fans to be less "heavy" than the mainstream. This is due less to musical differences than to their visual style, which is more flamboyant and androgynous than that of heavier metal.[28]

Androgyny has a long history in music; I have already mentioned problems of gender and representation in Baroque opera. (And one could also mention the seventeenth-century castrati, perhaps the most dedicated androgynes in history.) Recent examples of male androgyny outside heavy metal range from Liberace to Little Richard to Lou Reed, not to mention the androgynous glamour of many country-western stars.[29] Some of this history has faded through supercession: some thought the Beatles' hair, for example, threateningly androgynous in 1964. But in glam metal, androgyny has found popular success to a degree unique in the rock era. And it's a particular sort of androgyny; unlike the 1970s' great androgyne, David Bowie, heavy metal usually lacks ironic distance. It is this absence of irony more than anything else that leads rock critics to scorn glam metal, for the ridiculous seriousness of metal's gender constructions is at odds with the patriarchal premises undergirding the ideologies and institutions of rock.

Poison is a good example of a successful glam metal band: one that boasts millions of fans and no critical approval. "Nothin' but a Good Time," from Poison's multiplatinum album *Open Up and Say . . . Ahh!* (1988), is shot almost entirely as a performance video, one that presents the band as though actually performing the song we hear. It includes, however, two framing scenes, which I will describe and discuss briefly before focusing on Poison's androgyny. The opening scene shows us a young man, with a metal fan's long hair, washing dishes in the back of a restaurant. He is swamped with work, surrounded by dirty plates and hot steam, and he is alone except for a small radio, which is playing a song by Kiss, the founders of spectacular metal. Next we meet his boss, loud and rude, who has stomped back to apply a verbal whip; he threatens and insults the dishwasher, flipping off the radio as he leaves. Disgusted and exhausted, the kid sullenly turns the radio back on as soon as the boss leaves. Then he kicks open a nearby door, as though to grab a bit of air before returning to the grind. When the door opens, we are instantly plunged into a Poison performance, taking place just outside. "Nothin' but a Good Time" begins with that door-opening kick, and while it lasts, the framing narrative is suspended; we don't see the dishes, the washer, or the boss until the song is over. Afterward, we are returned to the same scene as at the beginning. Having heard the music, the boss storms back into the frame to lash again at the kid; he suddenly notices, however (at the same time that we notice it), that all of the dishes, miraculously, are clean. Confounded, he sputters and withdraws, as the dishwasher relaxes and smiles.

The framing scenes of this video call to mind culture critics' debates about class and resistance in popular culture. The issue is whether or not popular narratives such as that presented by this song and video contain any oppositional potential or critical perspective, whether they offer viewers anything more than an experience of rebellion that is ultimately illusory and inconsequential. We must be wary of simply dismissing such "unreal" resolutions of real social antagonisms; as Fredric Jameson has argued, although mass culture has conservative functions, though it commonly arouses utopian hopes but perpetuates their containment within hegemonic social forms, the very representation of social fantasies is risky, and maintenance of dominant ideologies is never complete.[30] However, the overt political lesson of the video's framing narrative may be far less important than the implications of the band's visual and musical styles for notions of authenticity and gender. "Nothin' but a Good Time" can serve as an example of those subcultural challenges to hegemony which, as Dick Hebdige has argued, are not issued directly but rather are "expressed obliquely, in style."[31]

In the "Nothin' but a Good Time" video, the song itself is framed as a fantastic experience. Reality is the world of the frame, the world of work, steam, sweat, and abuse; as in *The Wizard of Oz*, the real world is shot with its colors muted so as to enable the fantasy to seem more real. When the dishwasher kicks open the door, Poison explodes in color and musical sound and the real world, the one that supposedly includes the fantasy, vanishes; the fantasy takes over as a more real reality. Even the dishwasher himself disappears for the duration of the song, in a kind of dissolution of the ego in the flux of musical pleasure. This fantasy is credited with magical agency as well: at the end of the song, we are returned to gray reality to find the dishes done, the impossible task fulfilled. The boss's torrent of abuse is plugged; something has been put over on him, though he can't say what or how.

When combined with the song's lyrics, the video's message seems fairly simple self-promotion: the good time being sung about is something that can be accessed through Poison's music, no matter what the "real" conditions. As with many TV advertisements, Poison's fantasy is represented as more real than mundane reality, and the fantasy is to be enjoyed through involvement with a commercial product. Such an appeal, though, must evoke our desires for community and for greater freedom and intensity of experience than are commonly available in the real world. Poison, like Pepsi, uses narrative and image to arouse these longings and to present us with a particular kind of consumption as the means of satisfying them.

But it would be a mistake to exaggerate the importance of the narrative framing of the song; however obvious the "political" message of the framing narrative may seem, it may be less important than the gender politics of the song and its performance. Debates over the liberatory possibilites of mass culture all too often proceed in terms that neglect the gendered character of all social experience. Yet popular music's politics are most effective in the realm of gender and sexuality, where pleasure, dance, the body, romance, power, and subjectivity all meet with an affective charge. The significance of the musical section of the video may be overlooked because it seems to be simply a representation of a live performance, whereas the frame is more arbitrary and thus presumably more meaningful. But it is the band's performance that is privileged visually, through color, free movement, and spectacle—and through the transgressive energies of male display and flamboyance. Most tellingly, it is the performance rather than the framing narrative that benefits from the affective invigoration of the music. If the framing scenes address labor relations, they do so in a rather flat, pedantic way. It is the video of the song itself that deals with the issues of greatest importance to metal fans: the power, freedom, transcendence, and transgression that are articulated through fantastic, androgynous display. The young man we meet in the frame finds his release from drudgery in Poison's spectacular androgyny.

Significantly, the video's "live" performance of "Nothin' but a Good Time" is neither live nor a real performance, but a constructed fantasy itself. The musicians undergo impossibly frequent and sudden changes of costume, without narrative explanation, through the invisible, extra-diegetic powers of editing. Along with similar metamorphoses of the guitar player's instrument, which is a different model and color each time we see it, these unreal transformations contribute to the fantastic aura of the performance by offering an experience of freedom and plenitude. Moreover, there is no audience; the band "performs" in an abstract space, a contextless setting for pure spectacle. Such a location can serve as a "free space" for Poison's play of real and unreal, authenticity and desire, and the ambiguous subversiveness of androgyny, supported by the energy of the music.

The lyrics of the song are fairly simple: they combine a lament about overwork with a celebration of partying. The music is similarly straightforward, built around a vigorous rock beat and standard power chords on the scale degrees I, ♭VII, and IV. The musical mode is Mixolydian, quite commonly used in pop-oriented hard rock or metal, as it combines the positive affect of the major third with the "hard" semiotic value of the minor seventh. "Nothin' but a Good Time" derives much of its celebratory energy from the repeated suspension of the fourth scale degree over this major third, and the conventional move to ♭VII adds to the song's rebellious or aggressive tone. The visual narrative and the musically coded meanings are roughly parallel; the lyrics are supported by music that is energetic, rebellious, and flamboyant.

But in "Nothin' but a Good Time" we can also detect the association of androgynous visual styles with a particular set of musical characteristics. The song features compelling rhythmic patterns, it contains the requisite guitar solo, it utilizes the distorted timbres one would expect in the electric guitar and vocals of a metal song; in short, the song meets generic criteria in every way. It is, of course, successful music, exploiting discursive potentials with skill and effectiveness. However, one would be hard-pressed to find it very distinctive in any way; this is not especially innovative or imaginative music. Androgynous metal usually includes less emphasis on complexity and virtuosity than do other styles of metal, and many arguments among fans are provoked by the collision of visual spectacle and transgression with metal's dominant aesthetic valorization of sonic power, freedom, and originality. This alignment of androgynous spectacle with a musical discourse relatively lacking in sonic figurations of masculinity is crucial, for it signals the extent to which a linkage of "feminine" semiotic instability with monolithic, phallic power is deemed impossible.

To be sure, if the music of glam metal were separated from its visual context, it would still sound like hard rock. Compared to other kinds of popular music, glam rock is replete with constructions of masculine power. But within the context of heavy metal, glam metal's relative lack of virtuosity, complexity, and originality are aural contributors to androgyny. Fans link visual signs of androgyny with an abdication of metal's usual virtuosic prowess. "It seems like if you have the makeup you're thought of as less than a musician," complains Poison's guitarist C. C. Deville. "It seems because of the image we can't get past that hurdle. Now we try to stay away from the glam thing. When we first came out we were a little extreme." [32]

Indeed, when I attended a Poison concert I discovered that their drummer, Rikki Rockett, was actually an excellent musician, whose featured solo was marked by sophisticated polyrhythms and rhetorical intelligence. I was surprised by this because his playing on Poison's recordings had always been extremely simple, however accurate and appropriate. But Poison's simplicity is constructed, like that of much American popular music throughout its history. From Stephen Foster to Madonna (not to mention Aaron Copland), many musicians have used great skill to craft musical texts that communicate great simplicity. The musical construction of simplicity plays an important part in many kinds of ideological representations, from the depiction of pastoral refuges from modernity to constructions of race and gender. Poison succeeded in a genre dominated by virtuosity because their musical simplicity complemented their androgynous visual style and helped them forge a constituency. As Deville's comment indicates, the band now yearns to be respected musically as well, and though they have yet to make much progress toward this goal, they have drastically reduced the amount of makeup they wear, in pursuit of it.

"Real Men Don't Wear Makeup"

In the case of bands such as Poison, we might understand androgyny as yet another tactic for dealing with the anxieties of masculinity. Androgynous musicians and fans appropriate the visual signs of feminine identity in order to claim the powers of spectacularity for themselves. But while it is certainly important to understand heavy metal androgyny as patriarchal, metal takes part in a rock and roll tradition of Oedipal rebellion as well: the musical and visual codes of heavy metal may function to relieve anxieties about male power, but they are incompatible with the styles previous generations of men developed for doing the same thing. Teenage boys and young men chafe under patriarchal control even as women do, and boys often develop innovative ways of expressing control over women as simultaneous proof of their achievement of manhood and their rebellion against dominant men. This internal tension is never entirely manageable or predictable, and heavy metal transgresses against patriarchal control in ways that sometimes undermine, sometimes affirm its tenets.

Musicians themselves may notice how the ambiguities of androgyny provoke compensatory strategies. Aerosmith's hit song and video "Dude Looks like a Lady" (1987) confronts the gender anxieties aroused by androgyny, airing the problem with a tone of mock hysteria. And singer David Lee Roth self-reflexively connects his enthusiasm for bodybuilding and martial arts training to his "feminized" image on stage: "A lot of what I do can be construed as feminine. My face, or the way I dance, or the way I dress myself for stage. . . . But to prove it to myself, to establish this [his masculinity], I had to build myself physically. I had to learn to fight."[33] Roth's private regimen allows him to go on being androgynous in public. His personal anxieties about masculinity are shaped by conventional patriarchy, yet the attraction of androgynous transgression is also strong. Among the most leering of rock's lyricists, Roth seems neither personally nor artistically to have resisted sexist objectification of women, as is attested by his notorious paternity insurance policy and the video for his swaggering remake of the Beach Boys' "California Girls." Yet Roth has also publicly criticized the sexism of a society that discourages women from becoming professional musicians: "What if a little girl picked up a guitar and said 'I wanna be a rock star.' Nine times out of ten her parents would never allow her to do it. We don't have so many lead guitar women, not because women don't have the ability to play the instrument, but because they're kept locked up, taught to be something else. I don't appreciate that."[34] Roth's ideal of personal freedom is in conflict with the limitations of conventional gender definitions, though he doesn't grapple with the problem of how patriarchal power relations might be further strengthened by transgressions that rely on objectified representations of women.

In the journalism of heavy metal, the most heated debates are over "authenticity," which often implicitly revolves around issues of gender and sexuality. Fans frequently write to the letters columns of metal magazines to denounce or defend glam metal bands. Attackers label such musicians "poseurs," implying either that the band is all image with no musical substance or that they find androgyny fundamentally offensive, a perversion. As one female fan complained in a letter to a fan magazine, "real men don't wear makeup."[35] On the other side, defenders of glam metal are quick to respond, though they rarely defend androgyny per se: "This is to Kim of Cathedral City . . . who said that real men don't wear makeup. I have just one question: Do you actually listen to the music, or just spend hours staring at album covers? True, Metallica and Slayer kick f?!kin' ass and Megadeth rules—but Poison, Motley Crue and Hanoi Rocks f?!kin' jam too."[36] Unwilling to discuss gender constructions directly or lacking cultural precedents for doing so, fans usually defend the musical abilities of the band's members or argue for the intensity of experience provided by the group. But they may also respect the courage that is required of those who disrupt the symbolic order through androgyny, those who claim social space by having "the guts to be glam."[37]

Male fans of "harder" styles of heavy metal are often frantic in their denunciations of androgyny, seeing in it a subversion of male heterosexual privilege and linking it to the threat of homosexuality. On the cover of an album by MX Machine (*Manic Panic*, 1988), a picture of a grimacing boy with his fist in the air is accompanied by a sticker proclaiming "No Glam Fags! All Metal! No Makeup!" Both homosexuality and symbolic crossing of gender boundaries threaten patriarchal control, and they are thus conflated in the service of a rhetoric that strives to maintain difference and power. Musicians who wear makeup often compensate in private for their transgressions with homophobic banter, insulting each other in order to call masculinity into question and provide an opportunity for collective affirmation of heterosexuality.[38] An interview with Charlie Benante, drummer in the thrash metal band Anthrax, confirms that even instruments themselves are conventionally gender-coded, and that the use of a feminine-coded instrument in the context of heavy metal evokes the specter of homosexuality. When an interviewer asked, "Would you ever consider using keyboards as a major part of the song?" Benante replied, "That is gay. The only band that ever used keyboards that was good was UFO. This is a guitar band."[39]

However, since many "glam" metal performers appeal in particular to young women, an analysis of heavy metal that understands it only as a reproduction of male hegemony runs the risk of duplicating the exscription it describes. Heavy metal androgyny presents, from the point of view of women, a fusion of the signs specific to current notions of femininity with musically and theatrically produced power and freedom that are conventionally male. Colorful makeup; elaborate, ostentatious clothes; hair that is unhandily long and laboriously styled—these are the excessive signs of one gender's role as spectacle. But onstage in a metal show, these signs are invested with the power and glory normally reserved to patriarchy. As usual, women are offered male subject positions as a condition of their participation in empowerment, but the men with whom they are to identify have been transformed by their appropriations of women's signs. In their bid for greater transgression and spectacularity, the men onstage elevate important components of many women's sense of gendered identity, fusing cultural representations of male power and female erotic surface.[40] At the symbolic level, prestige—male presence, gesture, musical power—is conferred upon "female" signs, which, because they mark gender difference and are used to attract and manipulate, men pretend are trivial but take very seriously.

Feminist scholars have long been concerned with investigating the gendered aspects of the relationship of symbolic and political orders, and the long-standing linkage of women with ephemeral spectacle is highly relevant to metal videos. Kaja Silverman has pointed out that the instability of female fashion has historically marked women as unstable, while male sartorial conservatism represents the stable and timeless alignment of men with the symbolic and social orders.[41] Heavy metal androgyny challenges this "natural" alignment, drawing on the power of musical and visual pleasures. It is true that there is no inherent link between subversive textual practices and subversive politics, but the relationships I have delineated among the lyrics, music, images, fans, musicians, and ideologies of heavy metal, particularly with respect to gender, are intended to make the case for a conventional link.[42] Glam metal has prompted a great deal of thought and discussion about gender by demonstrating, even celebrating, the mutability of gender, by revealing the potential instability of the semiotic or symbolic realms that support current gender configurations. In some ways, heavy metal reflects the impact of what Jane Flax has called the greatest achievement of feminist theory, the problematization of gender.[43]

Metal replicates the dominant sexism of contemporary society, but it also allows a kind of free space to be opened up by and for certain women, performers and fans alike. Female fans identify with a kind of power that is usually understood in our culture as male—because physical power, dominance, rebellion, and flirting with the dark side of life are all culturally designated as male prerogatives. Yet women are able to access this power because it is channeled through a medium, music, that is intangible and difficult to police. Female performers of heavy metal can become enabled to produce and control very powerful sounds, if they meet other genre requirements and acquiesce in the physical display that is so sexist and widespread in society generally but may in fact seem less so in metal, where men similarly display themselves.[44] Thus, when metal guitarist and singer Lita Ford brags, "I wear my balls on my chest," she combines her seemingly inevitable status as an object of sexual spectacle with her metallic stature as a subject embodying the spectacle of power.[45]

Women's reception of these spectacles is complex, and female performers of heavy metal may be advancing provocative arguments about the nature and limits of female claims to power. I have observed and interviewed female fans who dress, act, and interpret just like male fans, for example, particularly at concerts of bands like Metallica—bands that avoid references to gender in their lyrics, dealing instead with experiences of alienation, fear, and empowerment that may cut across gender lines. Elements of rock music that had been coded as masculine, such as heavy beats, are negotiable, insofar as female fans are willing to step outside traditional constrictions of gender identity.[46] It may well be, then, that the participation of female metal fans reflects the influence that feminism has had in naturalizing, to a great extent, the empowerment of women. Even in the 1970s, fewer women would have been comfortable identifying with power, when power was more rigidly coded as male. The choice was between being powerful and being a woman, a dichotomy that has since eroded somewhat.

But female fans also maintain their own distinctive modes of engagement with heavy metal, including practices that are often too quickly dismissed as degrading adoration. Sue Wise has argued that the young women who screamed and swooned over Elvis were not so much worshiping him, as so many male rock critics have assumed, as *using* him. Instead of a subject who caused his helpless fans to go into frenzies, Elvis was for many women an object by means of which they explored their own desires and formed friendships.[47] Similarly, many female heavy metal fans take great pleasure in collecting, owning, and looking at pictures of male heavy metal musicians. Predictably, male fans tend to be scornful of the pin-up magazines and their devotees.[48] But the enthusiasm of young women for glam styles of heavy metal is not simply an example of masochistic submission to male idols. Such spectacle also infuses with power the signs of women's hegemonically constructed gender identity, offers visual pleasures seldom available to women, and provides them with opportunities to form their own subsets of the fan community.

The channeling of so much masculine prestige through feminine forms thus represents a risky sexual politics, one that is open to several interpretations. Heavy metal's androgyny can be very disturbing, not only because the conventional signs of female passivity and objectification are made dynamic, assertive, and transgressive, but also because hegemonic gender boundaries are blurred and the "natural" exclusiveness of heterosexual male power comes into question.[49] For all of its male rhetoric of supremacy—phallic imagery, macho posturing, the musical semiotics of male power—metal's rebellion and fantastic play offer its fans, both male and female, opportunities to make common cause against certain kinds of oppression, even as the same text may enable each gender to resolve particular anxieties in very different ways. The level of discussion of gender among heavy metal fans is impressive, in statements that reflect their awareness of the mutability of gender roles and other cultural constructions. Practically every issue of the fan magazine *RIP* in 1989 contained letters from fans protesting sexism, racism, and even homophobia.[50] Glam metal fostered greater perception of the conventionality of gender roles, and thus helped lead to greater participation in metal by women and to debates over gender stereotypes, masculinity, behavior, and access to power.

Androgyny offers male performers (and vicariously, male fans) the chance to play with color, movement, flamboyance, and artifice, which can be a tremendous relief from the rigidity expected of them as men. Philip Gordon argues that singer Dee Snider "grew his hair and wore women's clothes and make-up, not merely to assert a difference between himself and his parents (as if any sign of difference would be equally effective), but as a carefully constructed style signifying attractiveness, energy and opposition to authoritative restrictions on particular pleasures."[51]

Critics have not generally understood glam metal in this way. E. Ann Kaplan denies any significance to heavy metal's gender politics: "Unlike the genuine Bakhtinian carnival, the protest remains superficial: mere play with oppositional signifiers rather than a protest that emerges from a powerful class and community base."[52] But Kaplan can make such a statement only because she made no efforts to discover anything about the "class and community base" of heavy metal. There is nothing superficial about such play; fans and musicians do their most important "identity work" when they participate in the formations of gender and power that constitute heavy metal. Metal is a fantastic genre, but it is one in which real social needs and desires are addressed and temporarily resolved in unreal ways. These unreal solutions are attractive and effective precisely because they seem to step outside the normal social categories that construct the conflicts in the first place.

Like many other social groups, metal musicians and fans play off different possibilities available to them from mainstream culture, at the same time that they may draw upon the facts of a social situation that is not mainstream. Androgynous metal's bricolage of male power and female spectacle and its play of real and unreal are complex responses to crucial social contradictions that its fans have inherited. Heavy metal's fantastic representations clash with the visions of many other social groups in the cultural competition to define social reality, and like the tensions to which they are a response, metal's fantasies are themselves richly conflicted. If male heavy metal fans and musicians sometimes assert masculinity by co-opting femininity, what they achieve is not necessarily the same kind of masculinity that they sought, as the conflicting demands of masculinity and rebellion are mediated through new models and the free play of androgynous fantasy shakes up the underlying categories that structure social experience.

However, androgyny is by no means a purely utopian sign. Capitalism, after all, feeds on novelty as a spur to consumption, and mass culture may colonize existing tensions and ambiguities for consumer purposes rather than to prefigure new realities. As Fred Pfeil points out, mass audiences are increasingly offered "scandalously ambivalent pleasure," and the same "de-Oedipalization" of American middle-class life that makes androgyny possible, attractive, and thrilling can also block further development toward new collective social forms, beyond fragmentation.[53] Moreover, postmodern cultural "decentering" can serve capitalism by playing to sensual gratification in ways that deflect people from making the connections that might enable critique.

But postmodern disruptions also open up new possibilities and enable new connections and formulations to be made by delegitimating conceptual obstacles; androgynous metal's defamiliarization of social categories that are still thought normative by many must be given its due. Poison's music and images reflect a concern with shifting boundaries of gender and reality that cannot simply be disregarded as no more than inauthentic or commodified fantasies, for such fantasies are exercises in semiotic power, offering challenges at the level of both what representations are made and who gets to make them. Dismissing fantasy and escapism "avoids the vital questions of *what* is escaped from, *why* escape is necessary, and *what* is escaped to."[54]

Simon Frith and Angela McRobbie ended their early theorization of rock and sexuality with what they saw as a "nagging" question: "Can rock be nonsexist?"[55] The obvious answer would seem to be no, for there is no way to step outside the history of a discourse, and Frith and McRobbie's question begs for a kind of music that is recognizably— that is, discursively—rock, but that does not participate in the sexism that rock has articulated. Rock can never be gender-neutral because rock music is intelligible only in its historical and discursive contexts. Rock can, however, be antisexist; instead of dreaming of a kind of music that might be both "rock" and "nonsexist," we can spot many extant examples of rock music that use the powerful codings of gender available in order to engage with, challenge, disrupt, or transform not only rock's representations of gender but also the beliefs and material practices with which those representations engage. The point of criticism should not be to decide whether rock music is oppositional or co-optive, with respect to gender, class, or any other social category, but rather to analyze how it arbitrates tensions between opposition and co-optation at particular historical moments.[56]

I have ranged widely within heavy metal in this chapter, turning to a number of very different bands and to various visual and musical strategies for dealing with the contradictions inherent in gender roles in the 1980s. The range of examples is necessary, I think, to demonstrate that heavy metal as a genre includes a great variety of gender constructions, contradictory negotiations with dominant ideologies of gender that are invisible if one is persuaded by metal's critics that the whole enterprise is a monolithic symptom of adolescent maladjustment. In fact, it is those most responsible for the very conditions with which metal musicians and fans struggle—the contradictory demands of subordination and socialization, of "masculine" aggressiveness and communal harmony, the possibilites of transcendent pleasure and street pain—who insist on reading this music as impoverished and debased "entertainment."

Heavy metal, like virtually all cultural practices, is continually in flux, driven by its own constitutive contradictions. Patriarchy and capitalism form the crucible, but human experience can never be wholly contained within such a vessel: there are aspects of social life that escape the organization of one or the other; there are also aspects organized in contradictory ways by the pair. Culture cannot transcend its material context, but culture very often transcends hegemonic definitions of its context: heavy metal perpetuates some of the worst images and ideals of patriarchy at the same time that it stands as an example of the kinds of imaginative transformations and rebuttals people produce from within such oppressive systems. Masculinity is forged whenever it is hammered out anew through the negotiations of men and women with the contradictory positions available to them in such contexts. It is also forged because masculinity is passed like a bad check, as a promise that is never kept. Masculinity will always be forged because it is a social construction, not a set of abstract qualities but something defined through the actions and power relations of men and women—because, with or without makeup, there are no "real men."

CHAPTER FIVE

Can I Play with Madness?

Mysticism, Horror, and
Postmodern Politics

✳

Cradled in evil, that Thrice-Great Magician,
The Devil, rocks our souls, that can't resist;
And the rich metal of our own volition
Is vaporized by that sage alchemist.   —Baudelaire [1]

In his course on rhetoric, the Roman orator Quintilian included a ficti-
tious legal exercise in the politics of music and madness. He presented
the case of a musician who is accused of manslaughter because he played
in the wrong musical mode during a sacrifice; by playing in the Phrygian
mode, a piper allegedly caused the officiating priest to go mad and fling
himself over a cliff.[2] Quintilian used this story to support his argument
that musical training is essential for the development of oratorical skills,
but the problem of the musician's liability is also of interest because it
raises questions about the nature and power of music, about social mis-
trust of those whose rhetorical abilities find their outlet through musical
discourse. As the popularity of heavy metal grew in the late 1980s, it
came increasingly under fire from critics who accused its musicians of
"playing in the wrong mode," causing madness and death. In this chapter I will criticize a number of influential condemnations of heavy metal
and propose alternative explanations of the significance of mysticism,
horror, and violence in heavy metal.

Professing Censorship: The PMRC and its
Academic Allies Attack

The single most influential critic of heavy metal in the 1980s was
Tipper Gore, whose status as the wife of U.S. Senator Albert Gore, Jr.,

provided her with access to media attention and political muscle to support her cause. In 1985, Gore, along with several other wives of powerful government figures (among them Susan Baker, wife of then treasury secretary James A. Baker) established the Parents' Music Resource Center (PMRC). The PMRC has been quite successful in articulating a reactionary cultural agenda and accomplishing its political goals. Since its founding, the group has pressured record companies into placing warning stickers on recordings with "adult" lyrics and has underwritten partially successful campaigns to persuade state legislatures to censor certain types of music, chiefly rap and heavy metal. Through its conjugal connections with Capitol Hill, the PMRC was able to provoke congressional hearings, in September 1985, on the subject of what they called "porn rock." Though the PMRC and Congress described the hearings as neutral "fact-finding," others saw them as terrorism, since congressional interrogation of musicians and leaders of the music industry suggested implicit (and illegal) threats of legislation if the moralistic demands of the PMRC for "voluntary" censorship were not met.

Although the PMRC has been accused of not really being a "resource center" because its publications display little familiarity with the scholarly literature on popular music, it is unmistakably "parental."[3] The fullest articulation of the PMRC brief is Tipper Gore's *Raising PG Kids in an X-Rated Society*, published in 1987. In it, Gore takes care to establish her authority as a social and cultural critic by emphasizing that she is a parent; she dwells on the numbers and genders of the children of PMRC leaders, while neglecting to mention that her main opponents at the Senate hearings, musicians Frank Zappa and Dee Snider, are also concerned parents.[4] Her references to twenty-year-old "boys" mark her concern to represent heavy metal as a threat to youth, enabling her to mobilize parental hysteria while avoiding the adult word *censorship*. Objecting to eroticism and "lesbian undertones" in popular music, along with sadism and brutality, she conflates sex and violence, which have in common their threat to parental control.

It is clear from Gore's book that heavy metal participates in a crisis in the reproduction of values, that it is a threat because it celebrates and legitimates sources of identity and community that do not derive from parental models. For the PMRC, assuming the universality of "the American Family," an institution of mythic stature but scant abundance, provides an absolute norm that can be righteously defended. Gore attempts to naturalize her perspective by appealing to "common sense" universals, such as the "shared moral values" that underpin "our" society. She combines such grand claims with disingenuousness about her own political clout, as when she refers to "our friends (some of whom happen to hold public office)." Like so many recent appeals to "common sense" and "morality," Gore's book is a call for the imposition of official values and the elimination of cultural difference.[5]

To bolster her attack on heavy metal, Gore relies heavily on a pamphlet by a professor of music, "The Heavy Metal User's Manual" by Joe Stuessy.[6] Not only is Stuessy often cited in Gore's book; he was also called upon as an expert witness for the Senate hearings in 1985. In both his testimony and his pamphlet, Stuessy argued that heavy metal lyrics are violent and deviant and that metal music is artistically impoverished. "Most of the successful heavy metal," he testified, "projects one or more of the following basic themes: extreme rebellion, extreme violence, substance abuse, sexual promiscuity/perversion (including homosexuality, bisexuality, sadomasochism, necrophilia, etc.), Satanism."[7] In fact, heavy metal lyrics dealing with these topics are uncommon. For example, examination of eighty-eight song lyrics reprinted by *Hit Parader* reveals relatively little concern with violence, drug use, or suicide. Reduced to the crudest terms, the songs could be grouped thematically so:[8]

> Assertion of or longing for intensity: 27
> Lust: 17
> Loneliness, victimization, self-pity: 17
> Love: 14 (affirmation, 8; regret or longing, 6)
> Anger, rebellion, madness: 8
> Didactic or critical (antidrug, anti-Devil, anti–TV evangelism,
>   critique of the subversion of justice by wealth): 5

Moreover, when such transgressive lyrics do appear, it is in contexts where they often function in ways that are more complex and sophisticated than Stuessy recognizes, as we will see below.

Connections between heavy metal and drug use have certainly existed throughout the music's history, beginning perhaps with the success of Blue Cheer among San Francisco speed freaks in the late 1960s.[9] But drugs cannot explain a style of music, since the music, lyrics, and images of even heavily drug-influenced music cross the boundaries of subcultural scenes and make sense to people who are using different drugs or even no drugs at all. And because both music and drugs are involved in strategies for coping with particular social circumstances, criticism of one cannot depend on denunciation of the other; both must be located in the real world of material and cultural tensions.[10] Moreover, critics have failed to notice that as heavy metal became both individually and collectively more virtuosic during the 1980s, musicians increasingly confided that they could no longer afford to indulge in drugs and alcohol because their music would suffer too much.[11]

Finally, criticism of rock music because of drug use often implicitly relies upon an absurdly sanitized version of musical history. Many now-canonic nineteenth-century artists "confidently engaged in 'mad' behavior—debauchery, drinking, drug use, irrational thinking—hoping thus to stimulate their creativity. . . . the viewpoint prevailed that genius and madness are inseparable."[12] Berlioz made no bones about his use of opium; his program for the *Symphonie fantastique* explicitly connects opium use with the rhetorical splendor of his music. Abuse of alcohol is well documented for composers such as Schumann, Schubert, and Mussorgsky, and much more information about drugs and canonic composers would no doubt be available were it not for the musicological whitewashing of the lives of these musicians, which has retroactively enforced compulsory sobriety, heterosexuality, and Christianity. Berlioz's *Symphonie fantastique* is, of course, more than the random outcome of an opium dream that it pretends to be; it is a powerful metaphorical articulation, grounded in contemporary social currents and musical discourses. Contemporary popular music is made to seem especially vulnerable to certain kinds of critique because so much has been purged from our hagiological histories of music and so much is hidden by the assumptions about cultural hierarchy we take for granted.

Throughout his book, Stuessy pursues the simplistic argument that healthy minds don't think negative thoughts, and he alleges that heavy metal is socially unique in its glorification of violence, which network news shows, for example, merely report. But Steussy, like Gore, is being disingenuous, because struggles for power are hardly unique to youth culture or popular culture. From the Super Bowl to Monster Truck races, from Capitol Hill to corporate boardrooms (where handbooks of advice have titles like *Swim with the Sharks* and *Leadership Secrets of Atilla the Hun*), adult Americans (especially men) display their seemingly insatiable fascination with power and violence, a way of thinking that is continually affirmed by the brutality of American capitalism and government policy. From President Johnson's War on Poverty to President Bush's War on Drugs, American politicians have found military metaphors the most effective means of selling programs that might have been described in communal and compassionate terms. In this light, Stuessy's concluding recommendations for action against metal are patently hypocritical: "I think the attack on heavy metal must be waged on all fronts using every weapon at our disposal. . . . Warning labels and ratings might be helpful, but that is not the final solution. Printed lyrics would be helpful, but that is not the ultimate weapon."[13] Glorification of violence in American society is hardly deviant, as we see from Stuessy's own plan for a "final solution" to the problem of heavy metal.

Stuessy's status as a professor of music makes him a useful ally to those who would strip heavy metal of First Amendment protections as free artistic expression, for he is able to offer an aggressive twist on the usual mystification that elevates classical music and protects it from ideological critique, leaving popular musics more vulnerable to attack. Stuessy assures us that the process of artistic creation remains "shrouded in mystery," and the inspiration of composers like Beethoven was "mysterious and quite possibly divine"; but heavy metal, he argues, is merely cranked out according to a formula, which disqualifies it from protection under freedom of expression, making it instead subject to "consumer protection" regulation like other manufactured products.[14]

At the same time, the aesthetic tradition has been so successful in effacing the social meanings of culture that Stuessy found it necessary to argue at length that music can in fact affect us. He adopts, and Gore accepts from him, a "hypodermic model" of musical effects; music's meanings are "pounded" or "dumped" into listeners, who are helpless to resist. Young people in particular are thought to be more vulnerable, especially when repetitive listening and headphone use help create "a direct, unfettered freeway straight into the mind."[15] Stuessy's problem is to define music so that heavy metal can be held responsible for harming listeners without calling into question the violence in Beethoven's *Eroica*, for example, or the glorification of drugs, violence, and Satanism in the *Symphony fantastique*.[16] The solution is simply to assume that the meanings of classical music are essentially benign because they are art, whereas heavy metal ought to arouse our suspicions because it is popular and commercially successful. Those who embrace such a position seem undaunted by the elitism that is required to underpin it, or by the fact that what we now call "classical music" is and always has been "commercial."[17]

Another academic, this one a professor of religious studies at the University of Denver, has recently launched a full-scale attack on heavy metal. Like several earlier book-length denunciations of rock music, Carl A. Raschke's *Painted Black: From Drug Killings to Heavy Metal—the Alarming True Story of How Satanism Is Terrorizing Our Communities* is explicitly concerned with defending "the values of Christian civilization," which he presumes are shared by all right-thinking citizens.[18] The book "reveals" a national epidemic of Satanism, manifest in ritual crimes and supported by heavy metal music. Unlike Tipper Gore's book, which maintains a rather calm tone and clear documentation, Raschke's is a potboiler, filled with sensational claims backed by shoddy scholarship. On the one hand, he uses unsubstantiated and marginally coherent similes to suggest that heavy metal is a terrible threat: "The end result [of heavy metal] is to erode the nervous system with noise, as drugs destroy the cerebrum"; "A national epidemic of 'satanist-related' crime was growing faster than AIDS"; and, most puzzling: "Heavy metal belongs to a so-called avant-garde art form that has stayed veiled from the eyes of mass audiences, the style known as aesthetic terrorism."[19]

On the other hand, Raschke also pretends to have objective, scientific justification for his hysteria:

In 1985, the *Wall Street Journal* reported that a fat sheaf of neuro-psychological research has shown remarkable, and complex, relationships between music listening and brain organization. Roger Shepard, a professor at Stanford University, believes that certain kinds of music "mesh effectively with the deep cognitive structures of the mind." Heavy metal seems to mesh with the limbic brain, the most primitive and potentially violent stratum of cerebral processing.[20]

But the last, damning sentence of this passage is a deliberate fabrication, for heavy metal was never mentioned by Shepard. Raschke has tacked onto his summary of a quite uncontroversial report his own condemnation of heavy metal, carefully couched in scientific language ("limbic brain," "cerebral processing") so as to suggest that it is justified by the findings of Shepard's research. He misleads his readers in an attempt to whip up a repressive frenzy directed against metal musicians and fans. Raschke invokes science as part of his effort to essentialize what are in fact social tensions: "Heavy metal does more than dissolve the inherent inhibitions against violence. It actively fosters, configures, anneals, reinforces, and purifies the most vicious and depraved tendencies within the human organism."[21] When he describes both "inhibitions against violence" *and* "depraved tendencies" as inherent qualities rather than socially negotiated ones, Raschke wants to have it both ways: heavy metal dissolves the fragile bonds of repression that make civilization possible, *and* it unnaturally corrupts human nature itself.

The terrorism of Raschke and similar critics depends upon two tactics: anecdote and insinuation. Raschke himself cites a group of sociologists of religion who determined that there was "not a shred of evidence" that Satanism is a problem in America, directly contradicting the thesis of Raschke's book. The "evidence disintegrates as close examination occurs" whenever Satanism and crime are linked, according to J. Gordon Melton, director of the Institute for the Study of American Religion in Santa Barbara.[22] Raschke replies by recounting, in sickening detail, a few instances of crimes involving satanic symbols, without addressing the question of how significant this sort of crime is—how it compares statistically with, for example, crimes committed by clergy or suicides related to plant closings.[23] In Stuessy's book, in Raschke's, and in a lecture I heard by a touring campus crusader against rock music, I found the same handful of stories repeated rapidly and balefully so as to suggest that they stood as select examples of widespread trends rather than the bizarre and anomalous events they were. In the end Raschke waffles and hedges: "And if no one can blame rock music directly for the 300 percent rise in adolescent suicides or the 7 percent increase in teenage pregnancies, it *may surely* be more than a negligible factor."[24] With the word *may*, Raschke admits that no link can be made; with the word *surely*, he attempts to cover up that admission. Moreover, if we assume that rock music is to blame for that rise in suicides, do we then credit rap and heavy metal with causing the dramatic decrease in drug use among high school students in the 1980s, the decade during which those styles came to dominate musical culture?[25]

In fact, none of these critics is able to connect heavy metal directly with suicide, Satanism, or crime. Tipper Gore does provide information on Dungeons and Dragons, a fantasy role-playing game that has been attacked for the same reasons. According to her, over eight million sets of D&D have been sold in the United States; yet even the game's harshest critics can link it with fewer than fifty people involved in suicides or homicides.[26] As with metal, one might reasonably infer from such statistics that D&D is to be applauded as a stabilizing factor in many adolescent lives. If I have dwelt on these critiques longer than seems necessary, it is because they have in fact been extremely influential. The flimsiness of these arguments seems to escape readers who are predisposed to accept heavy metal as a convenient scapegoat; Raschke was given a complimentary "Portrait," for example, in *The Chronicle of Higher Education.*[27]

Gore and other critics also point to actual violence at heavy metal concerts as more proof of the music's malignancy. But such violence is greatly exaggerated by metal's critics; mayhem is no more common at metal concerts than at sports events—or at the opera in nineteenth-century Paris or performances of Shakespeare in nineteenth-century New York.[28] In fact, concert security guards report that crowds at country music concerts are far more difficult to manage than heavy metal crowds.[29] Culture is valued because it mobilizes meanings with respect to the most deeply held social values and the most profound tensions. Only by effacing cultural history can heavy metal be portrayed as singularly violent in thought or deed. But insinuations of metal's violent effects are also contradicted by a recent study that finds no correlations between teenagers' preferences in music and their likelihood of having "behavioral problems" at school.[30]

To be sure, Tipper Gore raises legitimate concerns about sexual violence in the lyrics and visual representations of metal shows. But she labors to portray such violence as an aberration of youth and commercial exploitation, scapegoating heavy metal musicians and fans for problems that are undeniably extant but for which she holds entirely blameless the dominant social systems, institutions, and moral values she defends. Calls for censorship serve to divert attention from the real social causes of violence and misogyny.

All of these critics share the notion that heavy metal is bad because it is perverse deviance in the midst of a successfully functioning society. They ascribe much too much importance to a transhistorical notion of "adolescence," which allows them to overlook the specific forms that culture takes in particular circumstances of power and pain. They believe that insisting that "healthy minds don't think negative thoughts" will make people overlook the devastation caused by deindustrialization and disastrous social policies. They imagine that fans are passive, unable to resist the pernicious messages of heavy metal, and thus they themselves commit the sort of dehumanization they ascribe to popular culture. They make fans into dupes without agency or subjectivity, without social experiences and perceptions that might inform their interactions with mass-mediated texts.[31] And they portray heavy metal musicians as "outside agitators," just as social authorities tried to blame civil rights violence on Communist troublemaking, as though poverty, joblessness, and police brutality weren't sufficient explanation. But heavy metal exists not in a world that would be fine if it were not marred by degraded culture, but in a world disjointed by inequity and injustice.

In his 1987 movie, *The Hidden*, director Jack Sholder satirized such portrayals of the horrific effects of heavy metal. The back of the videocassette release summarizes the plot: "a demonic extraterrestrial creature is invading the bodies of innocent victims—and transforming them into inhuman killers with an unearthly fondness for heavy metal music, red Ferraris and unspeakable violence."[32] *The Hidden* replicates precisely the understanding of heavy metal promoted by its harshest critics, linking metal with violence, and depicting it as a threat coming from elsewhere, with no connection to this world, working its evil on helpless, innocent victims. The arguments of critics like Gore, Stuessy, and Raschke depend upon denying fans subjectivity or social agency so that they can be cast as victims who can be protected through censorship. By depicting fans as "youth," an ideological category that lifts them out of society and history, these critiques manage to avoid having to provide any explanation of why fans are attracted to the specific sounds, images, and lyrics of heavy metal.

Suicide Solutions

The most celebrated public controversy over heavy metal to date revolved around a lawsuit against Judas Priest, tried in 1990. Five years earlier, two young men from Reno, Nevada—Ray Belknap, eighteen, and Jay Vance, twenty—had consummated a suicide pact by taking turns with a shotgun. Belknap was killed instantly; Vance survived to undergo three years of reconstructive surgery before dying of a drug overdose in 1988. Both men had been avid Judas Priest fans, and the suit alleged that subliminal messages embedded in the band's 1978 release, *Stained Class*, had created a compulsion that led to their deaths. According to the plaintiffs, one song contained commands of "do it" that were audible only subconsciously, and other songs, when played backward, exhorted "try suicide," "suicide is in," and "sing my evil spirit."[33] As with previous accusations of "backward masking" in rock music, the suit depended on the premise that such hidden messages can be decoded without conscious awareness and on the idea that they affect listeners more powerfully than overt communication.

The strategy of the defense was simple: they argued that the lives of Vance and Belknap had been such that no mysterious compulsion was required to account for their suicides. During the two years preceding the suicide pact, for example, Vance had run away from home thirteen times; his mother admitted beating him "too often" when he was young.[34] His father beat him, too, especially after he lost his job (when a GM plant closed in 1979) and began drinking heavily. Vance's violent behavior long predated his involvement with heavy metal; a school psychiatrist had expressed concern about his self-destructive behavior when Vance was in second grade, and his mother testified that he had tried to strangle her and hit her with a hammer while he was still in grade school.[35] He had even been institutionalized for attempted suicide in 1976, at age eleven.

Ray Belknap's background was just as bad. At the time of his suicide attempt, he had just decided to quit his job with a local contractor, after his boss had won his week's wages in a pool game. His mother, a born-again Christian whose religious beliefs increased the tension at home, had just separated from her fourth husband, "a reportedly violent man who had once been arrested for menacing Ray's mother with a gun" and who sometimes locked Ray in the garage and beat him with a belt.[36] Defense lawyers argued that in such circumstances, there was little need to postulate secret musical compulsions in order to account for suicidal thoughts. The prosecution replied that many people have bad home lives yet do not kill themselves—a risky line of reasoning, one would think, since their case depended on overlooking the millions of people who listen to heavy metal yet do not kill themselves.

The Judas Priest case hinged, though, on the question of the impact of subliminal commands, allegedly masked but made no less effective by being placed on the album backward. As part of the substantial media attention given the case, "Newsline New York" interviewed an "expert," Wilson Bryan Key, who claimed that such messages in heavy metal music lead to violence. (The host of the show neglected to mention that Key has in the past claimed to have found satanic or sexual messages on Ritz crackers, $5 bills, and Howard Johnson's placemats.)[37] Yet studies by psychologists have repeatedly shown that while intelligible messages can be found in virtually anything played backward, there is no evidence that listeners perceive or are affected by backward messages. "Even when messages are there, all they do is add a little noise to the music," says one researcher. "There is absolutely no effect from content."[38]

Lead singer Rob Halford may have tipped the scales of justice when he appeared for the last day of testimony with a tape containing backward messages *he* had found on the *Stained Class* album. Reversing the fragment "strategic force / they will not" from "Invader" yielded an intelligible, if cryptic, "It's so fishy, personally I'll owe it." Halford reversed "They won't take our love away," from the same song, and had the courtroom howling when they heard "Hey look, Ma, my chair's broken." Finally, he played his last discovery: "Stand by for exciter / Salvation is his task" came out backward as "I-I-I as-asked her for a peppermint-t-t / I-I-I asked for her to get one."[39]

The trial ended with Judas Priest cleared of all charges, for the judge remained unconvinced that the "subliminal" messages on the album were intentionally placed there or were necessary to explain the conduct of Vance and Belknap. There seemed no credible motive for the subliminal crimes of which the band was accused; as their lawyer put it, "In order to find for the plaintiffs here, you'd have to assume that there is at work out there an Evil Empire of the media and the artist who want to damage the people who are buying their works. You hafta be nuts to think that if Judas Priest had the capability to insert a subliminal message they would tell the fans who've been buying all their albums, 'Go kill yourselves.' "[40]

In the face of such evidence, why is it that accusations of subliminal compulsions persist? Those who condemn heavy metal often posit conspiracies in order to scapegoat musicians and fans, avoiding questions of social responsibility for the destructive behavior of people such as Vance and Belknap. But charges of secret messages may persist because we as a society have afforded ourselves no other ways of explaining music's power to affect us. Subliminal manipulation substitutes for a conception of music as a social discourse; since we are trained not to think of music, or any other art, as symbolic discourse, drawing its power from socially grounded desires and contestations, we fall back on a kind of mysticism to explain the effects that music undeniably produces. Such effects may be acceptable when they are created by dead "great" composers, but they are perceived as dangerously manipulative when produced by others, such as heavy metal musicians.

Another reason the Priest suit hinged on subliminal messages was that an important precedent had already been set in 1985, when a judge decided that overt lyrics about suicide were protected speech under the First Amendment. This earlier case was a suit against Ozzy Osbourne, whose song "Suicide Solution" (1981) was alleged to have promoted suicide in its lyrics and to have compelled nineteen-year-old John McCullom to shoot himself.[41] Osbourne's claim that the lyrics were inspired by the alchohol-related suicide of a friend and that the song is in fact antisuicide and antidrug in sentiment was dismissed as sham social conscience, feigned after the fact. Although this suit too was eventually dismissed, the case became a cause célèbre, for it was timely. The PMRC was in the midst of a campaign against Osbourne and other musicians that had just culminated in widespread discussion of regulation of the record industry and the infamous Senate hearings, and they were quick to use the McCullom suicide as yet another example of the evil effects of heavy metal.

But despite his reputation for transgression—he once bit the head off a live bat (which he thought was rubber) tossed onstage by a fan—Ozzy Osbourne's lyrics tend to be quite moralistic. His *Blizzard of Ozz* album (1981), which contains "Suicide Solution," also includes an anti-porn song, "No Bone Movies," which deplores the degradation caused by obsessive lust. "Revelation (Mother Earth)" is a plea for environmental responsibility, and "Crazy Train" attributes its craziness to the modern pressures faced by the "heirs of a cold war." "Steal Away (The

Night)" celebrates love; "Goodbye to Romance" mourns its loss. And in "Mr. Crowley," Osbourne's lyrics refer to the infamous English Satanist Aleister Crowley (1875–1947); but far from celebrating occult practices, the song taunts Crowley, displaying an ironic tone often used by Osbourne (and never noticed by his literal-minded critics). Osbourne evokes the fascination with the supernatural that Crowley represents— "Uncovering things that were sacred / manifest on this earth"—at the same time that he tweaks Crowley's nose:

> Mister Charming, did you think you were pure?
> Mister Alarming, in nocturnal rapport
>
> . . . .
> Mister Crowley, won't you ride my white horse?
> Mister Crowley, it's symbolic, of course.

Osbourne plays with signs of the supernatural because they evoke a power and mystery that is highly attractive to many fans, but his song offers an experience of those qualities and even a critique, not a literal endorsement of magical practices.

In chapter 3, I discussed in more detail how "Mr. Crowley" uses signs taken from Baroque music to evoke gloom and fatefulness. It is also musical semiotics, I would argue, that has led virtually everyone to reject Osbourne's defense of the lyrics of "Suicide Solution" as an antisuicide statement. The lyrics by themselves are perhaps ambiguous:

> Wine is fine but whiskey's quicker
> Suicide is slow with liquor
> Take a bottle, drown your sorrows
> Then it floods away tomorrows
>
> . . . .
> Where to hide, Suicide is the only way out
> Don't you know what it's really about?

But musically, "Suicide Solution" is very carefully crafted to produce an affect of despair and futility. The song is built around a syncopated power chord riff, played at a morose, plodding tempo. Pulsing bass notes propel each square phrase inexorably into the next, while Osbourne's whiny voice, double-tracked to blur its pitch, repeats sneering, descending lines. Other chords slide inevitably back to a power chord on A; in spite of their syncopated energy, they can never escape.

In the bridge section of the song, brutal, unexpected punches form an irrational, disorienting pattern, accompanying the lines " 'Cause you feel life's unreal and you're living a lie" in the first bridge and "Breaking laws, knocking doors, but there's no one at home" the second time. The harmonic motion of the guitar chords again is a struggle up away from the tonic pedal which is always defeated. Chords are suspended against the pedal, generating great tension, particularly during the section where the vocal sounds are panning back and forth. But the chords are always forced back to the tonic, accompanied by screams and moans. Throughout, the bass remains immutable, implacable, relentlessly pounding tonic downbeats.

The fact that there are no guitar solos in "Suicide Solution" represents a significant exception to the rule, for heavy metal songs almost invariably have them. Often a dialectic is set up between the potentially oppressive power of bass, drums, and rhythm guitar, and the liberating, empowering vehicle of the guitar's solo flights. The feeling of freedom created by the virtuosic guitar solos and fills can be at various times supported, defended, or threatened by the physical power of the bass and the temporal control of the drums. The latter rigidly organize and control time; the guitar escapes with flashy runs and other arrhythmic gestures. The solo allows the listener to identify with the controlling power without feeling threatened, because the solo can transcend anything. "Suicide Solution," however, gains in impact by frustrating this norm; there is power and intensity of existence but no freedom. The song depicts a situation (which the text attributes to alcoholism) of frustration, of intense need balked by no options for action save suicide.

"Suicide Solution" also ends unusually; indeed, I do not know of another song with a comparable ending. Heavy metal songs, in line with their concern with control, typically achieve complete, unambiguous closure; they end with a punch that is withheld slightly, to create desire, but always given. Fade-outs are less often used by metal bands; a fade-out is indeterminate, a way of suggesting that the music continues forever. In "Suicide Solution," guitar cries fade into the "distance" (reverb helps create an engineered sense of space) over a monotonously pulsing, static bass, which also slowly fades but not completely; the song does end with the obligatory punch but at reduced volume. Near the end, the bass line finally changes, moving to a heartbeat pattern. The guitar's activities are reduced to demented noise, crazed sounds from all over sonic space. A cry from the guitar is stifled at the very end. The ending suggests neither continuing forever through a standard fade-out nor assertive closure, the metal norm; it ends uncomfortably, snuffing itself.

Throughout the song, the timbre of Osbourne's voice is ironic, mocking. His vocals are sometimes quickly panned across the stereo field, from left to right and back again, a scary, disorienting effect, especially on headphones. Other metal songs, and other kinds of music, too, have made such use of space to construct a paranoid's experience of persecution.[42] All of these other details support the affect of the opening riff, as the guitar chords struggle up a couple of steps and then sink back down, all over a constant, unyielding bass note; they resonate with a particular experience of life—life with no social support, no ethical core, no future.

But to construct such an affect is not to condone or compel suicide. To talk about something is not the same as promoting it; metal has a critical conscience many of its critics lack.[43] Many young people are frustrated at the hypocrisy they perceive around them, at the lack of history and genuine politics in their educations and in their lives. Many fans value heavy metal because it deals with issues that are of great importance but that are too often swept under the rug. "Metal is the only thing that says how the world really *is*," said one fan who attended the Judas Priest trial. "They want us to say that the grass is green and the air is clean and everything is beautiful."[44] Judas Priest guitarist K. K. Downing reflected after the trial: "I do feel haunted when I hear about their lives, 'cause they were the same as mine. . . . These kids just didn't get to live long enough to put all that past them. . . . I do feel angry, though, when they play all that backward surf music and talk about the *harm* our music did these kids, 'cause I think it was the best thing they had."[45]

Suicide is a serious problem (some estimates report six thousand teenage suicides per year in the United States),[46] and that is why popular artists address it. But music does not simply inflict its meanings upon helpless fans; texts become popular when people find them meaningful in the contexts of their own lives. That is why a wide range of responses is possible; indeed, the evidence suggests that only a tiny minority of fans found "Suicide Solution" depressing rather than sobering and thought-provoking. One fan wrote to Metallica to thank them because he had decided *not* to kill himself after hearing their song about suicide, "Fade to Black."[47] The lead singer of Dark Angel described a song from their album *Leave Scars* (1989): "There's a song called 'The Promise of Agony' that covers the depression and anxiety of being an adolescent. Hopefully there will be kids who pick up the new album and realize from reading the lyrics that even in their darkest despair they really aren't alone."[48]

A study of patients hospitalized for contemplating suicide indicates that a feeling of helplessness is the strongest predictor of which of them would actually go on to kill themselves.[49] Nobody listens to heavy metal because it makes them feel helpless. Sociologists distinguish between fatalistic suicide, caused by overregulation, and anomic suicide, attributable to nonintegration. Donna Gaines points out that many young people are doubly vulnerable, since they feel both overregulated by adults and alienated from them.[50] It is possible that texts can resonate with such attitudes; Goethe's *The Sorrows of Young Werther* seems to have helped make suicide a Continental fad of the late 1770s. But although its explicit treatments of violence might make suicide seem more familiar, metal is attractive precisely because it offers a way of overcoming those feelings of loneliness and helplessness. Even when it models musical despair, heavy metal confronts issues that cannot simply be dismissed or repressed, and it positions listeners as members of a community of fans, making them feel that they belong to a group that does not regulate them.

The vast majority of heavy metal fans don't worship Satan and don't commit suicide; yet many fans enjoy that fraction of heavy metal songs that deals with such things. Heavy metal's critics have provided no credible explanations for this, for they deny fans the agency that is necessary for attraction to exist, preferring to believe that such images are inflicted rather than sought. To find this unsatisfactory is to open up the problem of explaining the attractiveness of mysticism and horror.

Mysticism and Postmodernism in Heavy Metal

"The occult" is the remaining thread of critics' condemnations of heavy metal that has not yet been addressed. Tipper Gore, Carl Raschke, and others condemn heavy metal muscians for even mentioning the Devil, as though there were something deviant about such mysticism. Yet a 1990 Gallup Poll found that 55 percent of the American public believes in the Devil, up from 39 percent in 1978; half believe that demonic possession sometimes takes place.[51] In light of these statistics, it is perhaps surprising that comparatively little heavy metal touches on satanic topics. But as with other transgressive icons, the Devil is used to signify and evoke in particular social contexts; he is not simply conjured up to be worshipped. Even King Diamond, heavy metal's most infamous "Satanist," is scornful of his critics' literal-mindedness: "Satan, for me, is not like the guy with two horns and a long tail. I don't believe in hell as being a place where you burn for eternity. That's not what Satan is all about. Satan stands for the powers of the unknown, and that's what I'm writing about."[52] Heavy metal engagements with occult symbols and legends are more complex than the flat hermeneutics of the PMRC would have it.

Iron Maiden is among the most mystical and philosophical of heavy metal bands; many of their lyrics, taking inspiration from the Bible, Romantic poetry, and various other mythologies, explore the meaning of life, the contingency of existence, and the mysteries of fate and death. Critics often label them a "satanic" group, citing lines such as these, from "The Number of the Beast":

> The ritual has begun, Satan's work is done
> 666 the number of the beast
> Sacrifice is going on tonight

But the lines that immediately follow (less often quoted) complicate the simple endorsement read by critics:

> This can't go on, I must inform the law
> Can this still be real, or some crazy dream?
> But I feel drawn towards the evil chanting hordes

The lyrics are less concerned with celebrating satanic rituals than with exploring tensions between reality and dream, evil and power. As one fan told me, adults tend to take everything too literally, not understanding more sophisticated allegorical or figurative meanings.[53] Just as important, criticisms of metal often emanate from those who strive to eliminate difference and ambiguity in order to enforce their own brand of morality.

Iron Maiden draws upon a variety of religious and philosophical traditions in order to explore and interrogate moralities. Sometimes their lyrics present explicit critique; for example, "Run for the Hills" evokes the horror of the genocide of Native Americans, and "Flight of Icarus" retells the Greek legend with a paranoid twist: the boy's father has encouraged him to fly high, deliberately setting him up for disaster.[54] More often, though, Iron Maiden's lyrics ponder the meaning and nature of existence, frequently by investigating the attractions of mysticism. Many songs also consider the contradictory significance of battle, which they usually portray as exciting because of its intensity but ultimately futile—both glamorous and horrible.[55]

Iron Maiden's *Seventh Son of a Seventh Son* (1988) is a song cycle. That is, as with nineteenth-century song cycles by composers such as Schubert and Schumann, the songs on this album constitute a literary and musical unit, related by poetic theme and drawn together by musical means such as related keys and thematic materials. The song cycle structure binds together a great variety of musical styles and moods within a narrative frame, and *Seventh Son of a Seventh Son* contains some very gentle, ethereal music, as well as power chords and heavy beats. Given metal's reputation among outsiders as a monolithic genre, violent and unimaginative, the variety and affective range of Iron Maiden's music is worth stressing. But all of the songs are concerned with the related topics of fate, clairvoyance, visions, and philosophical speculation. To address these subjects, Iron Maiden mobilizes a fantastic array of musical, literary, and visual allusions, combined in ways that might usefully be considered postmodern.

To begin with visual images, Iron Maiden has for many years featured at its concerts and on its albums and T-shirts a mascot named Eddie. Eddie's appearance has varied over the years, but he has rather consistently retained many of the horrible qualities of an animated corpse. Skinless but sinewy, sometimes part machine, corporeally incomplete but still functioning, both damaged and threatening, Eddie is an oxymoron of disintegration and power. He has appeared in a number of different contexts, from the *Live after Death* album, where he is emerging from a grave, to *Powerslave*, where he appears as an Egyptian pharaoh, to *Seventh Son of a Seventh Son*, where on the front cover he floats, incomplete, in a surreal, icy solid/liquid nowhere; on the inner sleeve he is an ominous seer.[56] During Iron Maiden's 1988 tour, the concert stage featured, besides Eddie, two pieces of Egyptian statuary (references to the band's past tropes) and a miscellany of mystical symbols painted on all available surfaces.[57]

The cover and liner art of *Seventh Son of a Seventh Son* also contains visual references to a variety of mythologies, religions, and alchemies. A crystal ball floats between candlesticks fashioned after an angel and a demon, enacting a suspension between dualities characteristic of many mystical traditions. And Iron Maiden's lyrics reflect a similar hodgepodge of referents. Many songs draw upon the Book of Revelation for images of heaven and hell, Babylon, seven seals, seven deadly sins, fallen angels, and whatnot. But biblical references rub up against the parareligious objects of astrology, alchemy, and witchcraft: crystal balls, Gemini, the undead, and mandrake roots. Old books and quill pens further suggest secret knowledge, obscure meanings of unspecified lineage.

How are we to make sense of these seemingly arbitrary juxtapositions, unconnected and unexplained? Many theorists of contemporary culture would seize on such practices as evidence of what Fredric Jameson has called "pastiche" or "blank parody," a primary feature of postmodern art, according to his very influential formulation.[58] Jameson argued that such postmodern assemblages are neutral mimicry, ultimately signifying nothing. Since Iron Maiden borrows only superficially from various historical traditions and doesn't attempt to articulate any logical reconciliation of these incongruities, their bricolage would be seen by many theorists of the postmodern as meaningless imitation of a past that is no longer understood.

Yet these are not arbitrary choices of referents. On the contrary, Iron Maiden's symbolic borrowings all have certain fundamental characteristics in common, not in terms of their "real" history, but rather in terms of their present significance. Christianity, alchemy, myth, astrology, the mystique of vanished Egyptian dynasties: all are available in the modern world as sources of power and mystery. Such eclectic constructions of power, which might usefully be called postmodern, are possible *only because* they are not perceived as tied to strict historical contexts. All can be consulted, appropriated, and combined, used to frame questions and answers about life and death. If religion functions both to explain the world—providing models for how to live, tenets of faith and empowerment, and comfort for when they don't work—and to offer a sense of contact with something greater than oneself, then heavy metal surely qualifies as a religious phenomenon. But mystical metal draws upon the power of religious traditions without obeisance to any. One sociologist, observing teenagers' use of metal to carve out social space and experience communion there, referred to Led Zeppelin as "liberation theology in vinyl."[59]

Significantly, all of the mystical traditions drawn upon by Iron Maiden offer resources that seem to exist outside hegemonic notions of economic and material power. The situation we call "youth" is in large measure constructed by the contradictory demands of subordination and culturation. Young people are bombarded with messages promoting material power, but their lives, typically, are carefully regulated to deny them opportunities for acquiring much of it. If many of the bands on MTV seem to celebrate consumption and thus fit well with the channel's primary mission of delivering a demographic to advertisers, mystical metal bands like Iron Maiden often draw upon the mystique of precapitalist cultures to construct their spectacles of empowerment. And despite their reliance on transgressive and horrific images such as Eddie, Iron Maiden's songs and concerts put relatively little emphasis on violence and excess. Instead of violence or acquisition as antidotes to powerlessness, Iron Maiden offers experiences of community and feelings of contact with mystical meaningfulness. Fans at a concert participate in an empowerment that is largely musically constructed, but which is intensified by ritualistic images that sanctify the experience with historical and mystical depth. The solitary listener to records, likewise, is in fact almost never solitary, since metal fans tend to have other metal fans as friends, and they build much of their lives and identities around various social forms of involvement with heavy metal. In concerts or with recordings, Iron Maiden fans can experience a utopia of empowerment, freedom, and metaphysical depth, constructed in part out of ideas that have been excluded from the utilitarian world of work and school.

The lyrics of "Seventh Son of a Seventh Son" ostensibly relate the legend of the magical healing powers possessed by a seventh son of a seventh son:

> Here the birth from an unbroken line
> Born the healer the seventh, his time
> Unknowingly blessed, and as his life unfolds
> Slowly unveiling the power he holds
>
> . . . .
>
> Then they watch the progress he makes
> The Good and the Evil, which path will he take?
> Both of them trying to manipulate
> The use of his powers before it's too late

But these lyrics have relatively little to do, I would argue, with promoting pagan mysticism, as the PMRC might have it. Rather, they engage with socially produced anxieties and fantasies about power, history, and morality. Similarly, another song on this album is less about literal madness than about madness as a trope for unconventional thought:

> Give me the sense to wonder
> To wonder if I'm free
> Give me a sense of wonder
> To know if I can be me
> Give me the strength to hold my head up
> Spit back in their face
> Don't need no key to unlock this door
> Gonna break down the walls
> Break out of this bad place
>
> Can I play with madness?

As medical historian Roy Porter has argued, the writings of the truly mad preserve important historical insights and perceptive critiques:

The mad highlight the hypocrisies, double standards and sheer callous obliviousness of sane society. The writings of the mad challenge the discourse of the normal, challenge its right to be the objective mouthpiece of the times. The assumption that there exist definitive and unitary standards of truth and falsehood, reality and delusion, is put to the test. . . . Mad people's writings often stake counter-claims, to shore up that sense of personhood and identity which they feel is eroded by society and psychiatry.

Such a form of critical madness can be a powerful model for those who feel alienated from dominant social logic, who feel decentered by the pressures of modernity.[60]

Musically, "Seventh Son of a Seventh Son" begins with a series of dramatic flourishes that sound decidedly nonmetallic. They are annunciatory, preparatory; although the harmonic progression C–D–E (♭VI–♭VII–I again) is common in heavy metal, this introduction only gradually acquires the regular heavy beat that typically undergirds rock songs. The mood is dark and ominous, largely due to the use of the Aeolian mode. There is also a vaguely angelic choir hovering overhead, in the form of a synthesizer, adding to the gravity and mystical air of this opening. After an introduction sufficiently portentous for the subject at hand, the music settles into an absolutely steady, relentless rhythmic groove. It is the galloping, repeated eighth-and-two-sixteenths figure that Iron Maiden often uses, with heavily distorted guitars muted with the picking hand to make them more percussive.[61] The harmony is static, holding on E while the vocalist begins his declamation. The verses and choruses alike are built around this rhythm and these same chords and mode, so the first part of the song seems grimly consistent and fateful. The singer has a powerful voice, and he uses heavy vibrato to add to the impression of urgency and gravity. After some of the stanzas, he interjects a long, drawn-out "Ooooh," which is especially effective when the harmony changes underneath the sustained note, redefining it from the stable fifth degree to the mournful minor third as he holds it. This first part of the song, then, is quite unified; it exploits a number of musical parameters in ways that quite consistently articulate an affect of power, dread, and awe.

After all of the lyrics have been delivered, the song moves into a lengthy series of instrumental sections. At the end of the last chorus, while the voice hangs onto its final syllable (another drawn-out "Ooohh"), one of the guitars jumps to a different, faster tempo, playing a Baroque figuration that the other guitar soon joins in harmony. Another abrupt cut follows, to a fast tempo set by the drums, with acoustic guitar outlining poignant sustained chords. Spiked by one guitar's distant (lots of reverb), crying fills, this section combines slow harmonic change with a frantic drumbeat, articulating decenteredness, lack of progress, and urgency all at once. The singer then delivers a dramatic recitation over this conflicted aural landscape.

Finally, the song returns to what sounds like a recapitulation of the beginning, pompous and stable. But a guitar solo suddenly bursts in, shifting to a completely new key, a driving rhythmic pattern, and a fast tempo. Perhaps most important, the musical mode shifts from Aeolian to Phrygian, which carries with it a more frantic, claustrophobic affect. After the short guitar solo, the music moves through a period of what sounds like utter breakdown. The tritone, Western music's most ambiguous interval, is emphasized, throwing tonal grounding up in the air, and with it any sense of experiential stability. The drumming becomes complex and uneven, and the structure of time similarly seems to come unglued. A second guitar solo leads to another change of tempo and beat, and so on. A series of variations over a short harmonic cycle, another Baroque derivation, leads to a truncated, tense version of the opening flourish, which decisively closes the song.

A kind of postmodern logic applies to Iron Maiden's music as well as to their use of mystical images and phrases. Affective stabilities and narrative implications are constantly being defused and subverted by sudden shifts into new keys and tempos within their songs. The organic unities one can usually assume in pop song forms are often calculatedly undermined. But it is important to avoid confusing constructions of disintegration with artistic anarchy. Iron Maiden, in order to accomplish such disruptive shifts, in order to articulate decenteredness, must be much more precise and coordinated than most bands. Their seemingly chaotic ruptures require extreme precision of conception and execution, like the coordination of lighting and choreography at their concerts that relies on rigorous timing to create the impression of casual, free movement.

Iron Maiden's songs are bound together by regular phrases and precise execution, no matter how disjunct they are formally, in the same way that their pastiche of mystical referents is ideologically consistent, no matter how anachronous its elements may seem. Moreover, the musicians' precision contributes crucially to the experience of their music. For at the same time that their ruptures evoke what we might call postmodern decenteredness and anxiety, the musicians' musical successes offer an experience of coping and control in the face of those difficulties. Iron Maiden articulates decenteredness but simultaneously enacts resistance to it. The precision of the ensemble evokes the complexity and overwhelming force of the threat, and at the same time offers the only hope of surviving it.

Thrash metal bands like Metallica and Megadeth have developed a musical discourse based on a similar agenda. Their songs are formally even more complex, filled with abrupt changes of meter and tempo that model a complex, disjointed world and displaying a formidable ensemble precision that enacts collective survival. Thrash guitar is even more distorted than in other kinds of heavy metal, and sonic energy is further shifted to high and low frequencies, yielding a crunchy, percussive sound. While usually less mystical than Iron Maiden, thrash bands very often address violence, death, and madness in their lyrics. Frequent use of the Phrygian mode; faster, sometimes frantic tempos; and a vocal style that is rough, percussive, and nonvirtuosic make thrash metal darker than other metal—angrier, more critical and apocalyptic. Megadeth's album release of 1990 includes these lines, which have been quoted by moralistic critics as evidence of Satanism: "Satan rears his ugly head, to spit into the wind; I spread disease like a dog." But the song from which they are excerpted is called "Rust in Peace . . . Polaris," an evocation of the horror of nuclear holocaust; the "I" that speaks is the weapon of "defense" itself. Megadeth uses the supernatural figure of Satan to strengthen their condemnation of horrors that are entirely real. If their imagery is horrible, it is intended—and understood by fans—as an honest reflection and critique of a brutal world.

The mystical fusions of Iron Maiden continue a long tradition in heavy metal, dating back to such founding documents as Led Zeppelin's "Stairway to Heaven." Musically, "Stairway" fuses powerful "authenticities," which are really ideologies. On the one hand, a folk/pastoral/mystical sensibility; on the other, desire/aggression/physicality. The song begins with the gentle sound and reassuringly square phrases of an acoustic guitar, complemented by the archaic hooting of recorders, suggesting a preindustrial refuge in the folk. Soon, Jimmy Page trades in his acoustic for the twangy punch of an electric guitar and, eventually, the raucous roar of heavy distortion. After a Hendrix-like guitar solo (blues-based, mildly psychedelic), Robert Plant's voice rises an octave, wailing over countless repetitions of a two-measure pattern, propelled by the band's frantic syncopations. The apotheosis/apocalypse breaks off suddenly, and the song ends with Plant's unaccompanied voice, a return to the solitary poignancy of the beginning. This narrative juxtaposition of the sensitive (acoustic guitar, etc.) and the aggressive (distorted electric guitar, etc.) has continued to show up in heavy metal, from Ozzy Osbourne to Metallica. It combines contradictory sensibilities without reconciling them, as do Led Zeppelin's lyrics and cover art, as much as Iron Maiden's.

The cover of the album containing "Stairway to Heaven" juxtaposes a photograph of a laboring peasant with a view of a modern city, complete with both high rises and crumbling tenements. The photo seems very old, but it is colorized and thus strangely displaced in time. Inside, a mysterious sage looks down on a slumbering town from his mountaintop; a bell-bottomed seeker of wisdom scales the rocks toward him. The runes that give the album its nickname ("ZOSO") appear on the liner, along with the enigmatic lyrics of "Stairway to Heaven." These images seem not to have any historical coherence, but they are all available in the present as sources of power and mystery; it is how they are used that makes them coherent.

We might better understand the associative powers of the famously enigmatic lyrics by breaking them up into categories. We encounter a number of mysterious figures: a lady, the piper, the May Queen. Images of nature abound: a brook, a songbird, rings of smoke, trees, forests, a hedgerow, wind. We find a set of concepts (pretty much summing up the central concerns of philosophy): signs, words, meanings, thoughts, feelings, spirit, reason, wonder, soul, the idea that "all are one and one is all." We find a set of vaguely but powerfully evocative symbols: gold, the West, the tune, white light, shadows, paths, a road, and the stairway to heaven itself. At the very end, we find some paradoxical self-referentiality: "to be a rock and not to roll."

These lyrics provide a very open text; like those of Don McLean's "American Pie" (also released in 1971), they invite endless interpretation.[62] Yet they are resonant, requiring no rigorous study to become meaningful. Like the music, they engage with the fantasies and anxieties of our time; they offer contact with social and metaphysical depth in a world of commodities and mass communication. "Stairway to Heaven," no less than canonized works of artistic postmodernism, addresses "decentered subjects" who are striving to find credible experiences of depth and community. It strains at mystery and promises utopia: "A new day will dawn," and "If you listen very hard / The tune will come to you at last."

Film historian Dana Polan has warned that postmodern art can "work in support of dominant power by encouraging a serialized sense of the social totality as something one can never understand and that always eludes one's grasp."[63] Yet art that ignores the complexities, the decentering forces of contemporary capitalism, remains unconvincing, especially to those who have grown up knowing nothing else. For example, one young Twisted Sister fan told me that she starts feeling paranoid when she hears the "easy listening" music favored by her mother, because it so obviously seems to lie to her about the world. The heavy metal of Iron Maiden and Megadeth, on the other hand, articulates the anxieties and discontinuities of the postmodern world, but not in a way that concedes to such experiences. In their free appropriation of symbols of power, and in their material enactments of control, of hanging on in the face of frightening complexity, such heavy metal bands suggest to many that survival in the modern world is possible, that disruptions, no matter how unsettling, can be ridden out and endured.

It is not surprising, then, that many of Iron Maiden's fans study the band's sources, actually buy and read the books referred to in the song lyrics: the Bible, Coleridge's "Rime of the Ancient Mariner," a bevy of histories of various times and places.[64] For the idea that school prepares adolescents for adulthood is increasingly perceived as an obsolete fantasy; too often, adolescence is but a "psychic holding pen for superfluous young people, stuck in economic and social limbo."[65] Leaping beyond what they might see as the boring reverence of their school curriculum and the shallow expediency of the working world, metal musicians and fans draw on the power of centuries' worth of imaginative writing to make sense of their own social experiences and to imagine other possibilities.

The loss of historical specificity we see in the bricolage of Iron Maiden is surely not something to celebrate in itself, but it is important to see that the loss of monovocal, hegemonic history enables other constructions and connections to be formed. Moreover, the reasons for this loss of history deserve examination, and they may be found, I will argue, in the operation of the very bourgeois ideals that are supposedly being resisted. After discussing horror more specifically, I will be shifting theoretical ground, from the notions of postmodernism evoked above to Marshall Berman's broader vision of a modernism that spans the nineteenth and twentieth centuries. For unlike most postmodern theory, Berman's formulation calls upon us to make enabling connections to past experiences of disruption and dislocation.

Horror and History

> The tale of the irrational is the sanest way I know of expressing the world in which I live. These tales have served me as instruments of both metaphor and morality; they continue to offer the best window I know on the question of how we perceive things and the corollary question of how we do or do not behave on the basis of our perceptions. —Stephen King[66]

Horror, manifest primarily in literature and film, has been one of the most popular artistic themes of the past two centuries. Horror originated with the Enlightenment, in late eighteenth-century tales and novels; in 1756, Edmund Burke published his theorization of the aesthetic category of the Sublime—which included horror, astonishment, pain, danger, and terror—thus legitimating the gothic. A variety of psychological explanations have been offered to explain the success of horror: it enables us to overcome safely the objects of our fears, it is the return of the repressed, it represents rites of passage to adulthood or reproductive sexuality.[67] But we must seek for more specific treatment of the social situations within which horrific texts are meaningful. For example, historians have noted that horror films have tended to resurge in popularity in cycles of ten or twenty years, coinciding with periods of social strain or disorder: the Expressionist horror films at a time of crisis in the Weimar Republic, the classical Hollywood monster films that first appeared during the Depression, their revival in the 1950s as metaphors for the Red Threat and other internal enemies, and their greatest popularity ever in the 1970s, another time of crisis of legitimacy for dominant institutions and the economy.[68]

The development of heavy metal in the late 1960s and its continuing popularity through the 1970s and 1980s coincides exactly with the period of the greatest popularity horror films and books have ever known. Founding films of modern horror, such as *Rosemary's Baby* in 1968 and *The Exorcist* in 1973, mark a transitional moment in American history: the end of the Pax Americana; new economic crises; corrupt leadership; powerful social movements challenging dominant policies on race, gender, ecology, and consumer rights; new challenges to the stability of social institutions such as the family; and redefinitions of political themes like freedom. Not surprisingly, historians have noted that horror films are very specific in the threats they evoke: most center on the family, children, political leadership, and sexuality.

As Michael Ryan and Doug Kellner argue, the horror film functions to restore "the sense of security undermined by the dysfunctions of capitalism and the crises of political confidence that corrupt leadership in an underdeveloped democratic context provokes. It is less an irrational phenomenon than a way of dealing with the irrationality of the American social system."[69] Both heavy metal and the horror film address the insecurities of this tumultuous era. Both provide ways of producing meaning in an irrational society; both explore explanations for seemingly incomprehensible phenomena.

The heavy metal audience is part of the first American generation that will be worse off economically than its parents. Many young people have accepted relative affluence as normative, yet society has no real role for its young, and their chances of attaining affluence in the future are fading. Due to factors that include deindustrialization, the decline of union jobs, and the rise of low-paid service jobs, the earnings of young white men dropped 18 percent between 1973 and 1986; those of male high school dropouts, 42 percent.[70] A congressional study indicates that 97 percent of the new jobs filled by white males in the 1980s paid less than $7,000 a year.[71] And while some of its citizens still take pride in its unmatched military strength, the United States now ranks nineteenth worldwide in quality of life, according to a United Nations survey measuring literacy, life expectancy, social services, and average income.[72] Much of the blame is rightly placed on the disastrous social policies of Reaganism, but the 1960s had already seen the greatest wave of mergers, conglomeration, and transnationalization ever, and the first effects of the domination of the economy by large corporations were felt in the 1970s. From their peak in 1973, overall real wages had fallen more than 16 percent by 1990.[73] The 1980s were the first time that "a middle-level income no longer guaranteed what we have come to think of as a middle-class lifestyle."[74]

Heavy metal is, among other things, a way of articulating and sustaining individual and communal identities that can survive such strains. Critics and outsiders like *U.S. News and World Report* continue to prattle that the "primary theme" of metal is nihilism, but heavy metal is rarely nihilistic.[75] Nihilism is frightening because it undermines the myths that sustain social order and struggle alike; it may serve to invite or justify authoritarian repression by making the world seem irrational. Heavy metal, on the contrary, is nearly always concerned with making sense of the world. If it offers opportunities for expressing individual rage, it is largely devoted to creating communal bonds that will help fans weather the strains of modernity. Fans rely on an alignment with that which is "other" but powerful as a way of making sense of their own situation and of compensating for it. Heavy metal explores the "other," everything that hegemonic society does not want to acknowledge, the dark side of the daylit, enlightened adult world. By doing so it finds distinction in scandalous transgression and appropriates sources of communal empowerment. Heavy metal cannot be simply dismissed as alien and aberrant; the meaningfulness of images of horror, madness, and violence in heavy metal is intimately related to the fundamental contradictions of its historical moment.

Historian Marty Jezer traces recent violence in youth culture back to the 1950s, locating its sources not in deviance but in the fundamental contradictions of mainstream ideology: "A rising rate of juvenile delinquency, along with a growing cult of violence, was the first indication that the socialization of young people was not going well. Or, put another way, it was going *too* well, and the young were learning the underlying values of postwar society while ignoring the glossy suburban image that supposedly represented the real thing."[76] John Fiske makes the same point about violence on television, pointing out that not all violence is popular, that popular violence is tightly organized in terms of prevalent social tensions:

Represented violence is popular (in a way that social violence is not) because it offers points of relevance to people living in societies where the power and resources are inequitably distributed and structured around lines of conflicting interests. . . . Violence . . . is popular because of its metaphorical relationship to class or social conflict. Popular representations of the relationships between the socially central or dominant and the deviant are violent because the social experience of the subordinate is one of conflict of interests, not of a liberal pluralist or ritualistic consensus. So it is no surprise to find that the United States, where the difference between the haves and the have-nots is extreme, has the most violent popular television, whereas Britian and Australia, whose welfare and taxation systems mitigate *some* of the socioeconomic differences, have fewer acts of violence per hour on their screens."[77]

The dark side of heavy metal is intimately related to the dark side of the modern capitalist security state: war, greed, patriarchy, surveillance, and control. The lyrics of many heavy metal bands articulate a variety of fantasies of empowerment in this context, but some of the songs of Judas Priest address these issues quite specifically.

"Electric Eye" appeared on Judas Priest's first platinum album, *Screaming for Vengeance* (1982), and it has remained a staple of their concert programs. In it, lead singer Rob Halford adopts the point of view of a spy satellite, a perfect metal governmental agent, omniscient and detached. The eye's persona is split: the first stanza is official and public, marked by Halford with measured, middle-range singing and by added chorus and reverb that suggest spatial power and social legitimacy:

> Up here in space
> I'm looking down on you
> My lasers trace
> Everything you do

These lyrics begin just after a sudden shift from the tonic established by the introduction, E, to the fourth degree, A; they are made to feel temporarily suspended above the tonic, adding to the sense of space.

But then, with an emphatic shift to reconfirm E, a different voice appears: high, thin, sneering, slightly crazed, lacking the support and resonance of studio effects. Now the eye openly taunts those below; it is intoxicated with pride in its metallic perfection and inescapable gaze.

> I take a pride in probing all your secret moves
> My tearless retina takes pictures that can prove

Driven by frenetic but precisely controlled music, the song evokes the paranoia of state surveillance and control, at the same time that the narrator's position as the electric eye offers the seductive experience of omniscience and near omnipotence, the pride of metallic, technological perfection.

I'm made of metal
My circuits gleam
I am perpetual
I keep the country clean

I'm elected electric spy
I'm protected electric eye

With a decisive, galloping beat and Aeolian power chords, "Electric Eye" semiotically calls up power and danger and offers identification with both sides: both the threat and the thrill of concentrated power. The guitar solo scrambles, seeming barely to keep up with the demands of the progression. The choruses are filled with syncopations, pushing against the solid metric organization and resetting with each line of text. The song ends with feedback and echo, like a science fiction movie soundtrack accompanying a view of space—vast, mysterious, and ineffable. With "Electric Eye," Judas Priest evokes a modern technological environment of high-tech energy and conflict; in their live concerts, computer-controlled laser beams flash around the stage with scary precision. The split address of the lyrics keeps intact the unresolvable tensions of fear and envy that such an environment can create. And the power of the music energizes both the representation of that danger and the fans who must survive it.

Many of Judas Priest's songs engage with similar tensions and fantasies. The title song from *Painkiller* (1990) offers a more mythical embodiment of power flying through the skies. The Painkiller is a "metal monster," "half man and half machine," again addressing anxieties about the collision of human beings and technology. "Metal Meltdown," from the same album, portrays the seduction and spectacularity of modern technological power while simultaneously stressing its tremendous dangers. "The Sentinel," from Judas Priest's *Defenders of the Faith* (1984) presents a knife-throwing hero as an epic figure; though his battlefield is urban, he is as awesomely capable at killing as Achilles, a more respectable culture hero. But like Arnold Schwarzenegger's popular Terminator character, he is impassive, unconflicted, supremely rational. The Sentinel's violence is justified; he is "sworn to avenge" (thus he is not the aggressor) and he never doubts that setting things right requires overwhelming power and violence.

Such a fantasy is nothing less than the logical result of the radical individualism demanded by contemporary capitalism, confounded by widespread disillusionment with the proper channels offered for individual success: corrupt government and a rhetoric of freedom and equality undermined by the obviously systematic maintenance of inequity.[78] More overtly "political" bands, such as Queensrÿche, whose lyrics call for educating the masses and overthrowing the control of the rich, are usually less popular than bands that avoid didacticism and find indirect ways to stage fundamental social contestations and alternatives. But if violence in heavy metal is not the nihilism decried by its foes, neither is it the Dionysian creativity claimed by some of its defenders, discussed below, for both of these interpretations lift metal out of history.

Guns N' Roses N' Marx N' Engels

The fullest attempt to explain heavy metal in terms of Dionysian revel is Danny Sugerman's *Appetite for Destruction: The Days of Guns N' Roses.*[79] In contrast to critics such as Gore, Stuessy, and Raschke, Sugerman has read widely and knows the music intimately. Most important, Sugerman is genuinely interested in understanding the appeal and power of heavy metal—although he is careful not to call it that because he wants to position Guns N' Roses at the center of the rock tradition. His analysis remains circumscribed, however, by a reluctance to historicize; both Sugerman and Guns N' Roses celebrate the central bourgeois values of individuality and dynamism as essential human traits.

Sugerman's explanation of the phenomenal success of Guns N' Roses —their debut album, *Appetite for Destruction* (1987), sold over ten million copies and remained in the *Billboard* Top Ten for over a year—is that the band taps into timeless and universal sources of power. Lead singer Axl Rose is a shaman, reviving the mad frenzy of Dionysus, Shiva, and the Romantic poets. The response of his audience is "instinctual," a function of their underlying "animal nature."[80] At a Guns N' Roses show, "ancient customs and rituals are being reenacted and the inherent powers still exist."[81] Sugerman rightly points to large-scale sources of alienation, such as the mind/body split or the loss for many people of meaningful ritual or credible myth. But his account essentializes and mystifies, stopping short of explanation of the specific sounds and sights of heavy metal as the activities of particular people at a certain historical moment. In their rhetoric, both Sugerman and Guns N' Roses reveal their fidelity to certain narratives about modernity that have been most successfully analyzed and critiqued by Karl Marx and Marshall Berman.[82]

Marxist criticism of popular music has usually focused on the music's mediation, the ways in which it is marketed and circulated. Less often, scholars have tried to analyze the meanings of popular music in societies shaped by the ideologies of capitalism, but even then the approach is usually marked by assumptions of class essentialism. That is, critics too often look only for articulations of a particular class position, which may then undergo interference and vitiation through the processes of mass mediation. But Marx himself was less interested in the culture of classes than in the culture of environments shaped by the dominance of particular classes. This is why the fact that heavy metal attracts fans from varied class positions does not confound Marxist analysis of that music. On the contrary, Marx's diagnosis of the strains of the era of bourgeois capitalism, particularly as Marshall Berman has extended it through a number of cultural moments, enables much fuller accounts of certain aspects of heavy metal's value to its audiences.

Marx's attitude toward the bourgeoisie was complex: he genuinely admired their accomplishments while criticizing unflinchingly the personal and social devastation they wrought; he endorsed their notion of individual and collective development at the same time that he hoped that the bourgeois project would self-destruct and be transcended. Berman summarizes the dialectical tension that has inspired so much modern art and thought:

In the first part of the *Manifesto*, Marx lays out the polarities that will shape and animate the culture of modernism in the century to come: the theme of insatiable desires and drives, permanent revolution, infinite development, perpetual creation and renewal in every sphere of life; and its radical antithesis, the theme of nihilism, insatiable destruction, the shattering and swallowing up of life, the heart of darkness, the horror. Marx shows how both these human possibilities are infused into the life of every modern man by the drives and pressures of the bourgeois economy.[83]

What Berman calls bourgeois society's "insatiable drive for destruction and development" Axl Rose calls the "Appetite for Destruction."[84] Both are awed by it, both are aware of the damage it does; but in some ways, what Berman finds in Marx is very much like what millions of fans have found in heavy metal:

Marx plunges us into the depths of this life process, so that we feel ourselves charged with a vital energy that magnifies our whole being—and are simultaneously seized by shocks and convulsions that threaten at every instant to annihilate us. Then, by the power of his language and thought, he tries to entice us to trust his vision, to let ourselves be swept along with him toward a climax that lies just ahead.[85]

As one of the most dynamic of contemporary performers, Axl Rose, too, plunges us into a maelstrom of energy and turbulence, offering the strength of his performance and the power of the music as the only guarantees of survival.

"Welcome to the Jungle" is Guns N' Roses' indictment of the environment in which they had to operate when they landed in Los Angeles with hopes of becoming stars. As Marx could have warned them, they found a world where there is "no other nexus between man and man than naked self-interest, than callous 'cash payment.' "[86]

> We are the people that can find
> Whatever you may need
> If you got the money honey
> We got your disease
>
> . . . .
> You can taste the bright lights
> But you won't get them for free
>
> . . . .
> You can have anything you want
> But you better not take it from me

The jungle of L.A. is not just a commercial environment; it is mercenary, hyped, cutthroat, and cynical. The song's sinuous, chromatic guitar and bass lines suggest instability and deception; sudden key shifts and pounding drums disorient the jungle's newest victims. Worst of all, the jungle remakes the inhabitants in its own cruel image. Axl Rose gloats at the plight of the newcomer: "You're in the jungle baby, you're gonna die. . . . I wanna watch you bleed." The only relief is through brief intoxication: at one point an undistorted guitar gently resolves 4–3 suspensions while Rose sings, "And when you're high you never, ever want to come down." But the rest of the music is either chaotic, brutal, or both, using headlong chromatic descents, forceful ♭VI–♭VII–I progressions, and heavy distortion to charge the air with menace.

Sugerman offers an explanation of Rose's success in this environment: "He refuses to compromise, insists on a divine right to be himself. . . . He not only survived, he did it on his terms."[87] But where did "his terms" come from, and why do communities form around such expressions of individual autonomy? By calling the principle of individualism "divine," Sugerman obscures its origins and places it beyond critique. What Berman points out about Marx is equally true of Axl Rose: for all of their invective against bourgeois society, both Marx and Rose embrace the ideals and personality structure that arise from the priorities of bourgeois economic development. "Our goal is to break down as many barriers as we can," says Axl Rose. "I mean not just musical, I mean we want to break down the barriers in people's minds, too."[88]

Sugerman rightly points out, as have others, that there are certain direct links between rock and Romanticism: Jim Morrison read Nietzsche, for example, and influenced many other rock musicians in turn. But if an attitude of rebellion can be said to link artists across time, there is still the question of what precisely is being rebelled against at each moment, and, just as important, what sort of vision is being offered in its place. The dynamism and individuality celebrated in so much rock music are not derived from nineteenth-century Romanticism, as some critics have argued.[89] Rather, both of these cultural moments engage in dialogue with strains of modernity they have in common; rock's response contains an admixture from African-American music and reflects a different emphasis on bodily pleasure and communality.

"Paradise City," another hit single from *Appetite for Destruction*, is a good example. In its verse sections, the song uses guitar and bass lines that are low, chromatic, repetitive, and menacing, reminiscent of "Welcome to the Jungle." The verses sketch an urban environment just as bleak and chaotic, and Axl Rose has called the song "just some more lyrics about the jungle."[90]

> Just a' urchin livin' under the street
> I'm a hard case that's tough to beat
>
> . . . .
> Ragz to richez or so they say
> Ya gotta-keep pushin' for the fortune and fame
>
> . . . .
> Strapped in the chair of the city's gas chamber
> Why I'm here I can't quite remember
>
> . . . .
> Captain America's been torn apart
> Now he's a court jester with a broken heart
> He said—
> Turn me around and take me back to the start
> I must be losin' my mind—"Are you blind?"
> I've seen it all a million times

But the song's chorus offers an escape from the jungle that had seemed impossible in the other song, a kind of transcendence reached through the gospel music of the black church. A choir of voices sings the chorus, representing the sort of communal participation in music making that can submerge individual alienation in what is literally social harmony. Above this group, Rose soars like the ecstatic sopranos of many gospel choirs, transcending even this collective transcendence. His delivery of the text is smoother, but no less passionate, than the jagged hysteria of the verses. The lyrics of the chorus are simple:

> Take me down
> To the paradise city
> Where the grass is green
> And the girls are pretty
> Take me home

If only the lyrics are considered, this vision of Paradise City is hardly a vivid one. Rose gives us few details; the important parts are the invocation of desire to be transported ("take me down") and the characterization of Paradise City as "home." Even these barely sketch the fantasy; only the music endows this vision of an ideal (male) social space with power and credibility. The gospel qualities are borrowed to energize this vision as they have so many others.[91] During the chorus, the note G rings out over the G–C–F–C–G progression like a guarantee of homecoming. At the end of the song the tempo doubles, and a guitar solo scrambles euphorically over countless repetitions of the chorus progression. As with many gospel performances, there seems to be too much energy to stop; Paradise City exists only as long as it is supported by collective effort, especially by the straining of Axl Rose's voice toward transcendence.

Appetite for Destruction's other hit single offers a different refuge from the jungle:

> Her hair reminds me of a warm safe place
> Where as a child I'd hide
> And pray for the thunder
> And the rain
> To quietly pass me by.

"Sweet Child o' Mine" is startlingly tender, with acoustic guitar blended with chorused electric and a haunting opening riff based on poignant 4–3 suspensions. As in nineteenth-century notions of the separate sphere of the "Angel in the House," women are understood as salve for the wounded man recuperating from the brutality of industry and commerce.

What is so remarkable, what calls us to reexamine the dichotomies of modern and postmodern, of elite and popular, of politics and culture, is that Berman's discussion of the "voice" of modernity applies just as well to Axl Rose as to the nineteenth-century philosophers and literati he is describing:

What is distinctive and remarkable about the voice that Marx and Nietzsche share is not only its breathless pace, its vibrant energy, its imaginative richness, but also its fast and drastic shifts in tone and inflection, its readiness to turn on itself, to question and negate all it has said, to transform itself into a great range of harmonic or dissonant voices, and to stretch itself beyond its capacities into an endlessly wider range, to express and grasp a world where everything is pregnant with its contrary and all that is solid melts into air. This voice resounds at once with self-discovery and self-mocking, with self-delight and self-doubt. It is a voice that knows pain and dread, but believes in its power to come through. Grave danger is everywhere, and may strike at any moment, but not even the deepest wounds can stop the flow and overflow of its energy. It is ironic and contradictory, polyphonic and dialectical, denouncing modern life in the name of values that modernity itself has created, hoping—often against hope—that the modernities of tomorrow and the day after tomorrow will heal the wounds that wreck the modern men and women of today.[92]

Certainly, Marx and Rose have lived in very different worlds, and I have argued throughout this chapter that heavy metal must be understood within the specific context of recent history. But critics of heavy metal have striven to suggest that artistic treatment of violence and madness is unique to today's popular culture and that it reflects a breakdown of values. Such critics depend upon the notion that horror is abnormal, is outside the system, in order to scapegoat heavy metal as deviant and threatening. Instead, I have tried to show how heavy metal can be understood as immanently social and historical, as action engaged with the deepest of contemporary desires and tensions. And such formations have roots; they do not belong to our moment alone.

Moreover, criticism of metal as deviance depends upon historical amnesia, for much of the respected culture of the past made use of similarly transgressive imagery, however much its present context of reception hobbles our recognition of its original force. For example, musicologist Richard Taruskin wrote recently of the "vast sanitizing project" that "has for nearly two centuries been keeping the essential Bach at bay." He cites examples such as Bach's text for Cantata 179, which includes images worthy of any thrash metal band: "My sins sicken me like pus in my bones; help me, Jesus, Lamb of God, for I am sinking in deepest slime."[93] Taruskin concludes:

Anyone exposed to Bach's full range . . . knows that the hearty, genial, lyrical Bach of the concert hall is not the essential Bach. The essential Bach was an avatar of a pre-Enlightened—and when push came to shove, a violently anti-Enlightened—temper. His music was a medium of truth, not beauty. And the truth he served was bitter. His works persuade us—no, *reveal* to us—that the world is filth and horror, that humans are helpless, that life is pain, that reason is a snare.[94]

Like Bach, but at the other end of the Enlightenment, heavy metal musicians explore images of horror and madness in order to comprehend and critique the world as they see it. Although they are continually stereotyped and dismissed as apathetic nihilists, metal fans and musicians build on the sedimented content of musical forms and cultural icons to create for themselves a social world of greater depth and intensity. They appropriate materials for their music and lyrics from the myriad sources made available to them by mass mediation, selecting those they can fuse into a cultural alloy that is strong and conductive.

They develop new kinds of music and new models of identity, new articulations of community, alienation, affirmation, protest, rage, and transcendence by "Running with the Devil."

Not all of heavy metal's formulations point toward a society that is more just and peaceful, though some do. If in some ways heavy metal replicates the ruthless individualism and violence that capitalism and government policy have naturalized, it also creates communal attachments, enacts collective empowerment, and works to assuage entirely reasonable anxieties. Heavy metal, like all culture, can be read as an index of attempts to survive the present and imagine something better for the future; it is one among many coherent but richly conflicted records of people's struggles to make sense of the contradictions they have inherited, the tensions that drive and limit their lives.

Heavy Metal Canons

✳

Hit Parader's Top 100 Metal Albums (Spring 1989; release dates added)

1. Led Zeppelin, *ZOSO [IV]*, 1971
2. Def Leppard, *Pyromania*, 1983
3. AC/DC, *Back in Black*, 1980
4. Mötley Crüe, *Theatre of Pain*, 1985
5. Van Halen, *Van Halen*, 1978
6. Judas Priest, *Screaming for Vengeance*, 1982
7. Kiss, *Destroyer*, 1976
8. Metallica, *. . . And Justice for All*, 1988
9. Deep Purple, *Machine Head*, 1972
10. Ozzy Osbourne, *Blizzard of Ozz*, 1981
11. Iron Maiden, *Powerslave*, 1985
12. Bon Jovi, *Slippery When Wet*, 1987
13. Aerosmith, *Rocks*, 1976
14. Black Sabbath, *Paranoid*, 1971
15. Led Zeppelin, *II*, 1970
16. Guns N' Roses, *Appetite for Destruction*, 1987
17. Kiss, *Alive*, 1975
18. Judas Priest, *British Steel*, 1980
19. AC/DC, *Highway to Hell*, 1979
20. Poison, *Open Up and Say . . . Ahh*, 1988
21. Alice Cooper, *Love It to Death*, 1971
22. Megadeth, *So Far So Good . . . So What!*, 1988
23. Ratt, *Out of the Cellar*, 1984
24. Ozzy Osbourne, *The Ultimate Sin*, 1986
25. Mötley Crüe, *Shout at the Devil*, 1984
26. Whitesnake, *Whitesnake*, 1987
27. Scorpions, *Love at First Sting*, 1984
28. Cinderella, *Long Cold Winter*, 1988
29. Rainbow, *Ritchie Blackmore's Rainbow*, 1975
30. Dokken, *Back for the Attack*, 1988
31. Quiet Riot, *Metal Health*, 1983
32. Def Leppard, *Hysteria*, 1987
33. Aerosmith, *Permanent Vacation*, 1987
34. Black Sabbath, *Heaven and Hell*, 1980
35. The Jimi Hendrix Experience, *Are You Experienced?*, 1967
36. Cinderella, *Night Songs*, 1986
37. Van Halen, *1984*, 1983
38. Slayer, *South of Heaven*, 1988
39. Iron Maiden, *Number of the Beast*, 1984
40. Europe, *The Final Countdown*, 1986
41. Saxon, *Wheels of Steel*, 1980
42. Anthrax, *State of Euphoria*, 1988
43. Bad Company, *Bad Company*, 1974
44. Dio, *The Last in Line*, 1984
45. Van Halen, *II*, 1979
46. Kiss, *Animalize*, 1984
47. Poison, *Look What the Cat Dragged In*, 1986
48. Scorpions, *In Trance*, 1976
49. Accept, *Restless and Wild*, 1982
50. Deep Purple, *Made in Japan*, 1972

51. Lita Ford, *Lita*, 1988
52. Mötley Crüe, *Girls, Girls, Girls*, 1987
53. Queensrÿche, *Operation: Mindcrime*, 1988
54. Dokken, *Tooth and Nail*, 1984
55. Metallica, *Master of Puppets*, 1986
56. Led Zeppelin, *Led Zeppelin*, 1969
57. Y&T, *Black Tiger*, 1982
58. UFO, *Lights Out*, 1977
59. Twisted Sister, *Stay Hungry*, 1984
60. Whitesnake, *Slide It In*, 1983
61. Rush, *2112*, 1976
62. Ted Nugent, *Ted Nugent*, 1975
63. Led Zeppelin, *Physical Graffiti*, 1975
64. Stryper, *In God We Trust*, 1988
65. Thin Lizzy, *Jailbreak*, 1976
66. Bon Jovi, *7800° Fahrenheit*, 1985
67. Angel, *Helluva Band*, 1976
68. White Lion, *Pride*, 1988
69. Metallica, *Ride the Lightning*, 1984
70. Great White, *Once Bitten*, 1987
71. Yngwie Malmsteen, *Odyssey*, 1988
72. Grand Funk Railroad, *Survival*, 1971
73. Uriah Heep, *The Magician's Birthday*, 1972
74. Iron Butterfly, *In-A-Gadda-Da-Vida*, 1968
75. Krokus, *Headhunters*, 1983
76. Aerosmith, *Aerosmith*, 1973
77. Montrose, *Montrose*, 1974
78. Tesla, *Mechanical Resonance*, 1987
79. Megadeth, *Peace Sells . . . But Who's Buying?*, 1986
80. Blue Öyster Cult, *Agents of Fortune*, 1976
81. Cream, *Disraeli Gears*, 1967
82. Starz, *Violation*, 1977
83. Blue Cheer, *Vincebus Eruptum*, 1968
84. Ted Nugent, *Cat Scratch Fever*, 1976
85. Mountain, *Climbing*, 1969
86. Motörhead, *Ace of Spades*, 1980
87. W.A.S.P., *Inside the Electric Circus*, 1986
88. Manowar, *Battle Hymns*, 1982
89. Kingdom Come, *Kingdom Come*, 1988
90. L. A. Guns, *L. A. Guns*, 1988
91. David Lee Roth, *Eat 'Em and Smile*, 1986
92. Stryper, *To Hell with the Devil*, 1986
93. Deep Purple, *In Rock*, 1971
94. Triumph, *Allied Forces*, 1981
95. Savatage, *Hall of the Mountain King*, 1987
96. Loudness, *Thunder in the East*, 1985
97. The Michael Schenker Group, *MSG*, 1981
98. Death Angel, *Frolic in the Park*, 1988
99. Warlock, *True as Steel*, 1986
100. Kix, *Midnite Dynamite*, 1986

"Heavy Metal: The Hall of Fame" (*Hit Parader*, December 1982)

AC/DC, *Back in Black*, 1980
Aerosmith, *Rocks*, 1976
Black Sabbath, *Paranoid*, 1971
Black Sabbath, *Master of Reality*, 1971
Blue Cheer, *Vincebus Eruptum*, 1968
Blue Öyster Cult, *Blue Öyster Cult*, 1972
Alice Cooper, *Love It to Death*, 1971
Cream, *Disraeli Gears*, 1968
Deep Purple, *In Rock*, 1971
Deep Purple, *Machine Head*, 1973
Grand Funk Railroad, *Survival*, 1970
The Jimi Hendrix Experience, *Are You Experienced?*, 1967
Judas Priest, *Hell Bent for Leather*, 1979
Kiss, *Destroyer*, 1976
Led Zeppelin, *Led Zeppelin*, 1968
Led Zeppelin, *II*, 1969
Led Zeppelin, *ZOSO [IV]*, 1972
Motörhead, *Ace of Spades*, 1980
Ted Nugent, *Cat Scratch Fever*, 1977
Queen, *Queen*, 1973
Rush, *Rush*, 1974
Scorpions, *In Trance*, 1976
UFO, *Lights Out*, 1977
Van Halen, *Van Halen*, 1978
Van Halen, *II*, 1979

APPENDIX 2

Heavy Metal Questionnaire

✳

ẞeaby Metal Queſtionaire

These questions are being asked for a book on Heavy Metal, being
written by a guitar player/musicologist/metal fan. If you listen to heavy
metal, your help would be appreciated.

How long have you been listening to heavy metal? _____ years

How many hours do you listen to metal each day? [circle one]
0   1   2   3   4   5   6   7   8+

How many hours do you listen to other music each day?
0   1   2   3   4   5   6   7   8+

What are your *three* favorite bands? _____   _____   _____

How many metal recordings did you buy last month?
0   1   2   3   4   5   6   7   8   9   10+

What do you usually buy?
A. albums   B. cassettes   C. compact discs

What other kinds of music do you like (if any)? _____

Are most of your friends into metal too?   yes   no

Do you know people who used to listen to metal but don't anymore?
yes   no

If yes, what do they listen to now instead of metal? _____

Which do you listen to more, radio or recordings?
A. radio more than records   B. both about the same
C. records more than radio

Do you play any musical instruments?   yes   no   If yes, what? _____

Do you own any musical equipment?   yes   no   If yes, what? _____

Do you sing along with metal songs?   yes   no

How important are these elements of metal?

	not important				very important
guitar solos	1	2	3	4	5
lyrics	1	2	3	4	5
powerful drums & bass	1	2	3	4	5
lead singer	1	2	3	4	5
special effects	1	2	3	4	5

How many hours do you watch TV each day, on the average?

0   1   2   3   4   5   6   7   8+

How much do you watch music videos?
A. none   B. 1–3 hr/week   C. 1 hr/day   D. 2–3 hr/day
E. 4–6 hr/day   F. more

Do you watch "Headbangers' Ball" on MTV?
A. no   B. once a month   C. twice a month   D. every week

What do you like about metal compared to other music? Check the ones you strongly agree with.

— It's the most powerful kind of music; it makes me feel powerful.
— It's intense; it helps me work off my frustrations.
— The guitar solos are amazing; it takes a great musician to play metal.
— I can relate to the lyrics.
— It's music for people like me; I fit in with a heavy metal crowd.
— It's pissed-off music, and I'm pissed off.
— It deals with things nobody else will talk about.
— It's imaginative music; I would never have thought of some of those things.
— It's true to life; it's music about real important issues.
— It's not true to life; it's fantasy, better than life.

What is heavy metal? *Circle* a few of the bands you think best define "Heavy Metal." *Cross out* the bands you think are not metal at all.

AC/DC	Aerosmith	Bon Jovi
Boston	Lita Ford	Heart
Hüsker Dü	Iron Maiden	Judas Priest
Kiss	Led Zeppelin	Yngwie Malmsteen
Megadeth	Metallica	Mötley Crüe
Ozzy Osbourne	Poison	Rush
Stryper	Twisted Sister	Van Halen
The Who	Frank Zappa	ZZ Top

Do you ever read heavy metal fan magazines?
A. never   B. occasionally   C. often   Which ones? _____

What is your age? _____   You are (circle one):   Male   Female

Education completed:
A. some high school   B. high school diploma   C. some college
D. college degree

Present employment:
A. unemployed   B. part-time   C. full-time   Occupation: _____

Your parents' employment:

Father: A. unemployed   B. part-time   C. full-time

Occupation: _____

Mother: A. unemployed   B. part-time   C. full-time

Occupation: _____

Would you be willing to be interviewed about metal?   yes   no

If yes, leave your name and phone number: _____

𝔗𝔥𝔞𝔫𝔨𝔰 𝔣𝔬𝔯 𝔶𝔬𝔲𝔯 𝔥𝔢𝔩𝔭 RAW 8/31/90

Notes

✳

Introduction (Notes to Pages ix–xviii)

1. Blayne Cutler, "For What It's Worth," *American Demographics*, August 1989, pp. 42–45, 61–62.

2. Richard Parker, "Some with a Fountain Pen," *The Nation*, 24 December 1990, p. 820.

3. Christopher Small, private communication, 21 February 1991.

4. For an example of recent musicological work that vividly illustrates this point, see Ellen Rosand, *Opera in Seventeenth-Century Venice: The Creation of a Genre* (Berkeley: University of California Press, 1991). For a collection of documents that helps restore such erased aspects of musical history, see Piero Weiss and Richard Taruskin, eds., *Music in the Western World: A History in Documents* (New York: Schirmer Books, 1984).

5. Janice Radway, *Reading the Romance: Women, Patriarchy, and Popular Literature* (Chapel Hill: University of North Carolina Press, 1984); Steven Feld, *Sound and Sentiment: Birds, Weeping, Poetics, and Song in Kaluli Expression*, 2d ed. (Philadelphia: University of Pennsylvania Press, 1990); John Fiske, *Understanding Popular Culture* (Boston: Unwin Hyman, 1989), and *Television Culture* (New York: Methuen, 1987); George Lipsitz, *Time Passages: Collective Memory and American Popular Culture* (Minneapolis: University of Minnesota Press, 1990); Susan McClary, *Feminine Endings: Music, Gender, Sexuality* (Minneapolis: University of Minnesota Press, 1991); Christopher Small, *Music of the Common Tongue: Survival and Celebration in Afro-American Music* (New York: Riverrun, 1987).

6. See Christopher Small, *Music of the Common Tongue*, p. 50. Small is a maverick, and although his work belongs to a tradition of ethnomusicological study of music in culture (and music as culture), his is the strongest statement of this perspective because he doesn't shy away from developing his critique along political and philosophical lines.

7. Concerts are crucial to heavy metal, and they were my main avenue of contact with fans. I attended mostly arena concerts, by groups such as Ozzy Osbourne, Blue Öyster Cult, Iron Maiden, Megadeth, Def Leppard, Tesla, Dokken, Metallica, Scorpions, Van Halen, Living Colour, Poison, Fates Warning, Slave Raider, Judas Priest, and Lynch Mob.

8. See Stuart Hall, "Notes on Deconstructing 'the Popular,'" in *People's History and Socialist Theory*, ed. Raphael Samuel (London: Routledge and Kegan Paul, 1981), pp. 227–40.

9. See Susan McClary and Robert Walser, "Start Making Sense: Musicology Wrestles with Rock," in *On Record: Rock, Pop, and the Written Word*, ed. Simon Frith and Andrew Goodwin (New York: Pantheon, 1990), pp. 277–92.

10. M. M. Bakhtin, *The Dialogic Imagination*, ed. Michael Holmquist (Austin: University of Texas Press, 1981); George E. Marcus and Michael M. J. Fischer, *Anthropology as Cultural Critique: An Experimental Moment in the Human Sciences* (Chicago: University of Chicago Press, 1986).

11. See Kaja Silverman, "Fragments of a Fashionable Discourse," in *Studies in Entertainment: Critical Approaches to Mass Culture*, ed. Tania Modleski (Bloomington: Indiana University Press, 1986), pp. 139–52.

12. Jon Pareles, "Metallica Defies Heavy Metal Stereotypes," *Minneapolis Star Tribune*, 13 July 1988, p. 12 Ew.

13. Dave Marsh has argued that too much attention to the categories of youth and rebellion has skewed rock history and criticism in general; see *The Heart of Rock & Soul: The 1001 Greatest Singles Ever Made* (New York: New American Library, 1989), pp. xxiii–xxv.

Chapter 1. Metallurgies (Notes to Pages 1–25)

1. Philip Bashe, *Heavy Metal Thunder: The Music, Its History, Its Heroes* (Garden City, N.Y.: Doubleday, 1985), p. viii.

2. *The Oxford English Dictionary*, 2d ed., s.v. "heavy."

3. Headbanging is vigorous nodding to the beat of the music. Usually only a fraction of a concert audience headbangs, but heavy metal fans often refer to themselves as headbangers.

4. Compare the discussion of punk band names in Dave Laing, *One Chord Wonders: Power and Meaning in Punk Rock* (Philadelphia: Open University Press, 1985), pp. 42, 48–49.

5. Musicians' attitudes are discussed in chapter 3. On structural and functional perspectives on genres, see Tzvetan Todorov, *Genres in Discourse* (Cambridge: Cambridge University Press, 1990), pp. 9–19.

6. Michel Foucault, "History of Systems of Thought," in *Language, Counter-Memory, Practice: Selected Essays and Interviews*, ed. Donald F. Bouchard (Ithaca, N.Y.: Cornell University Press, 1977), p. 199.

7. The class origins of heavy metal have become obscured by its tremendous popularity, but many of the leading musicians of early metal were from working-class backgrounds, and the music has always retained a core audience of working-class youth. Judas Priest came out of the English industrial center of Birmingham, and Ozzy Osbourne, heavy metal's most enduring performer, was the son of a steelworker and a factory worker in the same city.

8. Anthony DeCurtis, "The Year in Music," *Rolling Stone*, December 15–29, 1988, p. 14. In 1989, heavy metal became "the largest revenue-grossing musical genre in the world . . . , generating more than 40 percent of all money made from record sales, concerts and promotions" (*Spin*, August 1990, p. 47). Estimates vary a great deal. In 1985, *Billboard* reported that heavy metal accounted for 10–30 percent of retail volume at record stores (Moira McCormick, "Metal Boom Levels Off at Retail As Indies Again Take Torch," *Billboard*, 27 April 1985, pp. HM-6, HM-18). In her book on metal, Deena Weinstein accepts figures reported in *Rolling Stone*, claiming that metal comprised 15–20 percent of the music industry's revenues in 1988 (*Heavy Metal: A Cultural Sociology* [New York: Lexington Books, 1991], p. 189). In *The Clustering of America* (New York: Harper & Row, 1988), Michael J. Weiss claimed that during the late 1980s, 5.62 percent of Americans (about 15 million) were buyers of heavy metal recordings

(p. 130). This last figure seems rather high, but it provides no way of distinguishing the occasional purchaser of a metal record from the serious fan.

9. See Appendix 1 for some canons of metal music, published in major fan magazines.

10. For example, an advertisement for the Columbia Record and Tape Club hypes: "Make Way For More Metal: Take 12 Heavy Metal Hits For A Penny! If you're heavy into heavy metal, this offer will blow you away with hard rockin' metal mania." The ad lists nearly one hundred albums by thirty-five bands, plus a section called "The Roots of Metal" (Led Zeppelin, Hendrix, Woodstock, Deep Purple, Mountain, Clapton) and a more general selection of rock (*Creem*, March 1988, pp. 10–11).

Compare:

If you're willing to be enchanted, enraptured, bedazzled, bewitched and spellbound by some of the most fantastically beautiful music ever recorded, then we'd like to send you a state-of-the-art compact disc, cassette or LP that is sheer musical euphoria! . . . To demonstrate the seductive power of music and to induce you to acquint yourself with the Society's mesmerizing musical fare, its outstanding recordings and its unique recording program, we'd like to send you, for just $1.00 post-paid, classical masterpieces by Mozart performed by The Academy of St. Martin-in-the-Fields, conducted by Neville Marriner and available only to new members of Musical Heritage Society, that will have you in a heady state of ecstasy within moments! . . . Each year Musical Heritage issues about 200 new recordings of the music of such great masters as Albinoni, the Bachs, Beethoven, Berlioz, Buxtehude. . . . Its recordings traverse all musical periods in great depth" (Musical Heritage Society advertisement, c. 1980).

11. Greg Ptacek, "Majors Return to Nuts and Bolts of Pre-MTV Metal Marketing Days," *Billboard*, 27 April 1985, p. HM-3.

12. There is a lot at stake here; metal merchandise outsells that of any other genre (although highest per capita sales are generated by bands appealling to preteens, such as New Kids on the Block). See Ethlie Ann Vare, "Heavy Metal: Pounding It Out," *Billboard*, 27 April 1985, p. HM-16.

13. Dan Zarpentine, Spencerport, N.Y., "Letters," *Guitar for the Practicing Musician*, January 1984, p. 5.

14. Co-Co, "Chain Mail," *Metal Mania*, July 1989, p. 23.

15. For example, a female metal musician decries sexism in *RIP*, May 1989, p. 5; the letters column in *RIP*, June 1989 (pp. 5–6) includes letters advising safe sex, admonishing sexist musicians and fans, and attacking the racism of the latest Guns N' Roses album, *G N' R Lies* (1988). The August 1989 issue features as its "Letter of the Month" (p. 5) the complaint of a gay metal fan about the homophobia of musicians like Axl Rose and Zakk Wylde. See chapter 4 for more discussion of such letters.

16. For Judas Priest's statement, see *Musician*, September 1984, p. 53; on Def Leppard, see David P. Szatmary, *Rockin' in Time: A Social History of Rock and Roll* (Englewood Cliffs, N.J.: Prentice-Hall, 1987), p. 205.

17. Andy Secher, "Heavy Metal: The Hall of Fame," *Hit Parader*, December 1982, p. 26.

18. *Musician*, September 1984, p. 53.

19. FabioTesta, "Yngwie Malmsteen: In Search of a New Kingdom," *The Best of Metal Mania* #2, 1987, p. 35.

20. *Musician*, September 1984, p. 53.

21. Anne Leighton, "Rush: The Fine Art of Metal," *RIP*, June 1989, pp. 63, 97. Lee's perception was confirmed by the fans who filled out a questionnaire I

circulated at concerts. One section asked fans to circle the names of bands that best define "heavy metal" and to cross out the bands that are not metal. Many more fans rejected Rush as a possible metal band than accepted them.

22. The following sketch of the history of heavy metal draws upon Bashe, *Heavy Metal Thunder*; Wolf Marshall, ". . . And Justice for All," *Guitar for the Practicing Musician*, June 1989, pp. 81–86, 136–38; Nick Armington and Lars Lofas, "The Genesis of Metal," *Drums and Drumming*, August/September 1990, pp. 21–25, 62–64; Jas Obrecht, "The Rise of Heavy Metal," in *Masters of Heavy Metal*, ed. Jas Obrecht (New York: Quill, 1984), pp. 8–9; Ed Ward, Geoffrey Stokes, and Ken Tucker, *Rock of Ages: The Rolling Stone History of Rock & Roll* (New York: Rolling Stone Press, 1986); *Hit Parader's Metal of the 80's*, Spring 1990; and Elin Wilder, "Heavy Metal: A Fan's Perspective," *High Times*, August 1988, pp. 32–39.

23. See, for example, Bashe, *Heavy Metal Thunder*, p. 4; Donald Clarke, ed., *The Penguin Encyclopedia of Popular Music* (New York: Viking, 1989), p. 532; Ward et al., *Rock of Ages*, p. 399; Jon Pareles and Patricia Romanowski, eds., "Heavy Metal," in *The Rolling Stone Encyclopedia of Rock & Roll* (New York: Rolling Stone Press, 1983), p. 248; Jon Pareles, "Heavy Metal," in *The New Grove Dictionary of American Music*, ed. H. Wiley Hitchcock and Stanley Sadie (London: McMillan, 1986), vol. 2, pp. 358–59; Robert Duncan, *The Noise: Notes from a Rock 'n' Roll Era* (New York: Ticknor and Fields, 1984), p. 39. Thanks to Bruce Holsinger and Christopher Taylor for reading *Naked Lunch* to check me on this.

24. This error seems connected with rock criticism's fascination with authenticity. Of course, rock critics are not alone in mythologizing origins. As Foucault (quoting Nietzsche) reminds us: "The lofty origin is no more than 'a metaphorical extension which arises from the belief that things are most precious and essential at the moment of birth'" (Michel Foucault, "Nietzsche, Genealogy, History," in *Language, Counter-Memory, Practice*, ed. Donald F. Bouchard, p. 143). Foucault's method, which I have found useful, is to look for beginnings rather than origins, shifts in discursive formation rather than generic birthdays.

25. David Fricke, "Metal Forefathers," *Musician*, September 1984, p. 56.

26. See chapter 2 for an extended discussion of musical constructions of power.

27. Szatmary, *Rockin' in Time*, p. 205. It is tempting to add other landmark albums of 1970, such as The Who's *Live in Leeds*, but metal musicians themselves consistently trace the genre back to these three founding bands.

28. The first Led Zeppelin album included two songs by Willie Dixon and one by Howlin' Wolf; only one of these was properly credited. On their second album, "The Lemon Song" is an uncredited cover of Howlin' Wolf's "Killing Floor," with a bit of Robert Johnson's "Traveling Riverside Blues" mixed in. That album's last cut is a grotesque mimicry of Sonny Boy Williamson's recording of Willie Dixon's "Bring It On Home." Plant and Page claimed songwriting credit (and royalties) without even bothering to change the title.

29. See chapter 3 for discussion of the classical influence on heavy metal.

30. See Vare, "Heavy Metal," p. HM-1. Gold albums have certified sales of five hundred thousand units; platinum status is awarded for one million sales.

31. Lester Bangs, "Heavy Metal," in *The Rolling Stone Illustrated History of Rock & Roll*, 2d ed., ed. Jim Miller (New York: Random House, 1980), p. 335.

32. Szatmary, *Rockin' in Time*, p. 205.

33. Ptacek, "Majors Return," p. HM-15.

34. See chapter 3.

35. Ptacek, "Majors Return," p. HM-15. As late as 1984, the heavy metal

audience was 80 percent male, according to a survey of record buyers cited in Charles M. Young, "Heavy Metal," *Musician*, September 1984, pp. 40–44.

36. See chapter 4 for further discussion of Bon Jovi's "fusion."

37. Kim Freeman, "Heavy Metal Bands Are Rocking Top 40 Playlists," *Billboard*, 20 June 1987, p. 1.

38. Tom Hunter, VP/Music Programming for MTV, in *RIP*, March 1989, p. 6.

39. See Paul Grein, "Metal Bands Dominate the Albums Chart," *Billboard* 13 June 1987, pp. 1, 12; Robert Edelstein, "The Last Heroes of Rock 'n' Roll," *Gallery*, April 1989, p. 42; and "Heavyosity," *Rolling Stone*, 15–29 December 1988, p. 124.

40. For brief metal typologies, see Kim Freeman, "Pioneering Indies Undaunted by Majors' Stripmining of Heroes and Profits," *Billboard*, 27 April 1985, pp. HM-3, HM-14; or Glenn Kenny, "Heavy Metal," *Genesis*, January 1986, pp. 42–43, 100–102.

41. David Fricke, "Heavy Metal Justice," *Rolling Stone*, 12 January 1989, p. 46.

42. *Metal Mania*, July 1989, p. 28.

43. See Elianne Halbersberg, "Heavy Metal and Hard Rock," *Billboard*, 25 May 1991, pp. HM-1, HM-8, HM-16, HM-18.

44. Elianne Halbersberg, *Heavy Metal* (Cresskill, N.J.: Sharon Publications, 1985), p. 41.

45. Halbersberg, *Heavy Metal*, p. 7. For a critique of rock's myths about technology and authenticity, see Simon Frith, "Art Versus Technology: The Strange Case of Popular Music," *Media, Culture, and Society* 8 (1986), pp. 263–79.

46. "The headbangers of Salerno salute the headbangers of Florence." See note 3, above.

47. Moira McCormick, "Metal Still Rock's Top Road Warrior As Street-Level Boom Fills Concerts," *Billboard*, 27 April 1985, p. HM-19.

48. Michael J. Weiss, *The Clustering of America*, p. 130. Weiss gathered his information from 1985 to 1987, relying in part on earlier census data.

49. One demographic study concluded that no one spends more money on music than a teenage metal fan in Atlanta. However, the author regretfully noted that most advertisers are unwilling to target this market segment because they don't want to be associated with the music; see Blayne Cutler, "For What It's Worth," *American Demographics*, August 1989, pp. 42–45, 61–62. That much is true, but advertisers also avoid contact with heavy metal because many of its fans don't buy nonmetal products, for which they lack means.

50. Malcolm Dome and Mick Wall, "World View: Metal Crusade in Global Gear," *Billboard*, 27 April 1985, p. HM-12.

51. See my questionnaire in Appendix 2. Nearly everyone I approached returned a fully completed questionnaire, and I collected 136.

52. Charles M. Young, "Heavy Metal," *Musician*, September 1984, pp. 40–44. The age range of metal fans has since expanded; I interviewed fans in their early teens whose parents were metal fans too.

53. Teri Saccone, "Somewhere on the Light Side of the Moon," *Rock Scene*, July 1987, p. 65. On the other hand, Harris says that only 30–40 percent of British fans know all of the lyrics. Dan Spitz of Anthrax claims that almost every one of their fans knows every word of their lyrics (Andy Aledort, "Devil's Advocates," *Guitar for the Practicing Musician*, April 1989, p. 80). I criticize some of these academic studies later in this chapter for ignoring the effects of their research methods on the answers collected.

54. I later discovered that my survey responses were consistently confirmed by the data collected by Jeffrey Arnett, in "Adolescents and Heavy Metal Music: From the Mouths of Metalheads," *Youth & Society* 23:1 (September 1991), pp. 76–98.

55. Robert Duncan, *The Noise: Notes from a Rock 'n' Roll Era* (New York: Ticknor and Fields, 1984), pp. 36–37.

56. Marc Eliot, *Rockonomics: The Money behind the Music* (New York: Franklin Watts, 1989), pp. 247–48.

57. Paul Williams, *The Map: Rediscovering Rock and Roll (a Journey)* (South Bend, Ind.: and books, 1988), p. 237. Williams makes the latter point twice, on pp. 17 and 239.

58. See Jerry Adler with Jennifer Foote and Ray Sawhill, "The Rap Attitude," *Newsweek*, 19 March 1990, pp. 56–59. Compare Guy Garcia, "Heavy Metal Goes Platinum," *Time*, 14 October 1991, p. 85 ("wah-wah guitars"?). The ad for the issue on teenagers appeared in *Newsweek*, 14 May 1990, p. 71.

59. Duncan, *The Noise*, pp. 45–47.

60. Chuck Eddy, *Stairway to Hell: The 500 Best Heavy Metal Albums in the Universe* (New York: Harmony Books, 1991).

61. Charles Young, "Heavy Metal," *Musician*, September 1984, p. 44.

62. Bashe, *Heavy Metal Thunder*; see the articles by Wolf Marshall in *Guitar for the Practicing Musician*, several of which are cited elsewhere in this book.

63. See George Lipsitz, *Time Passages: Collective Memory and American Popular Culture* (Minneapolis: University of Minnesota Press, 1990).

64. Lorraine E. Prinsky and Jill Leslie Rosenbaum, "'Leer-ics' or Lyrics: Teenage Impressions of Rock 'n' Roll," *Youth & Society* 18:4 (June 1987), pp. 384–97. On the complexity of conversations between the powerful and the subordinate, see James C. Scott, *Domination and the Arts of Resistance: Hidden Transcripts* (New Haven, Conn.: Yale University Press, 1990).

65. Christine Hall Hansen and Ranald D. Hansen, "Schematic Information Processing of Heavy Metal Lyrics," *Communication Research* 18:3 (June 1991), pp. 373–411. Dozens of similar studies have been published. For an attempt to reclaim a very different notion of "objectivity," see Donna J. Haraway, "Situated Knowledges: The Science Question in Feminism and the Privilege of Partial Perspective," in *Simians, Cyborgs, and Women: The Reinvention of Nature* (New York: Routledge, 1991), pp. 183–201.

66. See Will Straw, "Characterizing Rock Music Cultures: The Case of Heavy Metal," *Canadian University Music Review* 5 (1984), pp. 104–22. Revised as "Characterizing Rock Music Culture: The Case of Heavy Metal," in *On Record: Rock, Pop, and the Written Word*, ed. Simon Frith and Andrew Goodwin (New York: Pantheon, 1990), pp. 97-110.

67. Marcus Breen, "A Stairway to Heaven or a Highway to Hell?: Heavy Metal Rock Music in the 1990s," *Cultural Studies* 5:2 (May 1991), pp. 191–203.

68. Deena Weinstein, *Heavy Metal: A Cultural Sociology* (New York: Lexington Books, 1991).

69. Weinstein, *Heavy Metal*, p. 295.

70. Weinstein, *Heavy Metal*, p. 4.

71. Weinstein, *Heavy Metal*, p. 124.

72. See Stuart Hall, "Notes on Deconstructing 'the Popular,'" in *People's History and Socialist Theory*, ed. Raphael Samuel (London: Routledge and Kegan Paul, 1981), pp. 227–40.

1. J. D. Considine, "Purity and Power," *Musician*, September 1984, p. 49.

2. Edward Van Halen, interview in *Musician*, February 1987, pp. 94–95.

3. Fredric Jameson, "Towards a New Awareness of Genre," *Science Fiction Studies* 28 (1982), p. 322; quoted in Michael Denning, *Mechanic Accents: Dime Novels and Working-Class Culture in America* (London: Verso, 1987), p. 75.

4. M. M. Bakhtin, "The Problem of Speech Genres," in *Speech Genres and Other Late Essays*, ed. Caryl Emerson and Michael Holquist (Austin: University of Texas Press, 1986), p. 91. See also Horace M. Newcomb, "On the Dialogic Aspects of Mass Communication," *Critical Studies in Mass Communication* 1 (1984), pp. 34–50.

5. Simon Frith, "Towards an Aesthetic of Popular Music," in *Music and Society: The Politics of Composition, Performance, and Reception*, ed. Richard Leppert and Susan McClary (Cambridge: Cambridge University Press, 1987), p. 145. See Wilfred Mellers, "God, Modality, and Meaning in Some Recent Songs of Bob Dylan," *Popular Music* 1 (1981), pp. 142–57. I don't think the problem is primarily at the level of the types of musical qualities that are investigated by musicologists, though the discipline does bring to bear biases in favor of harmonic and melodic characteristics. Rather, the problem is the elitist, "apolitical" formalism that has plagued the musicological study of all repertoires. As I understand Frith, his real objection to musicological analysis is that it has, so far, been formalist; it hasn't really told us much about how any music produces meaning or why people care about it.

6. I have written elsewhere about how musical innovations often result in discursive fusions that can best be approached with respect to the previous genres upon which they draw; see Robert Walser, "Bon Jovi's Alloy: Discursive Fusion in Top 40 Pop Music," *OneTwoThreeFour* 7 (1989), pp. 7–19.

7. See Michel Foucault, "History of Systems of Thought," in *Language, Counter-memory, Practice*, ed. Donald F. Bouchard (Ithaca, N.Y.: Cornell University Press, 1977), pp. 199–201.

8. John Fiske, *Television Culture* (New York: Methuen, 1987), pp. 110, 114.

9. Tzvetan Todorov, *Genres in Discourse* (Cambridge: Cambridge University Press, 1990), especially pp. 9–19.

10. Peter Wicke, *Rock Music: Culture, Aesthetics, and Sociology* (Cambridge: Cambridge University Press, 1990), p. 24.

11. Wicke, *Rock Music*, p. 25.

12. To those who would question a detailed analysis of heavy metal music by asking, "Yes, but do heavy metal musicians *know* what they're doing?" I would answer that in those terms, some do and some don't. (See chap. 3 for discussion of the various ways heavy metal musicians theorize their practices.) But how musicians conceive of their activities is only part of what it is they are doing, and there are many different ways of "knowing."

13. See Jean-Jacques Nattiez, *Music and Discourse: Toward a Semiology of Music* (Princeton, N.J.: Princeton University Press, 1990).

14. David Lidov, "Mind and Body in Music," *Semiotica* 66–1/3 (1987), pp. 69–87; Mark Johnson, *The Body in the Mind: The Bodily Basis of Meaning, Imagination, and Reason* (Chicago: University of Chicago Press, 1987); George Lakoff and Mark Johnson, *Metaphors We Live By* (Chicago: University of Chicago Press, 1980). See also Robert Walser, "The Body in the Music: Epistemology and Musical Semiotics," *College Music Symposium* 31:1 (forthcoming).

15. This argument is, of course, not Johnson's alone; many scholars have

contributed to an expanded view of metaphor. See Johnson's own bibliography and citations in *The Body in the Mind*.

16. Johnson, 196.

17. John A. Sloboda, *The Musical Mind: The Cognitive Psychology of Music* (Oxford: Clarendon Press, 1985), pp. 1–2. Unfortunately, Sloboda limits musical meaning to "emotions."

18. Elianne Halbersberg, *Heavy Metal* (Cresskill, N.J.: Sharon Publications, 1985), p. 41.

19. The Editors of *Rock & Roll Confidential, You've Got a Right to Rock* ([Los Angeles]: Duke and Duchess Ventures, 1989), p. 5.

20. Fiske, *Television Culture*, p. 85. This approach derives from the work of various sorts of literary reader-response critics (Barthes, Eco, Fish, Holland, Iser, Jauss, et al.). See Susan R. Suleiman and Inge Crosman, *The Reader in the Text: Essays on Audience and Interpretation* (Princeton, N.J.: Princeton University Press, 1980), particularly Suleiman's Introduction, for a lucid introduction to and typology of this work. I would argue that musical analysis in terms of discourse should not be counterposed to reception-oriented approaches. On the contrary, it actually helps us understand problems such as what has been called "distracted listening." If we recognize the power of music to communicate very specific affective experiences, we can see how varying degress of incomplete verbal reception should not lead us to underestimate either the music or its audience.

21. Mounting a similar argument in a different discipline, Norman Bryson emphasizes that visual art is not simply *affected* by social economics (patronage systems, etc.) but is itself constituted through social discourse. Signs are activated through social labor; combinations of signifiers must make contact with discursive formations actually operative in society in order to be generally intelligible. See Norman Bryson, *Vision and Pointing: The Logic of the Gaze* (New Haven, Conn.: Yale University Press, 1983). Bryson argues that painter and viewer do not "communicate": "they are *agents* operating *through labor* on the *materiality* of the visual sign" (p. 150, original emphasis). By this he means to stress the inherently social nature of artistic production and reception; the artistic work, though guided by discursive channels, is unavoidably subject to the variety of readings produced by the various social experiences of its viewers (or auditors).

22. For good examples of this sort of work, see Steve Chapple and Reebee Garofalo, *Rock 'n' Roll Is Here to Pay* (Chicago: Nelson-Hall, 1977); and Reebee Garofalo, ed., *Rockin' the Boat: Mass Music and Mass Movements*, Boston: South End Press, 1992. But such approaches frequently degenerate into studies that ignore the social exchange of meanings that underpins the exchange of musical commodities.

23. John Blacking, *How Musical Is Man?* (Seattle: University of Washington Press, 1973), pp. 45, 54, 107. Blacking accepted this truism even as he bravely challenged many others.

24. For fuller critical surveys of approaches to musical analysis that have particular relevance for popular music, see Richard Middleton, *Studying Popular Music* (Philadelphia: Open University Press, 1990); John Shepherd, *Music as Social Text* (Cambridge: Polity Press, 1991); and Bruno Nettl, *The Study of Ethnomusicology: Twenty-Nine Issues and Concepts* (Urbana: University of Illinois Press, 1983).

25. See Terry Eagleton, *The Ideology of the Aesthetic* (Cambridge, Mass.: Basil Blackwell, 1990).

26. See, for example, Theodor W. Adorno, *Prisms* (Cambridge, Mass.: MIT

Press, 1981), *Introduction to the Sociology of Music* (New York: Continuum, 1988), and *Philosophy of Modern Music* (New York: Continuum, 1985).

27. See, for example, Bernard Gendron, "Theodor Adorno Meets the Cadillacs," in *Studies in Entertainment: Critical Approaches to Mass Culture*, ed. Tania Modleski (Bloomington: Indiana University Press, 1986), pp. 18–36; and Max Paddison, "The Critique Criticized: Adorno and Popular Music," *Popular Music* 2 (1982), pp. 201–18. To compare the best and worst of Adorno's musical analysis, see "Bach Defended against His Devotees" and "Jazz—Perennial Fashion," in his *Prisms*.

28. Alan Lomax, *Folk Song Style and Culture* (New Brunswick, N.J.: Transaction Books, 1968), p. ix.

29. Lomax's study displays many of the features of the anthropological tradition of "rescue" scholarship: the mission of saving folk cultures from their destruction at the hands of global mass culture, as though other cultures have never had history, have existed in timeless purity until their twentieth-century contamination. Thus, African-American blues are not included in his data; presumably their origin in cultural fusion marks them as abnormal, as though intercultural influence had never occurred before European colonizations. For a contrasting view, see Bruno Nettl, *The Western Impact on World Music: Change, Adaptation, and Survival* (New York: Schirmer Books, 1985).

30. Bruno Nettl, *The Study of Ethnomusicology* (Urbana, IL: University of Illinois Press, 1983), 212.

31. Steven Feld, "Linguistics and Ethnomusicology," *Ethnomusicology* 18:2 (1974), 197–217.

32. John Miller Chernoff, *African Rhythm and African Sensibility* (Chicago: University of Chicago Press, 1979), p. 155.

33. Blacking, *How Musical*, p. 25.

34. Steven Feld, *Sound and Sentiment: Birds, Weeping, Poetics, and Song in Kaluli Expression*, 2d ed. (Philadelphia: University of Pennsylvania Press, 1990).

35. Judith and Alton Becker, "A Musical Icon: Power and Meaning in Javanese Gamelan Music," in *The Sign in Music and Literature*, ed. Wendy Steiner (Austin: University of Texas Press, 1981), p. 203.

36. See, for example: Susan McClary, *Feminine Endings: Music, Gender, Sexuality* (Minneapolis: University of Minnesota Press, 1991); Lawrence Kramer, *Music as Cultural Practice, 1800–1900* (Berkeley: University of California Press, 1990); Rose Rosengard Subotnik, *Developing Variations: Style and Ideology in Western Music* (Minneapolis: University of Minnesota Press, 1991); and Richard Leppert and Susan McClary, eds., *Music and Society: The Politics of Composition, Performance, and Reception* (Cambridge: Cambridge University Press, 1987).

37. Philip Tagg, *Kojak—50 Seconds of Television Music* (Göteborg, Sweden: Musikvetenskapliga Institutionen, 1979); "Analysing Popular Music: Theory, Method, and Practice," *Popular Music* 2 (1982), pp. 37–67; "Musicology and the Semiotics of Popular Music," *Semiotica* 66–1/3 (1987), pp. 279–98.

38. Tagg, "Analysing Popular Music," pp. 43, 65.

39. See the discussion of this point in chapter 1, and Stuart Hall, "Notes on Deconstructing 'the Popular,'" in *People's History and Socialist Theory*, ed. Raphael Samuel (London: Routledge and Kegan Paul, 1981), pp. 227–40. See also John Fiske's discussions of these models in his *Introduction to Communication Studies*, 2d ed. (New York: Routledge, 1990).

40. This is confirmed not only by these musicians' statements and by the opinions of the fans I interviewed but also by a recent survey of metal fans, which reported that 48 percent said they pay attention mostly to the music; 41 percent, to both music and lyrics; and only 11 percent, primarily to the lyrics.

See Jeffrey Arnett, "Adolescents and Heavy Metal Music: From the Mouths of Metalheads," *Youth & Society* 23:1 (September 1991), p. 82.

41. John Fiske and John Hartley, *Reading Television* (New York: Methuen, 1978), p. 124–25.

42. Compare David Lidov's distinction between the alliance of language with exosomatic space and the endosomatic flux of bodily experience in "Mind and Body in Music," *Semiotica* 66–1/3 (1987), pp. 69–87. See also Shepherd, *Music as Social Text*, pp. 79–95.

43. For example, critic J. D. Considine includes "Runnin' with the Devil" in his list of the ten best metal songs of all time ("Good, Bad, and Ugly," *Musician*, September 1984, p. 53).

44. Mack, quoted in Chris Gill, "Dialing for Distortion: Sound Advice from 10 Top Producers," *Guitar Player*, October 1992, p. 86.

45. For a full explanation of resultant tones, see Arthur H. Benade, *Fundamentals of Musical Acoustics* (New York: Oxford University Press, 1976), pp. 273–74.

46. Advertisement for Dean Markley's Overlord effects pedal in *Guitar for the Practicing Musician*, February 1989, p. 102.

47. Advertisement for DiMarzio pickups in *Guitar for the Practicing Musician*, December 1988, p. 121.

48. John Stix, "Up to Par," *Guitar for the Practicing Musician*, January 1989, p. 70.

49. Robert Duncan, *The Noise: Notes from a Rock 'n' Roll Era* (New York: Ticknor and Fields, 1984), p. 47.

50. See the long and interesting discussion of vocal timbre in rock music in Shepherd, *Music as Social Text*, pp. 164–73.

51. See chapter 3.

52. Wolf Marshall, "Music Appreciation: Iron Maiden," *Guitar for the Practicing Musician*, January 1989, p. 113. See chapter 3 for further discussion of metal musicians' use of modal theory.

53. For a discussion of the relationship of music theory and popular music scholarship, see Susan McClary and Robert Walser, "Start Making Sense! Musicology Wrestles with Rock," in *On Record: Rock, Pop, and the Written Word*, ed. Simon Frith and Andrew Goodwin (New York: Pantheon, 1990), pp. 277–92.

54. Musicians often put tunes into foreign musical discourses for pedagogical reasons or just for the pleasure of such play. In an article called "Headbanger's Vocabulary," Wally Schnalle altered the basic metal drumbeat by changing the size of the snare drum, increasing the tempo, and exchanging the accompanying instruments and turned it into polka time (*Drums and Drumming*, August/September 1990, p. 52). *The Billboard Book of Rock Arranging*, by Mark Michaels with Jackson Braider (New York: Billboard Books, 1990), discusses the necessary ingredients of "the hard rock arrangement" by transforming "Silent Night," step by step, into "Sylint Nyyte" (pp. 147–50). The author deals well with timbre, rhythm, lyrics, idiomatic bass lines, etc., but he unfortunately neglects to adjust the mode, which would have improved his example enormously.

55. Marshall, "Iron Maiden," p. 113. For a lengthier discussion of the affective and functional characteristics of modes, see Susan McClary, "The Transition from Modal to Tonal Organization in the Works of Monteverdi" (Ph.D. diss., Harvard University, 1976).

56. Jesse Gress, "Performance Notes," in *Joe Satriani: Surfing with the Alien*, ed. Andy Aledort (Port Chester, N.Y.: Cherry Lane Music Company, 1988), p. 8. This is the sort of technical analysis that rock critics have always liked to ridicule when academics have produced it. Now that musicians themselves write

this way, it's harder to be so dismissive. In any case, musicologists are not the only ones to resort to arcane terminology in an attempt to describe musical affect and signification. Rock critic Chuck Eddy writes of Black Sabbath's *Paranoid*: "The rhythms compress circular zero-chops wah-wah wank over steady tomroll marches, with secondary beat-apparatus from powerchord pulverizations constructed into pseudosymphonic forceswing headbang progressions" (*Stairway to Hell: The 500 Best Heavy Metal Albums in the Universe* [New York: Harmony Books, 1991], p. 26).

57. Edward T. Cone, *Musical Form and Musical Performance* (New York: W. W. Norton, 1968), p. 17. For a very influential theory of rhythm that completely ignores the body, see Grosvenor Cooper and Leonard B. Meyer, *The Rhythmic Structure of Music* (Chicago: University of Chicago Press, 1960).

58. For a theoretical model dealing with the social projection of dread onto the female, the racial other, and the insane, see Sander L. Gilman, *Difference and Pathology: Stereotypes of Sexuality, Race, and Madness* (Ithaca, N.Y.: Cornell University Press, 1985). See also McClary, *Feminine Endings*.

59. James D. Graham, "Rhythms in Rock Music," *Popular Music and Society* 1:1 (1971), p. 37.

60. The virtuosity of guitar solos in heavy metal will be discussed more fully in chapter 3.

61. Compare Richard Dyer's argument that entertainment shows us how utopia *feels*, instead of describing it (as Plato, for example, did). Dyer emphasizes that the pleasures of entertainment are dispensed only with respect to historically determined sensibilities; see his "Entertainment and Utopia," in *Movies and Methods*, vol. 2, ed. Bill Nichols, pp. 220–32 (Berkeley: University of California Press, 1985).

62. The affective characters of the various modes are clear from the circumstances of their deployment, in connection with lyrics, images, and other musical factors. But more explicit explanations are available from metal guitar players themselves; see, for example, Wolf Marshall, "Music Appreciation."

63. In chapter 5, I analyze a similarly anomalous song, Ozzy Osbourne's "Suicide Solution." In brief, I maintain that "Suicide Solution" uses a variety of musical means to construct a trapped, claustrophobic affect that would be burst open by a transcendent guitar solo.

64. Chapter 4 compares the negotiated reception by men and women, straight and gay, of the same texts in different ways.

Chapter 3. Eruptions (Notes to Pages 57–107)

1. A contemporary description of Franz Liszt from the *Allgemeine musikalische Zeitung* of May 1838, quoted in Piero Weiss and Richard Taruskin, eds., *Music in the Western World: A History in Documents* (New York: Schirmer, 1984), p. 363.

2. Malmsteen's first U.S. album, *Yngwie J. Malmsteen's Rising Force* (1984), had offered "special thanks" to Bach and Paganini.

3. John Stix, "Yngwie Malmsteen and Billy Sheehan: Summit Meeting at Chops City," *Guitar for the Practicing Musician*, March 1986, p. 59.

4. "Rock and soul" is Dave Marsh's term; by eliding "rock 'n' roll" and "soul," he underscores the fundamental connectedness of these musics, which are normally kept separate by historians, who have too readily accepted the racist marketing categories of record companies. In particular, Marsh uses the term to insist on the enormous debt owed by white rockers to black r&b and gospel artists. My favorite moment in Marsh's polemic on this point is when he dryly

refs to "the British Invasion" of the 1960s (the Beatles, Gerry and the Pace-makers, the Rolling Stones, etc.) as "the Chuck Berry Revival" (Dave Marsh, *The Heart of Rock and Soul: The 1001 Greatest Singles Ever Made* [New York: Plume, 1989], p. 3).

5. David P. Szatmary, *Rockin' in Time: A Social History of Rock and Roll* (Englewood Cliffs, N.J.: Prentice-Hall, 1987), p. 154. Glenn Tipton, guitarist with Judas Priest, offers a demonstration of the blues origins of heavy metal licks in J. D. Considine, "Purity and Power," *Musician*, September 1984, pp. 46–50.

6. For a recent and flagrant example of such musicological colonization of popular music, see Peter Van der Merwe, *Origins of the Popular Style: The Ante-cedents of Twentieth-Century Popular Music* (Oxford: Oxford University Press, 1989). See also my review of his book: Robert Walser, "Review of *Origins of the Popular Style*, by Peter Van der Merwe," *Journal of Musicological Research* 12/1–2 (1992), pp. 123–32.

7. Lawrence W. Levine, *Highbrow/Lowbrow: The Emergence of Cultural Hier-archy in America* (Cambridge, Mass.: Harvard University Press, 1988).

8. Christopher Small, *Music–Society–Education* (London: John Calder, 1980), and *Music of the Common Tongue: Survival and Celebration in Afro-American Music* (New York: Riverrun, 1987). See also Susan McClary, *Feminine Endings: Music, Gender, Sexuality* (Minneapolis: University of Minnesota Press, 1991); McClary generally works to reconstruct the lost signification and politics of classical music, instead of directly critiquing modern institutions, as Small does. But for a pointed criticism of academic modernism, see her "Terminal Prestige: The Case of Avant-Garde Music Composition," *Cultural Critique* 12 (Spring 1989), pp. 57–81.

9. Eric Hobsbawm and Terence Ranger, eds., *The Invention of Tradition* (New York: Cambridge University Press, 1983).

10. Mordechai Kleidermacher, "Where There's Smoke . . . There's Fire!" *Guitar World*, February 1991, p. 62.

11. See, for example, John Rockwell, "Art Rock," in *The Rolling Stone Illus-trated History of Rock & Roll*, ed. Jim Miller (New York: Random House, 1980), pp. 347–52.

12. Richard Middleton, *Studying Popular Music* (Philadelphia: Open University Press, 1990), p. 30.

13. Middleton, *Studying Popular Music*, p. 31.

14. See Wolf Marshall, "Ritchie Blackmore: A Musical Profile," *Guitar for the Practicing Musician*, March 1986, pp. 51–52.

15. Martin K. Webb, "Ritchie Blackmore with Deep Purple," in *Masters of Heavy Metal*, ed. Jas Obrecht (New York: Quill, 1984), p. 54; and Steve Rosen, "Blackmore's Rainbow," also in *Masters of Heavy Metal*, p. 62. Webb apparently misunderstood Blackmore's explanation, for what I have rendered as an ellip-sis he transcribed as "Bm to a D♭ to a C to a G," a harmonic progression that is neither characteristic of Bach nor to be found anywhere in "Highway Star." Blackmore was probably referring to the progression that underpins the latter part of his solo: Dm │ G │ C │ A.

16. For a discussion of the social significance of Vivaldi's concerto grosso procedures, see Susan McClary, "The Blasphemy of Talking Politics during Bach Year," in *Music and Society: The Politics of Composition, Performance, and Reception*, ed. Richard Leppert and Susan McClary (Cambridge: Cambridge University Press, 1987), pp. 13–62.

17. Nicolas Slonimsky, *Thesaurus of Scales and Melodic Patterns* (New York:

Coleman-Ross, 1947). On Slonimsky's influence on metal guitarists, see Andy Aledort, "Performance Notes," *Guitar for the Practicing Musician*, February 1989, p. 33. Alex Skolnick, guitarist in Testament, has called Walter Piston's *Harmony* "brilliant." He also studied jazz improvisation books by Jerry Coker and Jamey Aebersold (Brad Tolinski, "When Worlds Collide," *Guitar World*, February 1991, p. 32).

18. Steve Gett, "Basic Blackmore," *Guitar for the Practicing Musician*, February 1985, p. 68.

19. Webb, "Ritchie Blackmore," p. 57.

20. Mary J. Edrei, ed., *The Van Halen Scrapbook* (Cresskill, N.J.: Starbooks, 1984), p. 27. Jan Van Halen plays a clarinet solo on "Big Bad Bill (Is Sweet William Now)" on Van Halen's *Diver Down* (1982). Edward Van Halen is usually called Eddie by journalists and fans and Ed by his bandmates, but he makes a point of using Edward on his album credits, and I'll generally follow that example here.

21. Jas Obrecht, "Van Halen Comes of Age," in *Masters of Heavy Metal*, (New York: Quill, 1984), pp. 148–49.

22. Obrecht, "Van Halen Comes of Age," p. 155. Eric Clapton, Jimmy Page, and Jeff Beck, all white and British, became the most influential guitarists of the 1960s (along with Hendrix) by playing cover versions of the music of African-American blues guitarists like Muddy Waters, Howlin' Wolf, Buddy Guy, Albert King, Robert Johnson, and Blind Willie Johnson.

23. *Guitar World*, July 1990, pp. 51, 74.

24. This is described in, among other places, Obrecht, "Van Halen Comes of Age," p. 156.

25. Rodolphe Kreutzer was a contemporary of Beethoven, slightly older than Paganini. He was best known as a violinist and pedagogue, although he composed forty-three operas and many other works. His *40 Études ou Caprices* has been published in countless editions.

26. I have made a similar argument for the semiotics of the main theme of J. S. Bach's *Jauchzet Gott in allen Landen*; see Robert Walser, "Musical Imagery and Performance Practice in J. S. Bach's Arias With Trumpet," *International Trumpet Guild Journal* 13:1 (September 1988), pp. 62–77.

27. Wolf Marshall, "The Classical Influence," *Guitar for the Practicing Musician*, March 1988, p. 102.

28. See also Andy Aledort's inaugural "Guitar in the 80s" column on tapping, "The Bach Influence," *Guitar for the Practicing Musician*, May 1985, 30–31.

29. Carl Philipp Emanuel Bach and Johann Friedrich Agricola, "Obituary of J. S. Bach," in Hans T. David and Arthur Mendel, *The Bach Reader*, rev. ed. (New York: W. W. Norton, 1966), p. 223.

30. See Peter Bondanella's "Introduction" to Niccolò Machiavelli, *The Prince*, edited and with an introduction by Peter Bondanella (Oxford: Oxford University Press, 1984), p. xviii. Compare also this excerpt from the letter of a patron to a sixteenth-century artist: "I recognize that in this magnificent work you have tried to express both the love which you cherish for me and your own excellence. These two things have enabled you to produce this incomparable figure" (Lauro Martines, *Power and Imagination: City-States in Renaissance Italy* [Baltimore: Johns Hopkins University Press, 1988], p. 228).

31. Joseph Horowitz, *The Ivory Trade: Music and the Business of Music at the Van Cliburn International Piano Competition* (New York: Summit Books, 1990), p. 61.

32. This quotation is taken from an article Schumann wrote in 1840 for his

Neue Zeitschrift für Musik; it was reprinted in Robert Schumann, *Schumann on Music*, ed. Henry Pleasants (New York: Dover, 1965), pp. 157–58. My thanks to Susan McClary for calling my attention to this passage.

33. Bruce Pollock, "Rock Climbing: Baseball," *Guitar for the Practicing Musician*, March 1989, p. 12.

34. *Guitar World*, July 1990, p. 74.

35. Charles Shaar Murray, *Crosstown Traffic: Jimi Hendrix and the Rock 'n' Roll Revolution* (New York: St. Martin's Press, 1989), p. 194.

36. Murray, *Crosstown Traffic*, p. 216.

37. Marshall, "The Classical Influence," p. 98.

38. On Liszt, see Weiss and Taruskin, *Music in the Western World*, pp. 363–67. On Frescobaldi, see Carol MacClintock, ed., *Readings in the History of Music in Performance* (Bloomington: Indiana University Press, 1979), pp. 132–36.

39. See Wolf Marshall, "Randy Rhoads: A Musical Appreciation," *Guitar for the Practicing Musician*, June 1985, p. 57.

40. Jas Obrecht, "Randy Rhoads," in *Masters of Heavy Metal* (New York: Quill, 1984), p. 174.

41. Obrecht, "Randy Rhoads," p. 182.

42. For an analysis of several pieces in terms of the performative articulation of affect, see Walser, "Musical Imagery and Performance Practice." See also Frederick Wessel, "The *Affektenlehre* in the Eighteenth Century (Ph.D. diss., Indiana University, 1955), and Robert Donington, *Baroque Music: Style and Performance* (New York: Norton, 1982) on Baroque affect; see Terry Eagleton, *The Ideology of the Aesthetic* (Cambridge, Mass.: Basil Blackwell, 1990) for a thorough critique of the concept of "the aesthetic."

43. Levine, *Highbrow/Lowbrow*, p. 192.

44. See chapter 5 for an interpretation of this omission.

45. McClary, "The Blasphemy of Talking Politics," pp. 32–36.

46. Don Michael Randel, ed., *The New Harvard Dictionary of Music* (Cambridge, Mass.: Harvard University Press, 1986), p. 859.

47. The first (interior) solo in this recording of "Suicide Solution" also plays with the semiotics of irrationality by violating the norms of tonal syntax: Rhoads uses feedback, pickup interruptions, an ascending sequence of tritones, a descending chromatic sequence, groans and wailing with the whammy bar.

48. See Wolf Marshall, "Randy Rhoads," *Guitar for the Practicing Musician*, April 1986, p. 51.

49. One fan told me that he respected heavy metal more than other kinds of music because it has the most "advanced" guitar playing. Scott, interview with author, 30 June 1989.

50. *Guitar for the Practicing Musician*, May 1985, pp. 30–31.

51. My thanks to Christopher Kachian, professor of guitar at the College of St. Thomas, for discussing these issues and metal recordings with me.

52. Doug Smith, educational director, Music Tech, Minneapolis, telephone interview with author, 12 December 1990.

53. On Clark, see David Fricke, "Steve Clark: 1960–1991," *Rolling Stone*, 21 February 1991, p. 14. On Collins, see Elianne Halbersberg, "Doing the Def Leppard Family Proud," *Faces*, May 1989, p. 21. On Spitz, see Andy Aledort, "Thrashing It Out," *Guitar for the Practicing Musician*, March 1988, p. 64. On Vincent, see FabioTesta, "Vinnie Vincent: Rockin' the Eighties," *The Best of Metal Mania* #2, 1987, p. 22.

54. On Spitz, see *Metal Mania*, July 1989, p. 40. On Stradlin', see John Stix, "In the Classic Way," *Guitar for the Practicing Musician*, September 1988, p. 76. On Van Halen, see Obrecht, "Van Halen Comes of Age," pp. 146, 154.

55. Matt Resnicoff, "George Lynch," *Guitar World*, July 1990, p. 92 (originally published in *Guitar World*, April 1988).

56. Resnicoff, "George Lynch," p. 92.

57. Joe Lalaina, "Yngwie, the One and Only," *Guitar School*, September 1989, p. 125.

58. Matt Resnicoff, "Flash of Two Worlds," *Musician*, September 1990, p. 76.

59. Lalaina, "Yngwie," p. 15.

60. FabioTesta, "Yngwie Malmsteen: In Search of a New Kingdom," *The Best of Metal Mania* #2, 1987, p. 33.

61. Wolf Marshall, "Performance Notes: Black Star," *Guitar for the Practicing Musician Collector's Yearbook*, Winter 1990, pp. 26–27. See example 12 (pp. 96–97).

62. Compare Janet Levy's cautious but valuable exposé of the values implicit in the writings of academic musicologists, in "Covert and Casual Values in Recent Writings about Music," *Journal of Musicology* 6:1 (Winter 1987), pp. 3–27.

63. Andy Aledort, "Performance Notes," *Guitar for the Practicing Musician Collector's Yearbook*, Winter 1990, p. 6.

64. John Stix, "Yngwie Malmsteen and Billy Sheehan: Summit Meeting at Chops City," *Guitar for the Practicing Musician*, March 1986, p. 59. On the other side of his lineage, Malmsteen cites early Deep Purple as another moment of high musicianship, adding, "I think what people are doing today is far worse than early heavy metal. If you consider today's music involves two or three chords and players in some bands do even less. They could just as well be plumbers" (p. 64).

65. FabioTesta, "Yngwie Malmsteen," p. 35.

66. Stix, "Yngwie Malmsteen and Billy Sheehan," p. 57. Heavy metal bass players have, for the most part, simply laid down a solid foundation for the music. Bassists had not attempted to transform their instrument into a vehicle for virtuosic soloing until the recent success of Sheehan, who has been hailed variously as the "Eddie Van Halen of the bass" and the "Jaco Pastorius of heavy metal." Like Malmsteen, Sheehan cites among his main influences Bach, Paganini, and Hendrix.

67. Guitar players who are members of bands, however, are usually the leading composers of their groups, and the collaborative experience of working out songs and arrangements in a rock band is a type of musical creativity seldom enjoyed by classical musicians.

68. Jeff Loven, interview with the author, 9 February 1989, Minneapolis, Minn.

69. *Guitar for the Practicing Musician*, February 1989, p. 162. This description may sound exaggerated to some, but as someone who has known young practice fanatics in both classical and popular styles, I find it quite credible.

70. Matt Resnicoff, "The Latest Temptation of Steve Vai," *Musician*, September 1990, p. 60. Compare Milton Babbitt's "Who Cares If You Listen?" *High Fidelity*, February 1958, pp. 38–40, 126–27.

71. *Musician*, September 1990, p. 112.

72. The opposite story is told by Mark Wood, the first heavy metal violinist, who recalls having to unlearn the rigidity fostered by his classical training before going on to modify his instrument, imitate blues singers and guitarists, and experiment with distortion and power chords (Pete Brown, "Mark Wood," *Guitar for the Practicing Musician*, September 1991, pp. 161–66).

73. *Guitar World*, July 1990, p. 51. As Chris Kachian pointed out to me, Van

Halen always keeps his virtuosity lyrical, while Malmsteen inserts lyricism parenthetically among the virtuosic licks. Some of the new speed demons dispense with lyricism entirely.

74. Resnicoff, "Flash of Two Worlds," p. 126.

75. George E. Marcus and Michael M. J. Fischer, *Anthropology as Cultural Critique: An Experimental Moment in the Human Sciences* (Chicago: University of Chicago Press, 1986). For an interesting early example of "musicology as cultural critique," see Sidney Finkelstein, *Jazz: A People's Music* (New York: International Publishers, 1988 [orig. pub. 1948]), especially chapter 2, "The Sound of Jazz," which includes a section called "What Jazz Teaches Us About the Classics."

76. John Berger, Sven Blomberg, Chris Fox, Michael Dibb, and Richard Hollis, *Ways of Seeing* (London: British Broadcasting Corporation, 1972).

77. Ed Ward, Geoffrey Stokes, and Ken Tucker, *Rock of Ages: The Rolling Stone History of Rock & Roll* (New York: Rolling Stone Press, 1986), p. 608. Other histories discuss heavy metal briefly and musical virtuosity not at all. See Szatmary, *Rockin' in Time*, pp. 204–5; and Robert G. Pielke, *You Say You Want a Revolution: Rock Music in American Culture* (Chicago: Nelson-Hall, 1986), p. 202. See also the relevant entries in Jon Pareles and Patricia Romanowski, eds., *The Rolling Stone Encyclopedia of Rock & Roll* (New York: Rolling Stone Press, 1983); or Donald Clarke, ed., *The Penguin Encyclopedia of Popular Music* (New York: Viking, 1989). Pareles's entry on "Heavy Metal" in the *New Grove Dictionary of American Music*, ed. H. Wiley Hitchcock and Stanley Sadie (London: McMillan, 1986), mentions only Edward Van Halen's virtuosity, and that in passing.

78. Within the academy, one hears occasional calls for reforms that will respond to modern cultural, demographic, and technological changes; perversely, these often turn out to be pleas to bolster sagging attention to "serious" music in order to combat the moral evils and musical crudities of heavy metal and other popular musics. The 1990 conference of the National Association of Schools of Music, held 15–20 November in Indianapolis, was one recent occasion where such calls to arms dominated.

79. Anne Fadiman, "Heavy Metal Mania," *Life*, December 1984, p. 106.

80. Theodor W. Adorno, "Bach Defended against His Devotees" [1950], in *Prisms* (Cambridge, Mass.: MIT Press, 1981), p. 136.

81. See, for example, McClary, "The Blasphemy of Talking Politics."

82. Adorno, "Bach Defended," p. 146.

83. V. N. Vološinov, *Marxism and the Philosophy of Language* (Cambridge, Mass.: Harvard University Press, 1986), p. 23. This aspect of the work of Bakhtin and Vološinov has been developed into a theory of "articulation" in cultural studies. For example, see Stuart Hall, "The Rediscovery of 'Ideology': Return of the Repressed in Media Studies," in Michael Gurevitch, Tony Bennett, James Curran, and Janet Woollacott, eds., *Culture, Society, and the Media* (New York: Methuen, 1982), pp. 56–90.

84. Vološinov, *Marxism*, p. 23.

85. See Stuart Hall, "Notes on Deconstructing 'the Popular,'" in *People's History and Socialist Theory*, ed. Raphael Samuel (London: Routledge and Kegan Paul, 1981), pp. 227–40.

86. J. D. Considine, "Purity and Power," *Musician*, September 1984, pp. 46, 48.

87. Small, *Music of the Common Tongue*, p. 126.

88. I refer to Jennifer Batten, guitarist (with Michael Jackson and others) and columnist for *Guitar for the Practicing Musician*, and to Vernon Reid of

Living Colour, who has been featured on the cover and in the analyses of the same magazine.

Chapter 4. Forging Masculinity (Notes to Pages 108–36)

1. Guy Debord, *Society of the Spectacle* (Detroit: Black and Red, 1983), §4.

2. See Susan McClary, "Constructions of Gender in Monteverdi's Dramatic Music," in *Feminine Endings: Music, Gender, Sexuality* (Minneapolis: University of Minnesota Press, 1991), pp. 35–52.

3. John Fiske, *Television Culture* (New York: Methuen, 1987), p. 202. See also Fiske, "British Cultural Studies and Television," in *Channels of Discourse*, ed. Robert C. Allen (Chapel Hill: University of North Carolina Press, 1987), pp. 254–89.

4. See Arthur Brittan, *Masculinity and Power* (New York: Basil Blackwell, 1989), especially pp. 36–41.

5. Deena Weinstein believes that heavy metal "celebrates the very qualities that boys must sacrifice in order to become adult members of society"; see her *Heavy Metal: A Cultural Sociology* (New York: Lexington Books, 1991), p. 105. I argue the opposite of this: that although behavior changes, the same patriarchal ideals are largely held in common by both "boys" and "adult members of society."

6. E. Ann Kaplan, *Rocking around the Clock: Music Television, Postmodernism, and Consumer Culture* (New York: Methuen, 1987).

7. Kaplan, *Rocking around the Clock*, p. 107.

8. Laura Mulvey, "Visual Pleasure and Narrative Cinema," in *Movies and Methods*, vol. 2, ed. Bill Nichols (Berkeley: University of California Press, 1985), p. 308.

9. For a full discussion of this point, see Susan McClary, "Introduction: A Material Girl in Bluebeard's Castle," in *Feminine Endings*, pp. 3–34.

10. See Barbara Ehrenreich, *The Worst Years of Our Lives* (New York: Pantheon, 1990), pp. 251–57. It is crucial to recognize that exscription is not subcultural deviance but a mainstream ideological convention. Daniel Patrick Moynihan once proposed that the "character defects" of young black men be solved by removing them to a "world without women" in the military (Adolph Reed, Jr., and Julian Bond, "Equality: Why We Can't Wait," *The Nation*, 9 December 1991, p. 733).

11. Fiske, "British Cultural Studies," p. 263. Fiske properly discusses the links between such a concept of masculinity and its context of patriarchal capitalism.

12. Of course, some women also find such images attractive, as I will discuss below. But the point is that "the social definition of men as holders of power is translated not only into mental body images and fantasies, but into muscle tensions, posture, the feel and texture of the body" (not to mention the music) (R. W. Connell, *Gender and Power: Society, the Person, and Sexual Politics* [Cambridge: Polity Press, 1987], p. 85).

13. When I first started studying metal, a friend and I discovered we were reading a Judas Priest concert film in these two very different ways. Occasionally, the threat of homoeroticism is addressed directly, as by metal star Ted Nugent, who remarked during a concert, "I like my boys in the band, as long as they don't fucking touch me." On the theory of "negotiated" readings of popular texts, see Horace M. Newcomb, "On the Dialogic Aspects of Mass Communication," *Critical Studies in Mass Communication* 1 (1984), pp. 34–50.

14. Klaus Theweleit, *Male Fantasies*, vol. 2 (Minneapolis: University of Minnesota Press, 1989).

15. For example, many Judas Priest songs, such as "Hard as Iron" and "Heavy Metal," from *Ram It Down*, and the album cover art from *Ram It Down*, *Screaming for Vengeance*, and *Defenders of the Faith*.

16. Tipper Gore, *Raising PG Kids in an X-Rated Society* (Nashville, Tenn.: Abingdon Press, 1987), pp. 17–18; William Graebner, "The Erotic and Destructive in 1980s Rock Music: A Theoretical and Historical Analysis," *Tracking: Popular Music Studies* 1:2 (1988), pp. 8–20.

17. Joseph W. Slade, "Violence in the Pornographic Film: A Historical Survey," *Journal of Communication* 34:3 (1984), p. 153. See also Linda Williams, *Hard Core: Power, Pleasure, and the "Frenzy of the Visible"* (Berkeley: University of California Press, 1989).

18. All from the album *Back for the Attack* (1987); further examples of this type of song can also be found on earlier Dokken albums, such as *Tooth and Nail* (1984). "Looks That Kill" is from Mötley Crüe's *Shout at the Devil* (1983); "Still of the Night" is on Whitesnake's *Whitesnake* (1987).

19. On this reading of the presentation of women in nineteenth-century opera, see Catherine Clément, *Opera, or the Undoing of Women* (Minneapolis: University of Minnesota Press, 1988). See also Susan McClary, *George Bizet: Carmen* (Cambridge: Cambridge University Press, 1992).

20. See, for example, the E Minor Partita. As I argued in chapter 3, such comparisons are neither arbitrary nor coincidental: album liner credits, published interviews with musicians, and the musical analyses in guitarists' trade journals all make explicit the relation of Baroque musical discourse to that of heavy metal, a relationship resulting from the continuing circulation of classical music in contemporary culture and metal guitarists' conscious and meticulous study.

21. In a stunning projection of violence onto the victim, the lyrics of "Midnight Maniac," by Krokus (*The Blitz*, 1984), warn of a female sex maniac creeping about at night, breaking in and killing; the singer evokes the terror of the presumably male victim.

22. I have written elsewhere about the musical organization of this song; see Robert Walser, "Bon Jovi's Alloy: Discursive Fusion in Top 40 Pop Music," *OneTwoThreeFour* 7 (1989), pp. 7–19.

23. Rob Tannenbaum, "Bon Voyage," *Rolling Stone*, 9 February 1989, pp. 52–58, 132–33.

24. This is the ♭VI–♭VII–I progression discussed in previous chapters.

25. See Steven Neale, "Masculinity as Spectacle: Reflections on Men and Mainstream Cinema," *Screen* 24:6 (November–December 1983): pp. 2–16; and Mulvey, "Visual Pleasure and Narrative Cinema."

26. Susan Orleans, "The Kids Are All Right," *Rolling Stone*, 21 May 1987, pp. 34–38, 108–111.

27. Mulvey, "Visual Pleasure and Narrative Cinema," p. 309.

28. See the album cover photos in Poison's *Open Up and Say . . . Ahh!* and the even more androgynous look on their first album, *Look What the Cat Dragged In*. See Mötley Crüe's photos on the albums *Shout at the Devil*, *Theatre of Pain*, and *Girls, Girls, Girls*. Such images fill the pages of metal fan magazines like *Hit Parader*, *Metal Mania*, *Faces*, *Metal Edge*, and *RIP*.

29. See Steven Simels, *Gender Chameleons: Androgyny in Rock 'n' Roll* (New York: Timbre Books, 1985). In 1987 the same costume designer was employed by both the metal band W.A.S.P. and Liberace (Anne M. Raso, "Video: Behind the Reel," *Rock Scene*, July 1987, p. 68).

30. Fredric Jameson, "Reification and Utopia in Mass Culture," *Social Text* 1:1 (1979), pp. 130–48.

31. Dick Hebdige, *Subculture: The Meaning of Style* (New York: Methuen, 1979), p. 17.

32. John Stix, "Ready or Not," *Guitar for the Practicing Musician*, March 1989, p. 56.

33. Roberta Smoodin, "Crazy like David Lee Roth," *Playgirl*, August 1986, p. 43.

34. Dave Marsh, ed., *The First Rock & Roll Confidential Report* (New York: Pantheon, 1985), p. 165.

35. Kim of Cathedral City, *RIP*, February 1989, p. 6.

36. Ray R., Winter Springs, Fl., *RIP*, May 1989, p. 6.

37. Scott, interview with author, 30 June 1989, St. Paul, Minn.

38. Besides observing this behavior among members of various bands, I discussed it openly with musicians during two interviews. Such behavior is equally widespread among orchestral musicians; indeed, it occurs whenever men transgress against hegemonic norms of masculinity by acting expressive, sensitive, or spectacular.

39. George Sulmers, "Anthrax: Metal's Most Diseased Band," *The Best of Metal Mania #2* (1987), p. 24.

40. Sheryl Garratt has argued that women identify with androgynous male musicians because they can dress like them and act like them. See Sue Steward and Sheryl Garratt, *Signed, Sealed, and Delivered: True Life Stories of Women in Pop* (Boston: South End Press, 1984), p. 144.

41. Kaja Silverman, "Fragments of a Fashionable Discourse," in *Studies in Entertainment*, ed., Tania Modleski (Bloomington: Indiana University Press, 1986), pp. 139–52.

42. For a critical view of this position, see Rita Felski, *Beyond Feminist Aesthetics: Feminist Literature and Social Change* (Cambridge, Mass.: Harvard University Press, 1989). Felski's criticism of avant-garde strategies of textual disruption as political action rests on her perception of a conflation of gender and class: avant-garde art is as elitist as anything it might challenge. It is worth noting that the same problem hardly exists with heavy metal.

43. See Jane Flax, "Postmodernism and Gender Relations in Feminist Theory," in *Feminism/Postmodernism*, ed. Linda J. Nicholson (New York: Routledge, Chapman, & Hall, 1990), pp. 39–62.

44. Pat Benatar discusses the difficulty of creating her own hard rock image: "I never considered the character [I play] to be a sex symbol. I just was looking for extreme strength and self-assuredness. . . . I listened to a lot of male-dominated groups like the Stones and Led Zeppelin. There weren't a lot of women around to emulate, no one female figure, so I took a shot in the dark and tried to figure out a way to do this without looking stupid and victimized" (Joe Smith, *Off the Record* (New York: Warner Books, 1988), pp. 406–407). See also Lisa A. Lewis, *Gender Politics and MTV: Voicing the Difference* (Philadelphia: Temple University Press, 1990), especially chapter five.

45. Laurel Fishman, "Lita Ford," *Metal*, May 1988, pp. 36–38. One fan told me that she was contemptuous of Ford and other female metal musicians because they are "stupid sex objects" but that she also saw some of the male musicians the same way (Rita, interview with author, 30 June 1989).

46. For writings that focus on female reception of heavy metal and hard rock, see Daniel J. Hadley, "'Girls on Top': Women and Heavy Metal," paper presented at the Feminist Theory and Music Conference, University of Minnesota, June 1991, and Lisa Lewis, *Gender Politics and MTV*, especially pp. 149–71.

Both Hadley and Lewis discuss the fanzine *Bitch*, wherein female heavy metal fans debated the meanings of their own involvement with metal.

47. Sue Wise, "Sexing Elvis," in *On Record: Rock, Pop, and the Written Word* ed. Simon Frith and Andrew Goodwin (New York: Pantheon, 1990), pp. 390–98.

48. This was debated at length during the author's interview with Lisa, Tammy, and Larry, 30 June 1989.

49. From her cross-cultural study of androgyny, Wendy Doniger O'Flaherty asserts that the androgyne expresses "conflict between one sex's need for and fear of the other, . . . primarily the male's need for and fear of the female." She concludes: "Dangling before us the sweet promise of equality and balance, symbiosis and mutuality, the androgyne, under closer analysis, often furnishes bitter testimony to conflict and aggression, tension and disequilibrium" (*Women, Androgynes, and Other Mythical Beasts* [Chicago: University of Chicago Press, 1980], pp. 331, 334).

50. See, for example, the letter from "Hard Rockin' and Homosexual, Boston, Massachusetts," in *RIP*, August 1989, p. 5; and a letter decrying sexism in metal by a female musician in *RIP*, May 1989, p. 5.

51. Philip Gordon, "Review of Tipper Gore's *Raising PG Kids in an X-Rated Society* and *Dee Snider's Teenage Survival Guide*," *Popular Music* 8:1 (January 1989), p. 122.

52. Kaplan, *Rocking around the Clock*, p. 72.

53. Fred Pfeil, "Postmodernism as a 'Structure of Feeling,'" in *Marxism and the Interpretation of Culture*, ed. Cary Nelson and Lawrence Grossberg (Urbana: University of Illinois Press, 1988), pp. 381–403.

54. Fiske, *Television Culture*, p. 317. Moreover, such explorations are not unique to capitalist societies, nor are they reducible to epiphenomena of commerciality. From his study of the music of the Venda people of South Africa, ethnomusicologist John Blacking learned that fantastic music is not an escape from reality; it is a creative exploration of reality, and of other possibilities (*How Musical Is Man?* [Seattle: University of Washington Press, 1973], p. 28).

55. Simon Frith and Angela McRobbie, "Rock and Sexuality," *Screen Education* 29 (1978–79), pp. 3–19.

56. See George Lipsitz, *Time Passages: Collective Memory and American Popular Culture* (Minneapolis: University of Minnesota Press, 1990), p. 102.

Chapter 5. Can I Play with Madness? (Notes to Pages 137–71)

1. Charles Baudelaire, "To the Reader," in *The Flowers of Evil: A Selection*, ed. Marthiel and Jackson Mathews (New York: New Directions, 1958), p. 3; this translation is by Roy Campbell.

2. See the excerpt from Quintilian's writings in Piero Weiss and Richard Taruskin, eds., *Music in the Western World: A History in Documents* (New York: Schirmer, 1984), pp. 12–15.

3. See James R. McDonald, "Censoring Rock Lyrics: A Historical Analysis of the Debate," *Youth and Society* 19:3 (March 1988); pp. 294–313.

4. Tipper Gore, *Raising PG Kids in an X-Rated Society* (Nashville, Tenn.: Abingdon Press, 1987). Snider, the lead singer for the heavy metal band Twisted Sister, has even written a book to help adolescents cope with their problems: Dee Snider and Philip Bashe, *Dee Snider's Teenage Survival Guide* (Garden City, N.Y.: Doubleday, 1987).

5. Gore, *Raising PG Kids*, p. 19. Subcultures and countercultures are often seen as marking a crisis in authority; a more useful formulation conceives of

such crises as breakdowns in the "reproduction of culture-class relations and identities." See John Clarke, Stuart Hall, Tony Jefferson, and Brian Roberts, "Sub Cultures, Cultures, and Class," in *Culture, Ideology and Social Process: A Reader*, ed. Tony Bennett, Graham Martin, Colin Mercer, and Janet Woollacott (London: B. T. Batsford, 1981), p. 73.

6. Joe Stuessy, "The Heavy Metal User's Manual," 18 pages, photocopied and privately circulated. Stuessy is professor of music at the University of Texas at San Antonio. I wish to thank him for sending me copies of his pamphlet and his notes for his Senate testimony.

7. Joe Stuessy, notes for testimony to U.S. Senate Commerce Committee, 19 September 1985, p. 6.

8. This sample includes all of the lyrics printed in *Hit Parader's Metal of the 80s*, Spring 1990, and *Hit Parader's Top 100 Metal Albums*, Spring 1989. Of course, lyrics about drugs can be at once moralistic and celebratory, which is why I offer this survey of lyrics only to make a limited point about the sorts of topics that are typically addressed in metal songs. *Interpretation* of songs must be much more complex. But critics' hysteria notwithstanding, as Jon Pareles says, "In all of rock, there are probably fewer songs about bestiality than about molecular biology" (*New York Times*, 11 February 1990, p. H30).

9. Harry Shapiro, *Waiting for the Man: The Story of Drugs and Popular Music* (New York: William Morrow, 1988), p. 121.

10. See Paul E. Willis, "The Cultural Meaning of Drug Use," in Stuart Hall and Tony Jefferson, eds., *Resistance Through Rituals: Youth Subcultures in Post-War Britain* (London: Hutchinson, 1976), pp. 106–18.

11. See, for example, the comments by Accept's Stefan Kaufmann in *The Best of Metal Mania #2* (1987), p. 66, and by star drummer Tommy Aldridge in Andy Doerschuk, "The Big Heavy Picture," *Drums and Drumming*, August/September 1990, p. 47.

12. Peter F. Ostwald, *Schumann: The Inner Voices of a Musical Genius* (Boston: Northeastern University Press, 1985), p. 191.

13. Stuessy, "User's Manual," p. 16.

14. Stuessy, "User's Manual," p. 6.

15. Stuessy, testimony, p. 8.

16. Berlioz ends his symphony with the triumphant frenzy of a witches' Sabbath.

17. The creation of "classical music" and its aesthetic ideology have been discussed in previous chapters.

18. Carl A. Raschke, *Painted Black: From Drug Killings to Heavy Metal—the Alarming True Story of How Satanism Is Terrorizing Our Communities* (San Francisco: Harper & Row, 1990), p. 170. Compare Dan Peters and Steve Peters, with Cher Merrill, *Why Knock Rock?* (Minneapolis: Bethany House, 1984); Steve Lawhead, *Rock of This Age: The Real and Imagined Dangers of Rock Music* (Downers Grove, Ill.: InterVarsity Press, 1987); Bob Larson, *Larson's Book of Rock* (Wheaton, Ill.: Tyndale House, 1987).

19. Raschke, *Painted Black*, pp. 56, 170, 244.

20. Raschke, *Painted Black*, p. 170. Raschke incorrectly cites the source of the article.

21. Raschke, *Painted Black*, p. 175.

22. Raschke, *Painted Black*, p. 246. Another study has charged that right-wing and religious groups have manufactured the Satanist threat; its authors claim that there are fewer than one thousand actual Satanists in the United States, that they are members of a religion protected by the First Amendment, and that none of them has been linked to any ritual crimes. See David Alexan-

der, "Giving the Devil More Than His Due," *The Humanist*, March/April 1990, pp. 5–14, 34.

23. For a real cause of statistically significant suicide, we might look to deindustrialization: "In the aftermath of the Federal Mogul Corporation closing of its roller-bearing plant in Detroit, eight of the nearly 2,000 affected workers took their own lives. This macabre statistic is unfortunately not unusual. In their study of displaced workers, Cobb and Kasl found a suicide rate 'thirty times the expected number'" (Barry Bluestone and Bennett Harrison, *The Deindustrialization of America: Plant Closings, Community Abandonment, and the Dismantling of Basic Industry* [New York: Basic Books, 1982], p. 65).

24. Raschke, *Painted Black*, p. 164. Ephasis added.

25. See *Rock and Roll Confidential*, September 1991, p. 2.

26. Gore, *Raising PG Kids*, p. 118.

27. "Portrait," *The Chronicle of Higher Education*, 9 January 1991, p. A3.

28. See Jane Fulcher, *The Nation's Image: French Grand Opera as Politics and Politicized Art* (Cambridge: Cambridge University Press, 1987), pp. 38, 88, 101–2; and Lawrence W. Levine, *Highbrow/Lowbrow: The Emergence of Cultural Hierarchy in America* (Cambridge, Mass.: Harvard University Press, 1988), pp. 61–65, 91.

29. Deena Weinstein, *Heavy Metal: A Cultural Sociology* (New York: Lexington Books, 1991), p. 181.

30. Jonathon S. Epstein, David J. Pratto, and James K. Skipper, Jr., "Teenagers, Behavioral Problems, and Preferences for Heavy Metal and Rap Music: A Case Study of a Southern Middle School," *Deviant Behavior* 11 (1990), pp. 381–94.

31. For a striking ethnographic refutation of this view, see the forthcoming collection of interviews with a variety of people about how they use music in their lives: *My Music*, edited by Susan D. Crafts, Daniel Cavicchi, and Charles Keil, to be published in 1993 by University Press of New England.

32. Jack Sholder (director), *The Hidden* (New Line Cinema and Heron Communications, 1987).

33. Ivan Solotaroff, "Subliminal Criminals: Judas Priest in the Promised Land," *Village Voice*, 4 September 1990, pp. 24–34.

34. The Editors of Rock & Roll Confidential, *You've Got a Right to Rock* (Duke & Duchess Ventures, 1990), p. 21.

35. *Minneapolis Star/Tribune*, 18 July 1990.

36. Dean Kuipers, "Executioner's Song," *Spin*, November 1990, p. 66.

37. Doug Ireland, "Press Clips," *Village Voice*, 20 March 1990, p. 9. Key was taken very seriously by many people; he also appeared on CNN's Larry King Live and in Jack Anderson's syndicated column.

38. John R. Vokey and J. B. Read, "Subliminal Messages: Between the Devil and the Media," *American Psychologist* 40:11 (1985), pp. 1231–39. See also S. B. Thorne and P. Himelstein, "The Role of Suggestion in the Reception of Satanic Messages in Rock and Roll Recordings," *Journal of Psychology* 116 (1984), pp. 245–48.

39. Solotaroff, "Subliminal Criminals," p. 34.

40. Kuipers, "Executioner's Song," p. 66.

41. See *Variety*, 6 November 1985, p. 2. Another suit concerning the same song was filed in 1989, but as in the Judas Priest case, the plaintiff alleged that subliminal messages were at fault rather than lyrics.

42. Including Heinrich Schütz, who used antiphonal choirs to achieve precisely that effect in his "Saul, Saul, was verfolgst du mich?" from his *Symphoniae Sacrae III* of 1650.

43. In a typical display of "Let's be nice and not talk about bad things" reactionary politics, *The Rock Rating Report*, endorsed by the PMRC, gave Phil Collins an extremely negative rating for opposing homelessness (The Editors of Rock & Roll Confidential, *You've Got a Right to Rock*, pp. 20–21).

44. Kuipers, "Executioner's Song," p. 66.

45. Solotaroff, "Subliminal Criminals," p. 34.

46. Patrick Goldstein, "Is Rock a Scapegoat for Teen Suicide?" *Los Angeles Times Calendar*, Sunday, 8 May 1988, p. 98.

47. David Fricke, "Heavy Metal Justice," *Rolling Stone*, 12 January 1989, p. 77. Another fan told me that "Fade to Black" made him realize how stupid suicide would be and helped get him motivated to make something of his life.

48. Gene Hoglan, quoted in Mike Gitter, "The Hellish Thrash of Dark Angel," *RIP*, June 1989, p. 94.

49. *New York Times*, 10 February 1985, p. A23.

50. Donna Gaines, *Teenage Wasteland: Suburbia's Dead End Kids* (New York: Pantheon, 1990), p. 253.

51. George H. Gallup, Jr., and Frank Newport, "Belief in Paranormal Phenomena among Adult Americans," *Sceptical Inquirer* 15:2 (Winter 1991), pp. 137–46. Catholics and members of some other denominations, of course, are required to believe in the Devil.

52. Mary Toledo, "Roll Over Lugosi," *The Best of Metal Mania #2* (1987), p. 84.

53. Rita, interview with author, 30 June 1989, Maplewood, Minn.

54. Both of these songs appear on *Live after Death* (1985).

55. For the former, see "No Prayer for the Dying" and "Fates Warning" on *No Prayer for the Dying* (1990). On the topics of violence and combat, see, for example, "Tailgunner," "Run Silent," and "Assassin," from *No Prayer for the Dying* (1990), and "Aces High," "Flash of the Blade," and "The Duellists," from *Powerslave* (1984).

56. As he appears on the cover of *Seventh Son of a Seventh Son*, Eddie is the best illustration I've seen of what Deleuze and Guattari call "the body without organs"—or in this case, the body with organs à la carte.

57. Eddie made his usual appearance at the concert I attended in 1988, garbed this time in a mummy's rags, but the band seems to be tiring of him, and his manifestation was perfunctory that night.

58. See Fredric Jameson, "Postmodernism and Consumer Society," in *The Anti-Aethetic: Essays on Postmodern Culture*, ed. Hal Foster (Port Townsend, Wash.: Bay Press, 1983), pp. 111–25. Jameson has since retreated somewhat from this position; see his revision of this essay in his *Postmodernism, or, The Cultural Logic of Late Capitalism* (Durham, N.C.: Duke University Press, 1991), pp. 1–54. Jameson's earlier formulation remains influential, however.

59. Gaines, *Teenage Wasteland*, p. 183.

60. Roy Porter, *A Social History of Madness: The World through the Eyes of the Insane* (New York: E. P. Dutton, 1989), pp. 3, 25. Artists have often cultivated madness or its signs, particularly in the nineteenth century. Porter describes Robert Schumann's engagement with artistic madness:

> What first drew attention to him as a musician was his astonishing gift of improvising at the piano, especially his capacity to conjure up music which perfectly captured someone's mood or character. This he called "fantasizing" or "mad improvising." He would often describe such elation as a form of madness. As such it was a hallmark of his genius. This was not merely an affectation, an adolescent self-indulgence. Rather it was a crucial milepost in the attempt to establish an identity which would advance his career, win

acceptance and recognition, and fulfill his "promise." . . . It was [also] a way of coming to terms with a deep unease towards the world." (p. 66)

61. Wolf Marshall discusses this characteristic rhythmic pattern in "Music Appreciation: Iron Maiden," *Guitar for the Practicing Musician*, January 1989, pp. 112–16.

62. Dave Marsh has tried to convince me that there is only one possible interpretation of McLean's lyrics, but surely many people have enjoyed this song while understanding it "incorrectly"—me, for instance.

63. Dana Polan, "Postmodernism and Cultural Analysis Today," in *Postmodernism and Its Discontents: Theories, Practices*, ed. E. Ann Kaplan (New York: Verso, 1988), p. 53.

64. Teri Saccone, "Somewhere on the Light Side of the Moon," *Rock Scene*, July 1987, p. 64.

65. Gaines, *Teenage Wasteland*, p. 254.

66. Stephen King, *Four Past Midnight* (New York: Penguin, 1990), p. 608.

67. See James B. Twitchell, *Dreadful Pleasures: An Anatomy of Modern Horror* (New York: Oxford University Press, 1985), and Noël Carroll, *The Philosophy of Horror, or, Paradoxes of the Heart* (New York: Routledge, 1990).

68. See Michael Ryan and Douglas Kellner, *Camera Politica: The Politics and Ideology of Contemporary Hollywood Film* (Bloomington: Indiana University Press, 1988), p. 170. Stephen King makes the same point in his analytical history of horror, *Stephen King's Danse Macabre* (New York: Berkeley Books, 1981), p. 28.

69. Ryan and Kellner, *Camera Politica*, p. 170.

70. Barbara Ehrenreich, "Marginal Men," in *The Worst Years of Our Lives* (New York: Pantheon, 1990), pp. 208–12.

71. *Rock & Roll Confidential*, January 1989, p. 8. That metal audiences have been gender-balanced since the mid-1980s may owe something to the fact that many women are finding such economic statistics more directly relevant to their lives than ever before.

72. Alexander Cockburn, "Beat the Devil," *The Nation*, 18 June 1990, p. 846.

73. Tim Wise, "Accounts Payable," *The Nation*, 18 June 1990, p. 845.

74. Barbara Ehrenreich, *Fear of Falling: The Inner Life of the Middle Class* (New York: HarperCollins, 1990), p. 205. Needless to say, economic security and social well-being in the United Kingdom, the most important source and site of heavy metal culture after the United States, also have dwindled.

75. John Podhoretz, "Metallic Rock That's Designed to Shock," *U.S. News and World Report*, 7 September 1987, p. 50. There are exceptions; during one interview I conducted, discussion turned to nuclear war, and one fan's comments reflected a nihilism born of helplessness and alienation from those who have the power to "vaporize us any minute." "Just get it over with," he said; "I've often wanted them to do that; felt like, all right, push the button right now; it'd be cool." But the other fans in the group disagreed emphatically. (Five metal fans, interview with the author, Spring Lake Park, Minn., 7 July 1988). All the same, nihilism is a complex concept: "The true nihilists are the ones who oppose nihilism with their more and more faded positivities, the ones who are thus conspiring with all extant malice, and eventually with the destructive principle itself. Thought honors itself by defending what is damned as nihilism" (Theodor W. Adorno, *Negative Dialectics* [New York: Continuum, 1973], p. 381). Nihilism is always political; James C. Scott relates: "Alice Walker began a speech at a nuclear disarmament rally with . . . an effort to explain why many blacks were not much interested in signing nuclear freeze petitions. Their 'hope for revenge' made them look on nuclear destruction brought about by a white-ruled world with equanimity if not malevolent pleasure. One has, she implies,

no right expecting civic spiritedness from those whose experience of community has mostly been that of victims" (James C. Scott, *Domination and the Arts of Resistance: Hidden Transcripts* [New Haven, Conn.: Yale University Press, 1990], p. 43).

76. Marty Jezer, *The Dark Ages: Life in the United States 1945–1960* (Boston: South End Press, 1982), p. 237.

77. John Fiske, *Understanding Popular Culture* (Boston: Unwin Hyman, 1989), pp. 134–35.

78. Compare Jeffrey Arnett's finding that metal fans are best categorized politically as libertarian, in "Adolescents and Heavy Metal Music: From the Mouths of Metalheads," *Youth & Society* 23:1 (September 1991), p. 90.

79. Danny Sugerman, *Appetite for Destruction: The Days of Guns N' Roses* (New York: St. Martin's Press, 1991).

80. Sugerman, *Appetite for Destruction*, pp. 92, 96.

81. Sugerman, *Appetite for Destruction*, p. 108. For similar interpretations of rock music, see also Jerry Hopkins and Daniel Sugerman, *No One Here Gets Out Alive* (New York: Warner Books, 1980), and Oliver Stone's film, *The Doors* (1991). Deena Weinstein also mystifies and depoliticizes heavy metal in just this way in her book *Heavy Metal*, especially pp. 35–43.

82. It should not be but probably is necessary to state that by discussing and quoting Marx I am not signaling my endorsement of any of the social plans that have been proposed or attacked in his name. Every social/economic system has its hazards, and Marx's critique of capitalism still offers insights into the pains and joys of contemporary culture.

83. Marshall Berman, *All That Is Solid Melts into Air: The Experience of Modernity* (New York: Simon and Schuster, 1982), p. 102.

84. Berman, *All That Is Solid*, p. 118. Of course, Rose and Berman have different projects and intentions; I am bracketing them to see what we can learn by taking them equally seriously, for strict divisions between "high" and "low" culture (which are constructed categories serving particular interests) conceal more than they reveal.

85. Berman, *All That Is Solid*, p. 102.

86. Karl Marx and Frederick Engels, *Manifesto of the Communist Party* (1848; reprint, Moscow: Progress Publishers, 1971) pp. 34–35. Along with the difficulties faced by struggling bands everywhere, there is "pay-for-play" in L.A.— bands often have to pay club owners as much as $800 in exchange for the exposure gained from being allowed to play a 45-minute set at an important venue. This figure is drawn from my interviews with a number of L.A. metal bands; see also Janiss Garcia, "Guns N' Roses," *Guitar for the Practicing Musician*, February 1989, pp. 81–90.

87. Sugerman, *Appetite for Destruction*, pp. 93, 85.

88. Quoted in Sugerman, *Appetite for Destruction*, p. 63.

89. Sugerman dwells on this idea throughout his book. An earlier book tried to explain rock music entirely in these terms: Robert Pattison, *The Triumph of Vulgarity: Rock Music in the Mirror of Romanticism* (New York: Oxford University Press, 1987).

90. Sugerman, *Appetite for Destruction*, p. 102.

91. Examples abound in recent popular music; two of the most effective are Dolly Parton's "9 to 5" (1980) and Madonna's "Like a Prayer" (1989).

92. Berman, *All That Is Solid*, p. 23.

93. Richard Taruskin, "Facing Up, Finally, to Bach's Dark Vision," *New York Times*, 25 January 1991, p. 28.

94. Taruskin, "Facing Up," p. 28. Here Taruskin follows in the footsteps

of Theodor Adorno and Susan McClary, both of whom have published essays that strive to reclaim the noise and politics of Bach's music. See Theodor W. Adorno, "Bach Defended against His Devotees," in *Prisms* (Cambridge, Mass.: MIT Press, 1981), pp. 133–46; and Susan McClary, "The Blasphemy of Talking Politics during Bach Year," in *Music and Society: The Politics of Composition, Performance, and Reception*, ed. Richard Leppert and Susan McClary (Cambridge: Cambridge University Press, 1987), pp. 13–62.

Select Discography

❋

AC/DC. *High Voltage*. Atco, 1976.
———. *Highway to Hell*. Atlantic, 1979.
———. *Back in Black*. Atlantic, 1980.
———. *Dirty Deeds Done Dirt Cheap*. Atlantic, 1981.
———. *For Those About to Rock We Salute You*. Atlantic, 1981.
———. *Blow Up Your Video*. Atlantic, 1988.
———. *The Razors Edge*. Atco, 1990.
Accept. *Accept*. Passport, 1980.
———. *Balls to the Wall*. Portrait/CBS, 1984.
———. *Russian Roulette*. Portrait/CBS, 1986.
Aerosmith. *Rocks*. Columbia, 1976.
———. *Permanent Vacation*. Geffen, 1987.
Alice Cooper. *Love It to Death*. Warner Bros., 1971.
Anthrax. *State of Euphoria*. Megaforce/Island, 1988.
———. *Persistence of Time*. Megaforce/Island, 1990.
Black Sabbath. *Black Sabbath*. Warner Bros., 1970.
———. *Paranoid*. Warner Bros., 1970.
———. *Sabbath Bloody Sabbath*. Warner Bros., 1974.
———. *Never Say Die!* Warner Bros., 1978.
Blue Cheer. *Vincebus Eruptum*. Philips, 1968.

———. *Louder Than God*. Rhino, 1986.
Blue Öyster Cult. *Agents of Fortune*. Columbia, 1976.
Bon Jovi. *7800° Fahrenheit*. Mercury, 1985.
———. *Slippery When Wet*. Mercury, 1986.
———. *New Jersey*. Mercury, 1988.
Cacophony. *Speed Metal Symphony*. Shrapnel, 1987.
Celtic Frost. *"Into the Pandemonium."* Combat, 1987.
Cinderella. *Long Cold Winter*. Mercury, 1988.
Deep Purple. *Deep Purple in Rock*. Harvest, 1970.
———. *Machine Head*. Warner Bros., 1972.
———. *Perfect Strangers*. Polydor, 1984.
Def Leppard. *Pyromania*. Mercury, 1983.
———. *Hysteria*. Mercury, 1987.
Dio. *The Last in Line*. Warner Bros., 1984.
Dokken. *Tooth and Nail*. Elektra, 1984.
———. *Back for the Attack*. Elektra, 1987.
Ford, Lita. *Lita*. BMG, 1988.
Girlschool. *Screaming Blue Murder*. Mercury, 1982.
Guns N' Roses. *Appetite for Destruction*. Geffen, 1987.

———. *G N' R Lies*. Geffen, 1988.
Hendrix, Jimi. *The Essential Jimi Hendrix*. Reprise, 1989.
Impaler. *Rise of the Mutants*. Important, 1985.
Iron Butterfly. *In-A-Gadda-Da-Vida*. Atco, 1968.
Iron Maiden. *The Number of the Beast*. EMI, 1982.
———. *Powerslave*. Capitol, 1984.
———. *Live after Death*. Capitol, 1985.
———. *Seventh Son of a Seventh Son*. EMI, 1988.
———. *No Prayer for the Dying*. Epic, 1990.
The Jimi Hendrix Experience. *Are You Experienced?* Reprise, 1967.
Judas Priest. *Sin after Sin*. Columbia, 1977.
———. *Stained Class*. Columbia, 1978.
———. *Unleashed in the East*. Columbia, 1979.
———. *British Steel*. Columbia, 1980.
———. *Point of Entry*. Columbia, 1981.
———. *Screaming for Vengeance*. Columbia, 1982.
———. *Defenders of the Faith*. Columbia, 1984.
———. *Turbo*. Columbia, 1986.
———. *Ram It Down*. Columbia, 1988.
———. *Painkiller*. Columbia, 1990.
King Diamond. *Fatal Portrait*. Roadracer, 1986.
Kiss. *Alive*. Casablanca, 1975.
———. *Destroyer*. Casablanca, 1976.
Krokus. *One Vice at a Time*. Arista, 1982.
Led Zeppelin. *Led Zeppelin*. Atlantic, 1969.
———. *Led Zeppelin II*. Atlantic, 1969.
———. *Led Zeppelin III*. Atlantic, 1970.
———. *ZOSO [IV]*. Atlantic, 1971.
———. *Physical Graffiti*. Swan Song, 1975.
Living Colour. *Vivid*. Epic, 1988.
———. *Time's Up*. Epic, 1990.

Loudness. *Thunder in the East*. Atco, 1985.
Lynch Mob. *Wicked Sensation*. Elektra, 1990.
Megadeth. *Peace Sells . . . But Who's Buying?* Combat/EMI, 1986.
———. *so far, so good . . . so what!* Combat/Capitol, 1988.
———. *Rust in Peace*. Combat/Capitol, 1990.
Metallica. *Kill 'Em All*. Important, 1983.
———. *Ride the Lightning*. Megaforce/Elektra, 1984.
———. *Master of Puppets*. Elektra, 1986.
———. *. . . And Justice for All*. Elektra, 1988.
———. *Metallica*. Elektra, 1991.
Michael Schenker Group. *MSG*. Chrysalis, 1981.
Mötley Crüe. *Shout at the Devil*. Elektra, 1983.
———. *Theatre of Pain*. Elektra, 1985.
———. *Girls, Girls, Girls*. Elektra, 1987.
Motörhead. *Live: No Sleep 'til Hammersmith*. Mercury, 1981.
———. *No Sleep at All*. Enigma/GWR, 1988.
MX Machine. *Manic Panic*. Restless Records, 1988.
Nazareth. *2XS*. A&M, 1982.
Nugent, Ted. *Great Gonzos: The Best of Ted Nugent*. Epic, 1981.
———. *If You Can't Lick 'Em . . . Lick 'Em*. Atlantic, 1988.
Ozzy Osbourne. *Blizzard of Ozz*. Jet/CBS, 1981.
———. *Diary of a Madman*. Jet/CBS, 1981.
———. *The Ultimate Sin*. CBS, 1986.
———. *No Rest for the Wicked*. CBS, 1988.
———. *Just Say Ozzy*. CBS, 1990.
———. *No More Tears*. Epic Associated, 1991.
Ozzy Osbourne/Randy Rhoads. *Tribute*. CBS, 1987 [recorded in 1981].
Poison. *Look What the Cat Dragged In*. Enigma, 1986.

———. *Open Up and Say . . . Ahh!*
Enigma/Capitol, 1988.
Pokolgép. *Pokoli Szinjáték.* Start
(Hungary), 1987.
Possessed. *Beyond the Gates.* Combat, 1986.
Queensrÿche. *Operation: Mindcrime.*
EMI-Manhattan, 1988.
Quiet Riot. *Metal Health.* Pasha,
1983.
Racer X. *Street Lethal.* Shrapnel, 1986.
Rainbow. *Ritchie Blackmore's Rainbow.* Polydor, 1975.
———. *Difficult to Cure.* Polydor, 1981.
Ratt. *Out of the Cellar.* Atlantic, 1984.
Roth, David Lee. *Crazy from the
Heat.* Warner Bros., 1985.
———. *Eat 'Em and Smile.* Warner
Bros., 1986.
———. *Skyscraper.* Warner Bros.,
1988.
———. *A Little Ain't Enough.* Warner
Bros., 1991.
Rush. *Moving Pictures.* Mercury, 1981.
Satriani, Joe. *Surfing with the Alien.*
Relativity, 1987.
———. *Flying in a Blue Dream.*
Relativity, 1989.
Scorpions. *In Trance.* RCA, 1976.
———. *Love at First Sting.* Mercury, 1984.
———. *Savage Amusement.* Mercury, 1988.
Slave Raider. *What Do You Know
about Rock 'n Roll?* BMG, 1988.
Slayer. *South of Heaven.* Def Jam,
1988.
———. *Seasons in the Abyss.* Def
American, 1990.

Steppenwolf. *Steppenwolf.* Stateside, 1968.
———. *16 Greatest Hits.* MCA, 1973.
Stryper. *To Hell with the Devil.*
Enigma, 1986.
Testament. *Souls of Black.* Megaforce/
Atlantic, 1990.
Twisted Sister. *Under the Blade.* Roadrunner, 1982.
———. *Stay Hungry.* Atlantic, 1984.
UFO. *Obsession.* Chrysalis, 1978.
Van Halen. *Van Halen.* Warner
Bros., 1978.
———. *Van Halen II.* Warner
Bros., 1979.
———. *Diver Down.* Warner Bros.,
1982.
———. *1984.* Warner Bros., 1983.
———. *5150.* Warner Bros., 1986.
———. *OU812.* Warner Bros., 1988.
Vinnie Vincent. *Invasion.*
Chrysalis, 1986.
Virus. *Pray for War.* Metalworks,
1987.
Voivod. *Dimension Hatröss.* Noise
International, 1988.
W.A.S.P. *Live . . . in the Raw.* Capitol, 1987.
———. *The Headless Children.* Capitol, 1989.
Warlock. *True as Steel.* Mercury, 1986.
Whitesnake. *Whitesnake.* Geffen,
1987.
———. *Slip of the Tongue.*
Geffen, 1989.
Y&T. *In Rock We Trust.* A&M, 1984.
Yngwie J. Malmsteen's Rising Force.
Yngwie J. Malmsteen's Rising Force.
Polydor, 1984.
———. *Odyssey.* Polydor, 1988.

Select Bibliography

✳

Adorno, Theodor W. *Prisms*. Cambridge, Mass.: MIT Press, 1981.
Aledort, Andy. "The Bach Influence." *Guitar for the Practicing Musician*, May 1985, pp. 30–31.
———. "Thrashing It Out." *Guitar for the Practicing Musician*, March 1988, pp. 62–64.
Armington, Nick, and Lars Lofas. "The Genesis of Metal." *Drums and Drumming*, August/September 1990, pp. 21–25, 27, 62–64.
Arnett, Jeffrey. "Adolescents and Heavy Metal Music: From the Mouths of Metalheads." *Youth & Society* 23:1 (September 1991), pp. 76–98.
Bakhtin, M. M. *The Dialogic Imagination*. Austin: University of Texas Press, 1981.
———. *Speech Genres and Other Late Essays*. Edited by Caryl Emerson and Michael Holquist. Austin: University of Texas Press, 1986.
Bangs, Lester. "Heavy Metal." In *The Rolling Stone Illustrated History of Rock & Roll*, 2d ed., edited by Jim Miller, pp. 332–35. New York: Random House, 1980.
Bashe, Philip. *Heavy Metal Thunder*. Garden City, N.Y.: Doubleday, 1985.
Berger, John, Sven Blomberg, Chris Fox, Michael Dibb, and Richard Hollis. *Ways of Seeing*. London: British Broadcasting Corporation, 1972.
Berman, Marshall. *All That Is Solid Melts Into Air: The Experience of Modernity*. New York: Simon and Schuster, 1982.
Blacking, John. *How Musical Is Man?* Seattle: University of Washington Press, 1973.
Blanchet, Philippe. *Heavy Metal Story*. Paris: Calmann-Levy, 1985.
Bluestone, Barry, and Bennett Harrison. *The Deindustrialization of America: Plant Closings, Community Abandonment, and the Dismantling of Basic Industry*. New York: Basic Books, 1982.
Breen, Marcus. "A Stairway to Heaven or a Highway to Hell?: Heavy Metal Rock Music in the 1990s." *Cultural Studies* 5:2 (May 1991), pp. 191–203.
Brittan, Arthur. *Masculinity and Power*. New York: Basil Blackwell, 1989.
Chapple, Steve, and Reebee Garofalo. *Rock 'n' Roll Is Here to Pay*. Chicago: Nelson-Hall, 1977.
Chernoff, John. *African Rhythm and African Sensibility*. Chicago: University of Chicago Press, 1979.
Clifford, James, and George E. Marcus, eds. *Writing Culture: The Poetics and Politics of Ethnography*. Berkeley: University of California Press, 1986.

Considine, J. D. "Purity and Power." *Musician*, September 1984, pp. 46–50.

Duncan, Robert. *The Noise: Notes from a Rock 'n' Roll Era*. New York: Ticknor and Fields, 1984.

Eagleton, Terry. *The Ideology of the Aesthetic*. Cambridge, Mass.: Basil Blackwell.

Edelstein, Robert. "The Last Heroes of Rock 'n' Roll." *Gallery*, April 1989, pp. 40–45, 73.

Eddy, Chuck. *Stairway to Hell: The 500 Best Heavy Metal Albums in the Universe*. New York: Harmony Books, 1991.

Ehrenreich, Barbara. *Fear of Falling: The Inner Life of the Middle Class*. New York: Harper Collins, 1989.

———. *The Worst Years of Our Lives: Irreverent Notes from a Decade of Greed*. New York: Pantheon, 1990.

Epstein, Jonathon S., David J. Pratto, and James K. Skipper, Jr. "Teenagers, Behavioral Problems, and Preferences for Heavy Metal and Rap Music: A Case Study of a Southern Middle School." *Deviant Behavior* 11 (1990): 381–94.

Feld, Steven. *Sound and Sentiment: Birds, Weeping, Poetics, and Song in Kaluli Expression*, 2d ed. Philadelphia: University of Pennsylvania Press, 1990.

Fiske, John. "British Cultural Studies and Television." In *Channels of Discourse: Television and Contemporary Criticism*, edited by Robert C. Allen, pp. 254–89. Chapel Hill: University of North Carolina Press, 1987.

———. *Television Culture*. New York: Methuen, 1987.

———. *Understanding Popular Culture*. Boston: Unwin Hyman, 1989.

Foster, Hal, ed. *The Anti-Aesthetic: Essays on Postmodern Culture*. Port Townsend, Wash.: Bay Press, 1983.

Foucault, Michel. *Language, Counter-memory, Practice*. Edited by Donald F. Bouchard. Ithaca, N.Y.: Cornell University Press, 1977.

Frith, Simon. "Art Versus Technology: The Strange Case of Popular Music." *Media, Culture, and Society* 8 (1986), pp. 263–79.

———. *Sound Effects: Youth, Leisure, and the Politics of Rock 'n' Roll*. New York: Pantheon, 1981.

———. "Towards an Aesthetic of Popular Music." In *Music and Society: The Politics of Composition, Performance, and Reception*, edited by Richard Leppert and Susan McClary, pp. 133–49. Cambridge: Cambridge University Press, 1987.

Frith, Simon, and Andrew Goodwin, eds. *On Record: Rock, Pop, and the Written Word*. New York: Pantheon, 1990.

Frith, Simon, and Angela McRobbie. "Rock and Sexuality." *Screen Education* 29 (1978–79). Reprinted in Frith and Goodwin, eds., *On Record*, pp. 371–89.

Gaines, Donna. *Teenage Wasteland: Suburbia's Dead End Kids*. New York: Pantheon, 1991.

Garofalo, Reebee. "How Autonomous Is Relative: Popular Music, the Social Formation and Cultural Struggle." *Popular Music* 6:1 (January 1987), pp. 77–92.

———, ed. *Rockin' the Boat: Mass Music and Mass Movements*. Boston: South End Press, 1992.

Gore, Tipper. *Raising PG Kids in an X-Rated Society*. Nashville, Tenn.: Abingdon Press, 1987.

Gramsci, Antonio. *Selections from the Prison Notebooks*. Edited by Quinton Hoare and Geoffrey Nowell Smith. New York: International Publishers, 1971.

Greenberg, Keith Elliot. *Heavy Metal*. Minneapolis, Minn.: Lerner Publications, 1986.

Hadley, Daniel J. "'Girls on Top': Women and Heavy Metal." Unpublished paper, Department of Communications, Concordia University, Montreal, 1991.

Halbersberg, Elianne. *Heavy Metal*. Cresskill, N.J.: Sharon Publications, 1985.

Halfin, Ross, and Pete Makowski. *Heavy Metal: The Power Age*. New York: Delilah Books, 1982.

Hall, Stuart. "Notes on Deconstructing 'The Popular.'" In *People's History and Socialist Theory*, edited by Raphael Samuel, pp. 227–40. London: Routledge and Kegan Paul, 1981.

Hamm, Charles. *Music in the New World*. New York: W. W. Norton, 1983.

Harrigan, Brian. *HM A-Z: The Definitive Encyclopedia of Heavy Metal from AC/DC through Led Zeppelin to ZZ Top*. London: Bobcat Books, 1981.

Harrigan, Brian, and Malcolm Dome. *Encyclopedia Metallica*. London: Omnibus Press, 1986.

The Heavy Metal Photo Book. London: Omnibus Press, 1983.

Hebdige, Dick. *Subculture: The Meaning of Style*. New York: Methuen, 1979.

Hit Parader's Top 100 Metal Albums, Spring 1989.

Hobsbawm, Eric, and Terence Ranger, eds. *The Invention of Tradition*. New York: Cambridge University Press, 1983.

Jameson, Fredric. "Reification and Utopia in Mass Culture." *Social Text* 1:1 (1979), pp. 130–48.

Jasper, Tony, and Derek Oliver. *The International Encyclopedia of Hard Rock and Heavy Metal*. New York: Facts on File, 1983.

Johnson, Mark. *The Body in the Mind: The Bodily Basis of Meaning, Imagination, and Reason*. Chicago: University of Chicago Press, 1987.

Kaplan, E. Ann. *Rocking Around the Clock: Music Television, Postmodernism, and Consumer Culture*. New York: Methuen, 1987.

King, Stephen. *Stephen King's Danse Macabre*. New York: Berkeley Books, 1981.

Laing, Dave. *One Chord Wonders: Power and Meaning in Punk Rock*. Philadelphia: Open University Press, 1985.

Leggett, Carol. *The Heavy Metal Bible*. New York: Pinnacle Books, 1985.

Leppert, Richard, and Susan McClary, eds. *Music and Society: The Politics of Composition, Performance, and Reception*. Cambridge: Cambridge University Press, 1987.

Levine, Lawrence W. *Highbrow/Lowbrow: The Emergence of Cultural Hierarchy in America*. Cambridge, Mass.: Harvard University Press, 1988.

Lewis, Lisa A. *Gender Politics and MTV: Voicing the Difference*. Philadelphia: Temple University Press, 1990.

Lipsitz, George. "'Ain't Nobody Here But Us Chickens': The Class Origins of Rock and Roll." In *Class and Culture in Cold War America: "A Rainbow at Midnight,"* pp. 195–225. South Hadley, Mass.: Bergin and Garvey, 1982.

———. *Time Passages: Collective Memory and American Popular Culture*. Minneapolis: University of Minnesota Press, 1990.

Lomax, Alan. *Folk Song Style and Culture*. New Brunswick, N.J.: Transaction Books, 1968.

Marcus, George E., and Michael M. J. Fischer. *Anthropology as Cultural Critique: An Experimental Moment in the Human Sciences*. Chicago: University of Chicago Press, 1986.

Marcus, Greil. *Mystery Train: Images of America in Rock 'n' Roll Music*, rev. ed. New York: E. P. Dutton, 1982.

Marsh, Dave. *The Heart of Rock and Soul: The 1001 Greatest Singles Ever Made*. New York: Plume, 1989.

———, ed. *The First Rock & Roll Confidential Report*. New York: Pantheon, 1985.

Marshall, Wolf. ". . . And Justice for All." *Guitar for the Practicing Musician*, June 1989, pp. 81–86, 136–38.

———. "The Classical Influence." *Guitar for the Practicing Musician*, March 1988, pp. 98–99, 102.

———. "Music Appreciation: Iron Maiden." *Guitar for the Practicing Musician*, January 1989, pp. 112–16.

Martin, Linda, and Kerry Segrave. *Anti-Rock: The Opposition to Rock 'n' Roll*. Hamden, Conn.: Archon Books, 1988.

Marx, Karl. *Capital*, vol. 1. New York: International Publishers, 1967.

Marx, Karl, and Frederick Engels. *Manifesto of the Communist Party*. Moscow: Progress Publishers, 1971.

McClary, Susan. "The Blasphemy of Talking Politics during Bach Year." In *Music and Society: The Politics of Composition, Performance, and Reception*, edited by Richard Leppert and Susan McClary, pp. 13–62. Cambridge: Cambridge University Press, 1987.

———. *Feminine Endings: Music, Gender, and Sexuality*. Minneapolis: University of Minnesota Press, 1991.

McClary, Susan, and Robert Walser. "Start Making Sense: Musicology Wrestles with Rock." In *On Record: Rock, Pop, and the Written Word*, edited by Simon Frith and Andrew Goodwin, pp. 277–92. New York: Pantheon, 1990.

Middleton, Richard. *Studying Popular Music*. Philadelphia: Open University Press, 1990.

Mulvey, Laura. "Visual Pleasure and Narrative Cinema." In *Movies and Methods*, vol. 2, edited by Bill Nichols, pp. 303–15. Berkeley: University of California Press, 1985.

Murray, Charles Shaar. *Crosstown Traffic: Jimi Hendrix and the Rock 'n' Roll Revolution*. New York: St. Martin's Press, 1989.

Nattiez, Jean-Jacques. *Music and Discourse: Toward a Semiology of Music*. Princeton, N.J.: Princeton University Press, 1990.

Newcomb, Horace M. "On the Dialogic Aspects of Mass Communication." *Critical Studies in Mass Communication* 1 (1984), pp. 34–50.

Obrecht, Jas, ed. *Masters of Heavy Metal*. New York: Quill, 1984.

Pfeil, Fred. "Postmodernism as a 'Structure of Feeling.'" In *Marxism and the Interpretation of Culture*, edited by Cary Nelson and Lawrence Grossberg, pp. 381–403. Urbana: University of Illinois Press, 1988.

Pielke, Robert G. *You Say You Want a Revolution: Rock Music in American Culture*. Chicago: Nelson-Hall, 1986.

Porter, Roy. *A Social History of Madness: The World through the Eyes of the Insane*. New York: E. P. Dutton, 1987.

Prinsky, Lorraine E., and Jill Leslie Rosenbaum. "'Leer-ics' or Lyrics: Teenage Impressions of Rock 'n' Roll." *Youth & Society* 18 : 4 (June 1987), pp. 384–97.

Radway, Janice A. *Reading the Romance: Women, Patriarchy, and Popular Literature*. Chapel Hill: University of North Carolina Press, 1984.

Raschke, Carl A. *Painted Black: From Drug Killings to Heavy Metal—the Alarming True Story of How Satanism Is Terrorizing Our Communities*. New York: Harper and Row, 1990.

Ryan, Michael, and Douglas Kellner. *Camera Politica: The Politics and Ideology of Contemporary Hollywood Film*. Bloomington: Indiana University Press, 1988.

Secher, Andy. "Heavy Metal: The Hall of Fame." *Hit Parader*, December 1982, pp. 25–27.

Shapiro, Harry. *Waiting for the Man: The Story of Drugs and Popular Music*. New York: William Morrow, 1988.

Shepherd, John. *Music as Social Text*. Cambridge: Polity Press, 1991.

Silverman, Kaja. "Fragments of a Fashionable Discourse." In *Studies in Entertainment: Critical Approaches to Mass Culture*, edited by Tania Modleski, pp. 139–52. Bloomington: Indiana University Press, 1986.

Simels, Steven. *Gender Chameleons: Androgyny in Rock 'n' Roll*. New York: Timbre Books, 1985.

Small, Christopher. *Music–Society–Education*. London: John Calder, 1980.

————. *Music of the Common Tongue: Survival and Celebration in Afro-American Music*. New York: Riverrun, 1987.

Straw, Will. "Characterizing Rock Music Cultures: The Case of Heavy Metal." *Canadian University Music Review* 5 (1984), pp. 104–22.

Street, John. *Rebel Rock: The Politics of Popular Music*. New York: Basil Blackwell, 1986.

Stuessy, Joe. "The Heavy Metal User's Manual." Photocopied typescript, privately circulated, San Antonio, Texas, 1985.

Sugerman, Danny. *Appetite for Destruction: The Days of Guns N' Roses*. New York: St. Martin's Press, 1991.

Szatmary, David P. *Rockin' in Time: A Social History of Rock and Roll*. Englewood Cliffs, N.J.: Prentice-Hall, 1987.

Tagg, Philip. "Analyzing Popular Music: Theory, Method, and Practice." *Popular Music* 2 (1982), pp. 37–67.

————. *Kojak—50 Seconds of Television Music*. Göteborg, Sweden: Musikvetenskapliga Institutionen, 1979.

————. "Musicology and the Semiotics of Popular Music." *Semiotica* 66–1/3 (1987), pp. 279–98.

Todorov, Tzvetan. *Genres in Discourse*. Cambridge: Cambridge University Press, 1990.

Tolinski, Brad. "Speed Kills: A Thinking Man's Guide to Thrash." *Guitar World*, October 1989, pp. 66–77, 128–29, 138.

Vološinov, V. N. *Marxism and the Philosophy of Language*. Cambridge, Mass.: Harvard University Press, 1986.

Walser, Robert. "The Body in the Music: Epistemology and Musical Semiotics," *College Music Symposium* 31:1 (forthcoming).

————. "Bon Jovi's Alloy: Discursive Fusion in Top 40 Pop Music." *OneTwoThreeFour* 7 (1989), pp. 7–19.

————. "Eruptions: Heavy Metal Appropriations of Classical Virtuosity." *Popular Music* 11:3 (1992), pp. 263–308.

————. "Musical Imagery and Performance Practice in J. S. Bach's Arias with Trumpet," *International Trumpet Guild Journal* 13:1 (September 1988), pp. 62–77.

————. "Out of Notes: Signification, Interpretation, and the Problem of Miles Davis." *Musical Quarterly* (forthcoming).

————. "The Polka Mass: Music of Postmodern Ethnicity." *American Music* 10:2 (Summer 1992), pp. 183–202.

————. "Review of *Origins of the Popular Style*, by Peter Van der Merwe." *Journal of Musicological Research* 12/1–2 (1992), pp. 123–32.

————. "What It Really, Really Means." *Esquire*, November 1991, pp. 130–32.

Ward, Ed, Geoffrey Stokes, and Ken Tucker. *Rock of Ages: The Rolling Stone History of Rock & Roll*. New York: Rolling Stone Press, 1986.

Weinstein, Deena. *Heavy Metal: A Cultural Sociology*. New York: Lexington Books, 1991.

Weiss, Piero, and Richard Taruskin, eds. *Music in the Western World: A History in Documents*. New York: Schirmer, 1984.

Wicke, Peter. *Rock Music: Culture, Aesthetics, and Sociology*. Cambridge: Cambridge University Press, 1990.

Wilder, Elin. "Heavy Metal: A Fan's Perspective." *High Times*, June 1988, pp. 32–39.

Young, Charles M. "Heavy Metal." *Musician*, September 1984, pp. 40–44.

Index

✻

blues, 8, 17, 57–58, 63, 67–68, 93, 187n29
Bluestone, Barry, 200n23
Bon Jovi, 13, 14, 18, 63, 79, 105, 120–24,
173, 174, 176
Bon Jovi, Jon, 120, 123
Bondanella, Peter, 191n30
Boone, Pat, 47
"Born to Be Wild" (Steppenwolf), 8
Boston, 120, 176
Bowie, David, 124
Brahms, Johannes, 95, 101
Breen, Marcus, 23
Brittan, Arthur, 195n4
Brown, James, 9
Brown, Pete, 193n72
Bryson, Norman, 186n21
Burke, Edmund, 160
Burroughs, William S., 8
Bush, George, 140

Caccini, Giulio, 108
capitalism, 35, 134, 164–71
Carroll, Nöel, 202n67
censorship, xvi, 24, 138–45
Chapple, Steve, 186n22
Charles, Ray, 62
Chernoff, John Miller, 37, 49
Chopin, Frédéric, 101
Christian heavy metal, 13, 55
Cinderella, 2, 173
Clapton, Eric, 9, 10, 11, 58, 66, 67, 181n10,
191n22
Clark, Steve (Def Leppard), 92
Clarke, Donald, 182n23
Clarke, John, 199n5
class, 17–18, 180n7, 199n5
classical music, xv, 4, 18, 22, 30, 35, 38,
57–107, 116, 140–41
Clément, Catherine, 196n19
Cockburn, Alexander, 202n72
Coker, Jerry, 191n17
Coleridge, Samuel Taylor, 160
Collen, Phil (Def Leppard), 92
Collins, Phil, 201n43
concerts, arena, 14, 17, 80, 114
Cone, Edward T., 189n57
Connell, R. W., 195n12
Considine, J. D., 185n1, 188n43, 190n5,
194n86
Cooke, Sam, 62
Cooper, Alice, 11, 16, 78, 173, 174
Cooper, Grosvenor, 189n57
Copland, Aaron, 128

country music, 20, 24, 92, 124, 143
Cream, 9, 174
Crosby, Bing, 62
Crowley, Aleister, 148
cultural hierarchy, 58–62, 99, 107, 111, 140
Cutler, Blayne, 179n1, 183n49

Dark Angel, 150
Death Angel, 174
Debord, Guy, 108
Debussy, Claude, 68
DeCurtis, Anthony, 180n8
Deep Purple, 4, 10, 13, 47, 61, 64, 66, 173,
174, 181n10, 193n64
Def Leppard, 6, 10, 12, 92, 173, 179n7
Deville, C. C. (Poison), 128
Dickenson, Bruce (Iron Maiden), 6–7
"Difficult to Cure" (Rainbow), 66–67
DiMeola, Al, 66
Dio, 173
discourse, musical, xii, xiv–xv, 26–56, 113,
121–22, 147, 186nn20 and 21
discursive fusions, xv, 28, 58, 102, 120–
23, 185n6
distortion, 9, 15, 41–46
Dixon, Willie, 182n28
Doerschuk, Andy, 199n11
Dokken, 5, 12, 118–19, 173, 174, 179n7
Dokken, Don, 118
Dome, Malcolm, 183n50
Donington, Robert, 192n42
Downing, K. K. (Judas Priest), 66, 150
drugs, 139–41, 199n8
drums, 10, 128
Dufay, Guillaume, 105
Duncan, Robert, 20, 45, 182n23
Dungeons and Dragons, 143
Dyer, Richard, 189n61

Eagleton, Terry, 186n25, 192n42
Eddy, Chuck, 21, 189n56
Edelstein, Robert, 183n39
Edrei, Mary J., 191n20
Ehrenreich, Barbara, 115, 202nn70 and 74
"Electric Eye" (Judas Priest), 163–64
Eliot, Marc, 184n56
Ellington, Duke, 61
Elliot, Joe (Def Leppard), 10, 11–12
Elvis, 132
Emerson, Keith, 62
Emerson, Lake, and Palmer, 61–62
Engels, Frederick, 165, 203n86
Epstein, Jonathon S., 200n30

Index / 219

MUSIC / CULTURE

(series list continued from page ii)

Popular Music in Theory
by Keith Negus

Upside Your Head!
Rhythm and Blues on Central Avenue
by Johnny Otis

Singing Archaeology: Philip Glass's Akhnaten
by John Richardson

Black Noise:
Rap Music and Black Culture in
Contemporary America
by Tricia Rose

The Book of Music and Nature:
An Anthology of Sounds, Words, Thoughts
edited by David Rothenberg
and Marta Ulvaeus

Angora Matta:
Fatal Acts of North-South Translation
by Marta Elena Savigliano

Making Beats:
The Art of Sample-Based Hip-Hop
by Joseph G. Schloss

Dissonant Identities:
The Rock 'n' Roll Scene in Austin, Texas
by Barry Shank

Banda: Mexican Musical Life across Borders
by Helena Simonett

Subcultural Sounds: Micromusics of the West
by Mark Slobin

Music, Society, Education
by Christopher Small

Musicking:
The Meanings of Performing and Listening
by Christopher Small

Music of the Common Tongue: Survival and
Celebration in African American Music
by Christopher Small

Singing Our Way to Victory: French Cultural
Politics and Music During the Great War
by Regina M. Sweeney

Setting the Record Straight:
A Material History of Classical Recording
by Colin Symes

False Prophet:
Fieldnotes from the Punk Underground
by Steven Taylor

Any Sound You Can Imagine:
Making Music/Consuming Technology
by Paul Théberge

Club Cultures:
Music, Media and Sub-cultural Capital
by Sarah Thornton

Running with the Devil: Power, Gender, and
Madness in Heavy Metal Music
by Robert Walser

Manufacturing the Muse: Estey Organs and
Consumer Culture in Victorian America
by Dennis Waring

The City of Musical Memory:
Salsa, Record Grooves, and Popular Culture in
Cali, Colombia
by Lise A. Waxer

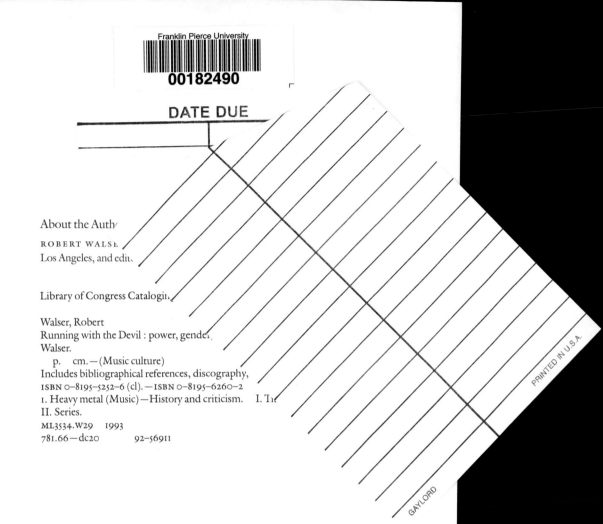
About the Auth/

ROBERT WALSE
Los Angeles, and edit

Library of Congress Catalogin

Walser, Robert
Running with the Devil : power, gende
Walser.
    p.   cm. — (Music culture)
Includes bibliographical references, discography,
ISBN 0-8195-5252-6 (cl). — ISBN 0-8195-6260-2
1. Heavy metal (Music) — History and criticism.   I. Ti
II. Series.
ML3534.W29   1993
781.66 — dc20   92-56911